4 Plays by
S. N. Behrman

☆ *by S. N. Behrman*

★ *Plays*

4 Plays BY S. N. Behrman

☆ THE SECOND MAN

★ BIOGRAPHY

☆ RAIN FROM HEAVEN

★ END OF SUMMER

Random House · New York

First Printing

Contents

☆

The Second Man

★

☆ | *to*
my brothers

The Second Man *was first presented by the Theatre Guild on April 11, 1927, at the Guild Theatre, New York, with the following cast:*

MRS. KENDALL FRAYNE	Lynn Fontanne
CLARK STOREY	Alfred Lunt
AUSTIN LOWE	Earle Larimore
MONICA GREY	Margalo Gillmore
ALBERT	Edward Hartford

DIRECTED BY Philip Moeller
SETTINGS BY Jo Mielziner

Scenes

The Scene is laid in Clark Storey's Apartment in West Fifty-sixth Street, New York City.

ACT ONE

SCENE: *The living-room of a duplex apartment of a studio-building on the West Side. The proscenium displaces the great windows typical of these apartments; midway up the rear wall is visible the railed landing of the stairs leading to the upper bedrooms. The great room is comfortably furnished, a slight preponderance of the "exotic" in furnishing. The walls are lined with bookshelves wherever convenient. There are books and magazines in profusion everywhere. On the right, near the fireplace, is a long, low, extremely comfortable looking armchair; leaning against it is an ordinary sewing board. On the other side of this chair is a low tabouret on which repose writing materials and a telephone. Not far from this armchair, also, just below the fireplace, is a small "portable" gramophone on a small stand.*

AT RISE: *MRS.* KENDALL FRAYNE *is discovered walking nervously about near the armchair. She is a tall, handsome, beautifully dressed woman, about thirty-five. She might be described as "majestic"; she has a fine face; her voice is beautifully modulated and restrained even when she speaks under the stress of deep feeling.*
She is nervous and angry. Keeps looking at her watch. Takes up the manuscript of a story on the tabouret, and drops it when she sees she has already read it. Finally she makes up her mind to leave; grasps her fur wrap, lying on a chair. At the door she stops, returns to the telephone. Her voice is calm as she asks for the number.

KENDALL (*At the telephone*) Gramercy 4304 please—yes—may I speak to Mr. Storey please?—I believe he lunched at the Club and I thought he might still be there—thank you so much—(*She holds the receiver to her ear, sitting on the arm of the chair*)—yes—about how long ago?—thank you.

5

(She takes up her wrap again with a sweeping gesture. This time she means really to go. She goes up-stage and disappears in the little hallway leading to the corridor. The telephone tinkles. She runs back, quite excited and answers the call)

KENDALL (*At phone*)   Yes. Yes, the line *was* busy—who?— no, Mr. Storey is not in—this—this is a friend of his—is there any message?—oh, Miss Grey—this is Mrs. Frayne— how do you do?—yes—he *was* here but stepped out—he'll be back in a few minutes—I'm leaving now but I'll leave the message for him. Not at all. Good-bye.

(She hangs up again. She is thoroughly angry, humiliated. She writes out message. Starts up-stage. CLARKE STOREY *rushes in)*

STOREY   Awfully sorry.

KENDALL   I'm leaving.

STOREY   Oh, come! I'm not *so* late.

KENDALL   Only an hour.

STOREY   The distinguished Englishman *insisted* on my drop- ping into his hotel with him. We got to talking—I told him his heroines were all neurotic and his heroes—

KENDALL   I've got to go.
(She tries to cross him)

STOREY   Honestly, Kendall, I rushed up here as fast as I could. Had a fight with one taxi-driver and it took me hours to find another. Please don't be angry. I'm full of things to tell you—

KENDALL   This always happens.

STOREY   Besides, I thought you'd be quite comfortable. I left my new story for you to read.

KENDALL   That took exactly fifteen minutes.

STOREY   Only that? Really, I must write a novel. Then I can be late with impunity. Great idea for a publisher's blurb: "This novel is so absorbing that a jealous woman, waiting for the author to keep an appointment, forgot all about him—"

KENDALL   Really, you've got to stop treating me like this!

STOREY   I swear I only stayed on so long because I thought it would amuse you to hear about the great English novelist. I kept saying to myself: "This will amuse Kendall—!"

KENDALL   Don't talk like that to me. It's all right for Monica Grey. It's transparent to me. She just telephoned you, by the way.

STOREY   What did she want?

KENDALL   You— It was humiliating. I had to say you had gone out. Of course she understood that I was waiting for you.

STOREY   Oh, well, everybody in town was at that luncheon. The great novelist is tall and thin and has a red beard. I suspect that if he shaved it would be discovered that he has no chin. And I was delighted to find what I had already suspected from reading his novels—he has no sense of humour.

KENDALL   Because he didn't find your flippancy amusing?

STOREY   It's as good a test as any.

KENDALL   He's a genius. It shows on nearly every page of his writing.

STOREY   I dare say he is a genius. Sad thing about geniuses—almost invariably lack humour. It's true. Genius is a sort of fanaticism—
    (*The telephone rings*)

KENDALL   I'm going.

STOREY   Please—just a minute— (*At phone*) You're doing it—who is this?—oh, hello there, Austin—what about?—Monica again?—I thought you were all set—oh, you take her too seriously—I'm busy right now—Mrs. Frayne—oh, sure—say twenty minutes—bye-bye. (*He hangs up*) Austin Lowe. Wants to weep on my shoulder. All burned up about Monica Grey.

KENDALL   And she's burned up about you.

STOREY   Nonsense. A baby. Doesn't know what she wants.

KENDALL   I think she does. (*Casually*) Why don't you marry her?

STOREY   I have other plans.

KENDALL   Meaning?

STOREY   Meaning you.

KENDALL   Why should you want to marry me? Outside of the fact that—you love comfort and I am—rich.

STOREY   Outside of the fact that I love comfort—and that you are rich—I like you very much. I like you enormously. You're the most intelligent woman I know.

KENDALL   Not so intelligent. I discovered that—just—now —waiting for you?

STOREY   How come?

KENDALL   I was—jealous.

STOREY   (*Wickedly*)   Of the celebrated English novelist? You misunderstand me, Kendall.

KENDALL   Jealous of your self-sufficiency. Your independence of me. I saw you there talking, enjoying yourself, revelling in your own fluency. I realised perfectly well that you must have forgotten me or, if you did think of me, that you must be saying: "Oh, she'll wait—" I was jealous, Storey.

STOREY   You too! My last hope is gone.

KENDALL   You see, Storey, you aren't in the least bit in love with me.

STOREY   I feel a much rarer, more stable emotion—friendliness and all sorts of affection and—

KENDALL   I know.

STOREY   I was hoping we—you and I—might demonstrate the triumph of the loveless marriage.

KENDALL   How old are you, Storey?

STOREY   What did I tell you last time you asked me?

KENDALL   I believe you said twenty-eight.

STOREY   I lied. I'm thirty.

KENDALL   I'm thirty-five.

STOREY   Delightful age.

KENDALL   When I'm forty-five you won't be any older than you are now.

STOREY   Won't I!

KENDALL   Suppose you fall in love?

STOREY   I'm through with that sort of thing.

KENDALL   You sound so young sometimes—so naïve.

STOREY   But I've been through that sort of thing. I know.

KENDALL   I can't imagine you really in love.

STOREY   But I assure you I was. It lasted two years. I suffered. I agonised.

KENDALL   Who was she?

STOREY   No one you know. She's married now. Has children and a dull husband, a dull home. I see her occasionally. And I wonder at myself. Was it for her I felt that base emotion— jealousy? Was it for her I used to wait in a torment of anxiety and anticipation? It seems impossible now. Such a nice, unimaginative, plodding creature. I see her and I wonder.

KENDALL   It may happen again—without warning.

STOREY   I doubt it. I'm fed up with love. It's a mirage, an illusion, a sort of pathology, feeds on being unsatisfied, rejected. Attain love and it vanishes—vanishes into the thin air or solidifies into such things as comfort and affection— things which you and I would have from the start, my dear.

KENDALL   (*Doubtfully*)   All this is very pretty—
    (*The phone rings*)

STOREY   That damn telephone— (*Taking it up*) Yes— hello, Monica—how are you?—yes, Mrs. Frayne told me—I'd just stepped out to buy her a magazine with a poem of mine in it—oh, a trifle—not one of my major works—you've got to see me?—Austin just called me and told me the same thing—what've you been doing to him?—now don't be a silly child—you're lucky to have him—it's no good you're coming to see me—I shan't coddle you—no, don't come; I shan't be here—I— (*She has put down the receiver on him. In disgust*) Crazy kid!

KENDALL   Gracious! You *are* pursued by women!

STOREY   Now there's a case—Monica Grey! Poor as a church mouse. Mother at her wit's end to keep up the pretence of a conservative gentility. And here's Austin Lowe absolutely dotty about her. A millionaire and a great man to boot—

KENDALL (*Gently*)   He is dull, Storey.

STOREY   Dull! One of the most promising young chemists in America. Under thirty and he's actually discovered something new—a new way of doing something or other. He's an F.R.S.!

KENDALL   Yes. And a B-O-R-E.

STOREY   If there's one man on earth I envy it's Austin Lowe. If I had his money and his brain—the vices I'd encourage— the secrets I'd explore—!

KENDALL   In that case I'm glad you haven't his money and I'm certainly glad you haven't his brain.

STOREY   Just because he's not glib, like I am!

KENDALL   He never has anything interesting to say—

STOREY   I can talk, can't I? And that impresses you. But Austin's a great man who's made a contribution to science while I'm an imitative poet and a second-rate short-story writer.

KENDALL   You *are* a dear, Storey.

STOREY   Well, it's true!

KENDALL   I'll make a great sacrifice: Monica can have the great man. I'll take the second-rate short-story writer.

STOREY   You'll get your preference. Austin can't see anyone in the world but Monica.

KENDALL   She doesn't care much for him, though.

STOREY   She will. I'll let you in on a little secret—

KENDALL   Yes?

STOREY   Austin and Monica are engaged.

KENDALL   Really? It's not announced, is it?

STOREY   It just happened yesterday. Austin telephoned me in a perfect ecstasy.

KENDALL   I gather he's in less of an ecstasy today—

STOREY   Oh, Monica's a crazy kid. And being completely in love with her Austin's at her mercy.

KENDALL   Miss Grey is rather adorable. Likes to be—audacious—doesn't she?

STOREY   Really an innocent. A Tennysonian ingénue with a Freudian patter.

KENDALL   Something appealingly wistful about her.

STOREY   Actually she has all the picture-book illusions of a *Saturday Evening Post* heroine—but she's picked up the vocabulary of the intelligentsia. Don't let it deceive you.

KENDALL   Are you urging her to marry Austin?

STOREY   Urge her? My dear, I insist on it.

KENDALL   Why?

STOREY   Why? Because Austin'll make an admirable husband for her. She'll settle down and have babies and live in luxury. Her mother'll spend her old age in comfort. And—so shall I!

KENDALL   You're incorrigible.

STOREY   I have enormous respect for money. You can't appreciate it. It can only be felt by those whose past was poverty-stricken and whose present—is precarious.

KENDALL   You could make a fortune if you worked harder.

STOREY   I doubt it. I'm too intelligent to write commercial truck and incapable of writing great stuff. It's unfortunate. No, my dear. The only solution for me is to persuade you to marry me.

KENDALL   Would you want to marry me if I were poor?

STOREY   That would be presumptuous.

KENDALL   Presumptuous?

STOREY   Only the rich should offer to marry poor girls. They are the only ones who can afford it.

KENDALL   You're awfully mercenary.

STOREY   I'm mature. But I am honest as well as mercenary. If you do marry me—I promise—I absolutely promise—not to live above your income—

KENDALL   (*Amused*)   I can't be angry with you.

STOREY   Why should you be angry with me?

KENDALL   Keeping me waiting an hour.

STOREY   At least I wasn't with another woman.

KENDALL   I suppose that will come too.

STOREY   I'll always come back to you.

KENDALL   You make me feel like a—

STOREY   Like a terminal?

KENDALL   Honestly, I wish I'd never met you.

STOREY   You don't mean that. Think of the nice times we've had together.

KENDALL   I feel you'll make me very unhappy.

STOREY   Only momentarily. And never wilfully.

KENDALL   Anyway, I wish I weren't in love with you.

STOREY   You won't be—long.

KENDALL   It's lasted now—three years.

STOREY   But most of that time your husband was alive.

KENDALL   (*After a moment*)   Storey—outside of being in love with you—I'm very fond of you. I feel such fine things in you. If only you wouldn't waste yourself so, if only you'd make the effort to live up to the best in you—

STOREY   Oh, now, Kendall, don't you be fooled too. I'm living up to the best in me, right now.

KENDALL   But you potter so. You're not concentrated on anything.

STOREY   But I've a talent for pottering.

KENDALL   I feel you could do great work—

STOREY   Now don't you go on having illusions about me. I have a certain facility for turning out pretty stuff—

KENDALL   I'm sure you could do great things.

STOREY   You are mistaken. I know my limitations. Nor have I any craving for immortality. When I'm rich—when I'm married to you—I probably shan't write at all. I'll be— what I've always wanted to be—a prosperous dilettante.

KENDALL   I never can tell when you're joking—

STOREY   I assure you I'm perfectly serious now. What this country needs is a dilettante class, interested in art with no desire to make money out of it. Why shouldn't there be an amateur class in art, as there is in sport?

KENDALL   Is this a pose?

STOREY   I assure you it isn't. Quite the contrary. At least you can't say afterwards that I married you under false pretences. I tell you now I'm an adventurer—intellectually and morally—an *arriviste* with one virtue—honesty.

KENDALL   Well, I've got you on my hands. I suppose I'll have to make the best of you.

STOREY   You'd better— (*He rises—kisses her lightly—folds her coat about her*)

KENDALL (*Turns and watches him—amused*)   I gather you're dismissing me.

STOREY   Well, I have to do some work. (*With a gesture toward the manuscript*)

KENDALL (*Laughing*)   What?

STOREY   I haven't touched that since this morning. And Austin's coming in—

KENDALL   And Miss Grey.

STOREY   You heard me tell her I wouldn't be home.

KENDALL   I heard her say she was coming.

STOREY   What can one do? It'll be a relief to me when these two are married off.

KENDALL   To me, too.

STOREY   Are you going out tonight?

KENDALL   I don't think so.

STOREY   Suppose I ring you—5:30ish. You might dine here. I'll order dinner from downstairs.

KENDALL   All right. By the way, Storey—

STOREY   Yes?

KENDALL   It's—the end of the month. If you're a bit short —I might lend you a little.

STOREY   Ken, you demoralise me.

KENDALL   Here's a check. You can pay me when your ship comes in. (*She gives* STOREY *the check. He puts it on table*)

STOREY   You *are* a darling! I suppose it's dreadful to take money from a woman. But why it's worse than taking it from a man I don't know. Do you?

KENDALL   It all depends—

STOREY   Really, Kendall, you've got to marry me right away—to save my self-respect.

KENDALL   What do you want your self-respect for?

STOREY   I haven't the least idea—

KENDALL   (*Slapping him*)   Half-wit . . .

STOREY   (*Affectionately*)   Darling . . . (*He walks out with her, returns a moment later. Goes to telephone*) Restaurant, please—Mr. Storey speaking—I want dinner for two for to-night—seven-thirty—up here. Oysters, small ones—clear soup—supreme of chicken with mushrooms—salad—yes—yes—thank you, Frederic—

> (*He hangs up, takes off his coat, puts on dressing-gown, an elaborate one, yellow silk-lined with wide sleeves and brilliant sash. Settles himself into the easy chair, puts the sewing board across its arms, making a bridge on which he puts the writing paper and starts to create. Inspiration is halting; he lights a cigarette. The lamp is too bright. He pins a piece of newspaper over it. Something in paper attracts his attention. He takes out the pin—leans back in chair and reads it. The doorbell rings. He gets up and goes to door admitting* AUSTIN LOWE. *Leaves him and comes back to his chair.* AUSTIN *is fattish, serious, woebegone.* STOREY'S *manner to him is extremely friendly*)

STOREY   (*With a wave toward his work*)   I was in the middle of an immortal sentence . . .

AUSTIN   I'm sorry, old man. I *had* to see you.

STOREY   You look seedy.

AUSTIN   Didn't sleep a wink last night.

STOREY   Cocktail?

AUSTIN   (*Miserably*)   Nothing.

STOREY   Do you good.

AUSTIN   I couldn't really. Couldn't even eat my lunch.

STOREY   What's the matter? Don't tell me that discovery you made turned out to be old stuff.

AUSTIN   It's nothing to do with that.

STOREY   There's an idea. Scientist works twenty years on a scent—finally gets it. Rushes to the Science Club or wherever scientists rush when they've found something. When he gets there the boss tells him: "Sorry, old man, but Professor Funkenwangler got this yesterday—here's his cable—"

AUSTIN (*Irritably*) I tried to get you twenty times today. Last night, too. Where the devil've you been?

STOREY Been? Let's see—where the devil have I been? Oh, last night I went to a party. Then on to Charmian Drew's. Know her?

AUSTIN No.

STOREY Very pretty girl. Got back at six this morning. Got up in time to go to lunch to meet Stryker Collins, the English novelist. Know his stuff?

AUSTIN No.

STOREY Vastly overrated, if you ask me. The heroines're always throwing things at the heroes. Never saw such nasty women.

AUSTIN I'm awful low today, Storey, old man.

STOREY (*Affecting surprise*) Low? Really? You seem so gay—
  (AUSTIN *gives him a woeful look*)

AUSTIN It's about Monica.

STOREY Monica?

AUSTIN She's thrown me over.

STOREY Nonsense.

AUSTIN Says she won't marry me.

STOREY You take that child too seriously, Austin.

AUSTIN But she means it this time, Storey. Told me last night. Says it's all over. Gave me back—the ring. See. Here—
(*Shows him the ring which he fumbles miserably*)

STOREY (*Looking critically at the ring*) I'm glad she did. Never was crazy about that ring. Neither was Monica, I imagine. You can return it now and get her something less—conventional. I'll go with you to Cartier's. The other day I saw a stunning oblong emerald—

AUSTIN But don't you see! She doesn't want my ring. Any ring. She doesn't want me.

STOREY   What's her reason? For suddenly—

AUSTIN   Said when she promised to marry me she yielded to outside pressure—

STOREY   Her little mother.

AUSTIN   Said she acted against her better nature. Now she says she realises she doesn't love me—that she never could love me. What shall I do now, Storey?

STOREY   Leave her alone for a week and—try again.

AUSTIN   The worst of it is—

STOREY   What?

AUSTIN   She loves somebody else.

STOREY   She said so?

AUSTIN   Yes.

STOREY   Who?

AUSTIN   Wouldn't tell me.

STOREY   I don't believe it.

AUSTIN   Why not?

STOREY   She'd have told *me*.

AUSTIN   You think so?

STOREY   Certainly.

AUSTIN   She would, unless—

STOREY   Unless what?

AUSTIN   Unless the man she loves—is you.

STOREY   I? You're crazy, Austin.

AUSTIN   (*Breathless*)   She likes you. She likes you better than me, that's plain. It's a wonder to me you *don't* marry her.

STOREY   Austin, you're losing your sense of humour. Fancy my being married to Monica. She'd leave me in six months. By which time I should certainly have left her.

AUSTIN   (*Wanting to be contradicted*)   I don't see why.

STOREY   She's penniless, for one thing. She couldn't stand the poverty of my ménage and—neither could I.

AUSTIN   I can't understand it. You're not in love with her?

STOREY   There speaks the eternal lover. I think it strange you *are* in love with her. She's pretty—I grant you that. But, great Heavens, man—so *young*.

AUSTIN (*Rapt*)   She *is* young.

STOREY   And so full of spirits!

AUSTIN   Isn't she?

STOREY   Always laughing. Like the constant ringing of chimes.

AUSTIN   It is like chimes.

STOREY   You've certainly got it bad, Austin.

AUSTIN   I can't think of anything else. It—it—obsesses me.

STOREY (*A bit wickedly*)   After all, you have your science.

AUSTIN   You think that means anything to me now? When I've lost her? I tell you I can't work since I've known Monica.

STOREY   Your researches?

AUSTIN   They're all nothing. I can't do a thing. I don't give a damn. It's only—Monica.

STOREY (*Shaking his head*)   What an illusion that is about the cold mastery of scientific men! Look at you—helpless as a baby.

AUSTIN   And the worst of it is there's nothing to do. It's not like a problem—that you can work at. She just doesn't love me. And that's all there is to it. I'm sunk.

STOREY   If you want her—really want her—you can get her.

AUSTIN   That's what you always say. But it's not true.

STOREY (*Lighting a cigarette*)   No doubt about it. I'm sure.

AUSTIN   But she told me—last night—

STOREY   She doesn't in the least know what she wants. Won't till after she's married. That's up to you—

AUSTIN   But she's not attracted to me.

STOREY   She doesn't understand you. She has no appreciation of your intellectual gifts.

AUSTIN (*Sadly*)   That's true. My work means nothing to her.

STOREY   Why don't you make it mean something to her? Teach her to see how wonderful it is. Go on about the marvellous delicacy of your experiments.

AUSTIN   If I could only talk like you.

STOREY   That's easy.

AUSTIN   How?

STOREY   Cultivate superficiality.

AUSTIN   If she only understood me—as you do!

STOREY   She shall be made to.

AUSTIN   How?

STOREY   (*Lighting another cigarette*)   Maternal pressure. I'll wager you anything a starved writer can pay that Mrs. Grey doesn't know Monica's refused you.

AUSTIN   What if she did?

STOREY   She'd raise hell. You see the old lady's dreadfully afraid—of guess what?

AUSTIN   What?

STOREY   That Monica will marry *me*.

AUSTIN   There, you see. Even she's noticed it.

STOREY   A good thing, too. Might be a fine thing to persuade Mrs. Grey that *I* want to marry Monica. She'll never rest then until Monica's married to you.

AUSTIN   What makes you think so?

STOREY   Monica's mother's perfectly cracked about the idea of having you for a son-in-law. Oh, it's not your scientific eminence. It's not even your family, though of course that has something to do with it. It's your money, my friend, your lucre, your multitudinous boodle—

AUSTIN   I can hardly believe—

STOREY   Sorry, but that's what it is. The Greys are mighty hard up. Monica's been dressing shamefully of late—

AUSTIN   (*Truculently*)   She looks better—

STOREY   I know. Niftier in gingham than a fine lady in velvet.

AUSTIN   She looks wonderful in anything.

STOREY How extraordinary that a little girl like Monica can make a man like you talk like a hack writer!

AUSTIN (*Bristling*) Look here, I don't quite like your tone about Monica!

STOREY Don't misunderstand me. Oh, I'm awfully fond of her. But she *is* a spoiled little minx, shallow as a platter. Her lack of appreciation of you proves that.

AUSTIN (*Pathetically*) Well, she's only twenty. Sometimes I think I'm too old for her.

STOREY You're only twenty-nine.

AUSTIN It's not that alone. She's so gay, so full of fun. I can't—prattle, Storey. I don't follow her small talk.

STOREY Her talk is not small. It is infinitesimal. Your microscopic training should help you.

AUSTIN I don't do the things she likes—dance, play tennis —you know.

STOREY (*Regarding him judicially*) You're not a jazz figure, Austin. But you'd better marry her anyway. If you don't she'll run away with a tenor or something.

AUSTIN You keep telling me to marry her as if I didn't want to. Damn it, Storey, I'd give my soul—

STOREY I don't think that will be necessary. But you might make some other sacrifices.

AUSTIN I'll do anything—

STOREY Take this thing more lightly, can't you? You've fallen in love like an awkward schoolboy—not like a man of the world.

AUSTIN But I'm not a man of the world.

STOREY Can't you act the base rôle? When Monica's around you get positively tongue-tied. All you can do is silently register adoration.

AUSTIN I know it. I can't help it. When I do think of something to say it sounds so inadequate to me that I don't say it.

STOREY If you'd only remember that everything's on your side. You've so much to offer.

AUSTIN I wish I thought so.

STOREY If you persist, you'll win her, as the military men say, by attrition. (*"Attrition" is a good word for future use. He makes notation on Ms.*)

AUSTIN She told me not to try to see her, not to call her on the telephone. I tell you, Storey, I don't know what to do with myself.

STOREY (*Shaking his head*) You're a great argument against celibacy, Austin, old boy.

AUSTIN You know, Storey, I used to think—before I met Monica—that I'd never marry a girl unless she wanted me as much as I wanted her. But that was before I wanted anybody —as I want Monica. (*Passionately*) I'd marry her on any terms, you understand? It's beyond—pride. You understand?

STOREY Of course I understand. And I'll do everything I can to help you, believe me.

AUSTIN (*Fervently*) You're a brick, Storey.

STOREY Now, look here. I've got to do a little work. Why don't you go around the corner to the Chemist's Club, look over some of those fascinating magazines full of algebraic formulas and come back here to dine?

AUSTIN That's awfully good of you, Storey, really. I hate to be alone.

STOREY I know.

AUSTIN You're the only person I can talk to.

STOREY Come back—say twenty minutes. I'll order dinner from downstairs.

AUSTIN You make it so easy for your friends to impose on you, Storey. You're swell.

STOREY Don't deceive yourself, old boy. I get a sadistic pleasure out of watching you writhe. And your pathetic reliance on me gives me a sense of superiority.

AUSTIN Always joking!

STOREY It's the grim truth.

AUSTIN You're the finest—

STOREY (*Hustles him to door*) Come now, Austin, run along. See you in twenty minutes.

AUSTIN (*At door*)   Er—there's something else.

STOREY   Yes.

AUSTIN   I've been wanting to speak to you about it for some time.

STOREY   Well, spit it out.

AUSTIN   It's about money.

STOREY   My favourite subject.

AUSTIN   Er—your writing. Does it—I mean to say—does it bring you in very much?

STOREY   Not what it should. I'm caviare to the general, Austin.

AUSTIN   That's what I thought. Well—you see—I mean to say—you see—well, damn it all, I'm so rich, Storey. Won't you let me help you out occasionally?

STOREY   Of course I will.

AUSTIN   (*Reaching eagerly into his pocket*)   That's fine—I—

STOREY   Oh, not now. I've got a check on the table now—I don't even know how much it is— (*Goes to the table and unfolds check* MRS. FRAYNE *has left*) Five hundred.

AUSTIN   For a story?

STOREY   Yes.

AUSTIN   That's more than we chemists get—

STOREY   But next time I'm broke—it'll probably be next week—I'll let you know.

AUSTIN   Any time. It'll be a pleasure.

STOREY   It's a pleasure I shan't deny you. So long, Austin.

AUSTIN   Good-bye, old man. Awfully good of you to let me come back.

STOREY   Don't mention it. (AUSTIN *goes out.* STOREY *goes to his armchair. There is a smile on his lips. After a moment of meditation he reaches for the telephone*) Regent 2772—please—Mrs. Frayne—Mr. Storey—hello, Ken—I've changed my mind about dining here—let's go out somewhere—yes, I did order it but I'm going to let two other people eat it—and—Kendall—will you call me up in about twenty minutes

—never mind what I say—just phone me. Comedy, my dear —tell you later—I'll come to your place about six-thirty— shan't dress, no—yes, I'm working now—oh, pretty well— not many sentences but distinguished. Good-bye, Mrs. Frayne, see you later. (*He hangs up, puts board across the arms of his chair, as before, begins to write. He sees "attrition" on his Ms. Goes to dictionary. Finds it. Goes back to his board, spelling it. Writes a few lines. Doorbell rings. He ignores it. It rings again, four short rings. Then, shouting*) Door's open!

MONICA (*Bursting in*)   Hello, darling. Working? (*She is young, vibrant, utterly charming*)

STOREY   Trying to.

MONICA   Sorry I came?

STOREY (*Drily*)   Well—!

MONICA   I don't care in the least. I'm delighted to see you. (*She puts her face against his cheek*)

STOREY   Don't muss me.

MONICA   Just had to see you, Storey. The one person in the world I wanted to see.

STOREY   Everybody's told me that today. I begin to feel like a Father Confessor.

MONICA   Glad to see me? Tell the truth.

STOREY (*Grumbling*)   Been trying to work all afternoon—

MONICA   You fib. You *are* glad. You know you are.

STOREY (*Writing*)   Oh, I don't mind you.

MONICA   I bet you're more than glad. I bet you're thrilled, excited.

STOREY   Modest creature.

MONICA   I'm confident you're in love with me, Storey, but you're too big a fool to tell me so.

STOREY (*Continuing writing*)   I thought we'd settled all that.

MONICA   You thought you did. You thought I'd quietly suc- cumb and marry Austin.

STOREY   Oh, you're staying!

MONICA   But I'm not going to. Hear that, Storey? I'm not going to—

(*He finishes a page and starts a fresh one, putting the finished one on the tabouret beside him*)

MONICA (*Taking finished page*)   Oh, may I?

STOREY   Be through in a minute.

MONICA (*Reading*)   Don't stop on my account.

STOREY (*Grimly*)   Oh, well, enough of creation— (*He throws down his pen*)

MONICA (*Absorbed*)   Oh, this is awfully interesting.

STOREY (*Same tone*)   Think so, do you? (*He sounds suddenly weary*)

MONICA   I love it. (*She reads*) "They had been dancing and he asked her to go outside with him. They stepped out through the open French windows, crossed the lawn and walked down a narrow path between high poplars. . . . The treetops made hedges in the sky between which the stars grew like buttercups. Buttercups. . . ." That's lovely.

STOREY   Go on.

MONICA   "It was a most curious moon, red-bronze in colour, wafer-thin, exquisitely curved, a shaving of a moon. Courtney allowed himself to speculate to the girl beside him. 'God,' he said. Oh, excuse me, 'God,' he said, 'must be a curious person to fashion such a moon, a butcher with artistic leanings. Or was he an artist suffering from a sadistic atavism?' Which did she think? The girl thought it was slightly chilly and hadn't they better go back to the ballroom?" Oh, I think that's wonderful. So—ironic!

STOREY   You think it's wonderful?

MONICA   I think everything you write is wonderful.

STOREY   I'm sorry I can't agree with you. Scented dishwater, that's what it is. Dishwater with eau de Cologne in it.

MONICA   What a funny mood you're in!

STOREY   It annoys me to have you keep prattling that my stuff's wonderful. What do you know about it? Have you ever read anything except movie magazines? Have you—?

MONICA   Oh, now, Storey, please don't scold me. Not today. Today I want you to be nice to me.

STOREY (*Rising*)   What's this about you and Austin?

MONICA   I can't go through with it, Storey. That's all.

STOREY   But you told me—you definitely told me—you'd made up your mind to marry him.

MONICA (*Whimpering a bit*)   You're not a bit nice today.

STOREY   You're such an awful dumbbell, Monica.

MONICA   I'm not. You're a dumbbell. Here—sit down and let me get comfy—and I'll tell you all about it . . . I'm going to sit on your lap. (*She does it*)

STOREY (*Groaning*)   You're the bane of my existence, Monica.

MONICA   Now, we'll talk.

STOREY   Well?

MONICA   Storey—tell the truth—wouldn't you rather have me sitting on your lap this way than Mrs. Frayne?

STOREY   Don't get fresh, Monica. Besides, the query is totally irrelevant.

MONICA   It isn't at all. It's got everything to do with everything. I can't imagine Mrs. Frayne sitting on anybody's lap. She's too—dignified.

STOREY   No one requires you to imagine that, my dear.

MONICA (*Defiantly*)   I don't like Mrs. Frayne.

STOREY   She likes you.

MONICA   I don't believe it. I'm sure she says nasty things about me.

STOREY   She doesn't discuss you. She thinks you're very pretty but adolescent.

MONICA (*With a wicked smile*)   I may be young but my thoughts are mature.

STOREY (*Pretending to be shocked*)   Monica!

MONICA   No, I don't like Mrs. Frayne. She's a bad influence on you.

STOREY   Will you please stop chattering about Kendall and tell me about you and Austin?

MONICA   You hate to have me criticise her. I know it.

STOREY   I'm really very busy, Monica.

MONICA   Busy! Bless your heart, you never do a thing.

STOREY   I might if you'd marry Austin and save me worrying about you.

MONICA   (*Incredulously*)   Would you really let me marry him?

STOREY   Let you! My God! I pray for it.

MONICA   You'd go to church—and—watch it happen?

STOREY   Why not?

MONICA   And go home and rub your palms and say "That's that," I suppose.

STOREY   (*Touched*)   Oh, now, Monica! You know I'll always be awfully fond of you.

MONICA   *Fond*—!

STOREY   Mighty lucky for you I'm not in love with you.

MONICA   Oh, I wish you were. I'd be awfully happy if you were.

STOREY   We'd probably marry and that would be the end of us. The end of you at any rate.

MONICA   Why? We'd be a charming couple.

STOREY   (*Abruptly*)   Tell me about you and Austin.

MONICA   (*Cuddling to him*)   I will.

STOREY   Well?

MONICA   Don't hurry me, darling. I'm going to stay here a long time.

STOREY   Unfortunately—

MONICA   (*Putting her hand over his mouth*)   Unfortunately, nothing. I'm going to stay here and dine with you and then we'll have a long talk and after that—we'll take a walk—

STOREY   And after that?

MONICA   I'll come back with you if you like. Storey, if you ruin me will you make an honest woman of me?

STOREY   I won't marry you, Monica, no matter what you do.

MONICA   (*Sighing*)   Gee, Storey, you're hard to get.

STOREY   You *are* a sweet child. I'm not as indifferent to you as I pretend.

MONICA   Aren't you?

STOREY   Of course I'm not.

MONICA   Don't you want to kiss me? (*He does. She kisses him passionately*) Oh, Storey, I'm so unhappy. (*She buries her head on his shoulder, crying*)

STOREY (*Stroking her hair*)   Why, darling?

MONICA (*Muffled*)   Because nobody loves me.

STOREY   Austin loves you. He's crazy about you.

MONICA (*Getting up and stamping her foot*)   Oh, don't talk to me about Austin.

STOREY   Why shouldn't I?

MONICA   Because he bores me. He bores me to death. I never want to see him again.
    (*There is a pause*)

STOREY   Monica, I want to tell you something. Listen. (*He draws her to him again*) Listen. I intend to be honest about Austin. You get me, don't you? He's so helpless—that I don't intend to take advantage of him. Besides, he's a fine fellow. Awfully sincere. Awfully honest—

MONICA   He bores me. I don't like him.

STOREY   He's inarticulate, but he's a fine brain.

MONICA   But I love you, Storey.

STOREY   Now don't be a silly child. What sort of life do you suppose we should have together?

MONICA   Cosy.

STOREY   And what'll we live on?

MONICA   I'll work.

STOREY   At what?

MONICA   I'll typewrite.

STOREY   What?

MONICA   Your stories. I'll go in the movies! I have a friend who's a director.

STOREY   Your mother would be delighted!

MONICA   By the way—I've told Mother.

STOREY   You've told Mother what?

MONICA   That I can't marry Austin because I'm in love with you.

STOREY   You didn't—!

MONICA   Mother despises you, Storey.

STOREY (*Very angry*)   And you're fool enough to tell her—!

MONICA (*Misunderstanding*)   It doesn't matter to me that she doesn't like you. It just makes me love you all the more—

STOREY   That's not the point. How dare you—

MONICA   Oh, that's not all I told her.

STOREY   It's quite enough—

MONICA (*In one breath*)   I told her you loved me too, and that you'd asked me to marry you and that I'd said yes. I intend to make quite a campaign, you see.

STOREY   I've a good mind to spank you!

MONICA   I thought that if I told Mother you'd asked me that you would be—sort of compromised. You see, I'm trying to get it spread around—that we're engaged. (*He starts to speak*)

STOREY   Now look here, Monica.
   (*She puts her hand over his mouth to stifle his protest*)

MONICA   For once don't talk and listen to me. The fact is that I'm doing all this for your good.

STOREY   Thank you!

MONICA   For your good, Mr. Storey.

STOREY   Would you mind telling me—!

MONICA   Of course I'll tell you. You see I know, I'm just certain—that way down deep it's me you love—and not Mrs. Frayne or anybody else. Since you love me you ought to marry me.

STOREY   You've been reading again.

MONICA   You admit that the only reason you *don't* ask me is because you're poor and you think I want all sorts of frivolous things. It's just like you—you're so splendid and always thinking of other people—

STOREY (*In despair*) Good God!

MONICA But you misjudge me, Storey. Honestly you do. I could be awfully happy on just what you have.

STOREY Perhaps. But *I* couldn't.

MONICA You ought to marry a poor girl, Storey. It would stimulate you, make you work harder.

STOREY Are you quite through?

MONICA Not quite. I just got an idea. I think I'll phone an announcement of our engagement to the newspapers.

STOREY (*Really frightened*) You'll do no such thing.

MONICA (*Laughing joyously*) I've got you, Storey—I've got you at last.

STOREY Come here. Now, come here.

MONICA No way out of it for you, Storey. You're cooked.

STOREY Come here! (*Leading her to sofa*) Now sit down like a lamb and concentrate on what I'm going to tell you.

MONICA (*Demurely*) All right, teacher.

STOREY How old are you, Monica?

MONICA You know perfectly well. I'm twenty.

STOREY Now listen—this is serious. I'm thirty-one.

MONICA Nice age for a man.

STOREY Eleven years older than you. Just think, when I'm forty-one—that's middle-aged, you know, Monica—

MONICA I'll be thirty-one. Think how attractive I'll be.

STOREY Of course you will. And I'll be—bald and wrinkled and— Oh, I know that's been said before.

MONICA No, you won't. Your hair'll be just touched with grey. You'll look very distinguished.

STOREY I'm too old for you, Monica.

MONICA And yet you want me to marry Austin. He's as old as the hills.

STOREY He's two years younger than I am.

MONICA Well, he seems lots older. He's so correct—like an old deacon.

STOREY You talk outrageously when he's around.

MONICA   I love to shock him. He's such a Puritan!

STOREY   You've got to stop reproaching me, before him, for not having an affair with you. It gets on my nerves.

MONICA   I believe I shock you, too, Storey.

STOREY   Not in the least. But I hate to see the poor fellow suffer.

MONICA   Austin's so literal. Absolutely no glimmering of humour. Oh! This will make you laugh—wait till I show you! (*She runs back to get her bag, dredges in it*)

STOREY   Nobody in love has a sense of humour!

MONICA   (*Holding up magazine*)   Look what he sent me—

STOREY   (*Taking the austerely covered pamphlet*)   Proceedings of the American Chemical Society—

MONICA   With an article by Austin in it—look—here—

STOREY   (*Reading*)   "A new method of separating atoms and ions which are chemically similar but have different weights by diffusion—including the separation of radium from the barium residues." Tells you what to expect, doesn't it?

MONICA   Now whatever do you think Austin—!

STOREY   (*Intent on the article*)   This is very touching, Monica.

MONICA   I know, but—why, it's nearly all figures—it would take an expert to—
    (*He hasn't removed his eyes from the article; she stands looking at it with him*)

STOREY   Has a brilliant climax, this thing.

MONICA   Climax! Where?

STOREY   There. It's an *equation*—can't you see!

MONICA   O, Storey, come now! I don't believe you have the faintest idea what it's all about.

STOREY   Of course I haven't. I've had a shallow literary education. But I *can* see this—that in this chaos here in the first part of his article—you see—in this abracadabra—this forest of figures—Austin had scented somewhere, an equation lurking. And he's found it, damn him, dredged it out of the morass, lifted it into clear light—and there it is!

MONICA   Oh, Storey!

STOREY I'm perfectly serious, Monica. And I think it was very sweet of him to send you this—if you had any imagination you'd see—it's a tender, a beautiful gesture—this (*Tapping paper*) this is *his lyric,* Monica.

MONICA I prefer lyrics that rhyme.

STOREY An equation is a rhyme—a perfect rhyme, subtler and harder to find than any you'll see in *my* effusions— (*Flinging the thing away*) How do you know what hope for the future is hidden in this little prose-poem?

MONICA You're so generous about others, Storey. I love you for it!

STOREY Don't be too sure of my motive. Perhaps it's because I want to get conveniently rid of *you!*
   (MONICA *presents herself before him, shaking her head stubbornly, her hands crossed behind her back*)

MONICA It's no good, Storey! You might as well give up!

STOREY Now please be serious, Monica. Austin'll make you a wonderful husband. You're lovely and his money will provide you with the exquisite background your beauty requires. . . . And he's *good!*

MONICA (*Sitting on sofa, piteously*) I just can't do it, Storey. Please don't ask me to.

STOREY He won't bother you. Spends ages in his laboratory, you know.

MONICA I'm sure he doesn't sleep in the laboratory.

STOREY Oh, now, Monica. Really, you're impossible.

MONICA Am I so terrible, Storey? Don't *you* love me at all?

STOREY I'm frightfully fond of you—crazy about you.

MONICA Then why do you keep me in suspense like this?

STOREY Monica, you're so young. I know so much more about life than you do. I know what would happen—I know this feeling you have for me now—won't last.

MONICA But I swear—I'll never love anybody else. If you don't marry me—I'll go into a convent. I swear.

STOREY I'm going to marry Mrs. Frayne—if she'll have me.

MONICA (*Passionately*)   Just because she's rich! You know you wouldn't think of marrying her if she weren't—the trouble with you is—you're damned selfish.

STOREY   Of course I am.

MONICA   Just admitting it doesn't do any good. You like to go around and be petted by people. And your silly little comforts. You see, I know, deep down, you're fonder of me than of anyone. Just as I know that I'm fonder of you than I ever shall be of anyone— (*He makes a sudden move toward her; is irresistibly attracted, stops*) Obey that impulse.

STOREY   It's ridiculous. Impossible. Ridiculous.

MONICA   Why not?

STOREY   You're a silly child. You don't know anything about anything. You don't know what you want, really.

MONICA   Yes, I do know.

STOREY (*Disturbed*)   I warn you, Monica—if you keep this up I *will* marry you.

MONICA   You won't be sorry if you do, Storey. I swear it's for you as much as for myself. I want to save you.

STOREY   Save me?

MONICA   I want you to live up to the best that's in you.

STOREY   My God, Monica, I believe you have the makings of a good woman.

MONICA   You ought to marry me for the sake of your art. If you marry Mrs. Frayne you'll be so comfortable you won't write a thing.

STOREY   I am thirty-one and in full possession of my senses. It would be positively immoral for me to marry you.

MONICA   But it would be more moral than anything else you could do to me.

STOREY (*Looking at her with perplexity. The doorbell rings*) Thank God! Austin. (*He jumps up*)

MONICA (*Terrified*)   Austin!

STOREY   Well, I think it's Austin. (*The bell rings again*)

MONICA   Don't answer. He'll go away.

STOREY   I couldn't do that.

MONICA   Did you know he was coming?

STOREY   I wasn't sure.

MONICA   Promise you'll get rid of him—promise.

STOREY   I'll do what I can— (*Bell rings*) Why doesn't he come in? The door's open.
(*He goes out.* MONICA *walks about petulantly. She flings a pillow violently into a corner.* AUSTIN *comes in followed by* STOREY)

MONICA   Hello, Anti Genesis.

STOREY   Anti what?

MONICA   Don't you know my little pet-name for Austin? Anti Genesis.

STOREY   How come? Eh?

AUSTIN   Monica actually believed the world began in the Garden of Eden.

MONICA (*Slyly*)   Austin disillusioned me about the Book of Genesis.

AUSTIN (*Seriously*)   She'd never heard of the nebular theory.

STOREY   Monica!—Oh, well, you mustn't mind her, Austin. It's the fashion nowadays to be flippant. Monica gets it from me. The difference is—my flippancy is a sort of defence. Monica's is a boast. The nice thing though about Monica is she doesn't know anything. Gives one a pleasant sense of omniscience— (*The phone rings.* STOREY *answers it*) Yes— oh, hello—waiting for me?—why, our engagement was for Tuesday, wasn't it?—Dear me, is *this* Tuesday?—How awfully stupid of me—the truth is I've been so lost in my work —yes, I can make it easily by seven—I'll be right over— Good-bye. (*He hangs up*) Certainly lucky you dropped in, Austin.

MONICA (*Sensing something*)   What's happened now?

STOREY   The fact is, my dear, I can't dine with you after all.

MONICA (*Furious*)   Oh, can't you?

STOREY   I had no idea it was Tuesday. I thought it was Monday.

MONICA   Of course when one works as hard as you do one is apt to forget the day of the week!

STOREY (*To* AUSTIN) I've ordered dinner for two. Would you mind dining with Monica instead of me?

AUSTIN (*Overjoyed*) Right here?

STOREY I've ordered a delicious dinner from downstairs.

AUSTIN I'd love to. That is, if Monica—

MONICA (*Mechanically*) Of course.

STOREY I've really got to dash. Austin, mind lending me a dollar for taxi fare? Don't believe I've got a cent with me.

AUSTIN Of course. (*He takes out a bill and hands it to* STOREY)

STOREY One thing about Austin. He's not one of those millionaires who never has any money with him.

AUSTIN Can give you more. Here's a twenty.

STOREY Well, perhaps I'd better. (*Takes it*) So long, children. (*To* AUSTIN) You'll find everything ready for a cocktail in the kitchenette.

MONICA Are you coming back?

STOREY Might. I'll phone you.

AUSTIN I'm not very good at mixing cocktails.

STOREY And you a chemist—!

MONICA This is a dirty trick, Storey.

STOREY (*To* AUSTIN) You'll find a recipe in the kitchenette.

AUSTIN Will I? You'll have to help me, Monica. (*He goes past* STOREY *into hallway*)

MONICA (*White with anger*) You're dining with Mrs. Frayne.

STOREY Yes. In five years you'll thank me. In less—

MONICA All right for you, Storey—

STOREY Good-bye, darling. Be nice to him.
(*He goes out. He can be heard saying* "So long, Austin," *as he exits.* MONICA *moves down-stage;* AUSTIN *reappears with a cocktail shaker*)

AUSTIN It doesn't say how much absinthe or how much vermouth— (MONICA *says nothing. Her face is set in misery.*

AUSTIN *comes down a little. He stands awkwardly holding the cocktail mixer by the neck. Wistfully*) I don't know —do you put absinthe or do you put vermouth—? (*She turns away impatiently. The curtain falls*)

CURTAIN

ACT TWO | Scene One

SCENE: *The same.*

TIME: *8:30. Two hours after the fall of the first act curtain.*

AT RISE: AUSTIN *and* MONICA *are discovered at the gate-legged table, finishing dinner.* MONICA *dallies with a dessert.* AUSTIN *watches her, wondering what to say.*

AUSTIN (*Finally*)   Will you have some more coffee?

MONICA   No, thanks.
(*There is another pause*)

AUSTIN (*Mournfully*)   It's—it's jolly to be sitting here and eating like this.

MONICA (*Mechanically*)   Isn't it?

AUSTIN   It is for me, anyway. (*As she says nothing*) I suppose you're—bored.

MONICA   Why, I'm not.

AUSTIN   I wish I knew how to amuse you, Monica.

MONICA   You're a dear, Austin. You're far too nice for me.

AUSTIN   Too nice for *you*. . . .

MONICA   You are, really. You're a great man. And awfully modest and nice. I'm just a restless little nobody who doesn't know what she wants.

AUSTIN   You're fairly certain about what you don't want—

MONICA   I'm afraid I know what I want too, Austin.

AUSTIN   I wish I were fluent, like Storey. I wish I could talk, like Storey.

MONICA   What would you say?

AUSTIN   I'd tell you I love you.

MONICA   But you've told me that. And I've told you that I don't admire your choice.

AUSTIN   I know.
(*There is a pause*)

MONICA   There's no reason why we can't be friends.

AUSTIN   That's like telling a starving man—there's no reason he can't look at the food in a baker's window.

MONICA   Why, Austin, you're brilliant tonight.

AUSTIN   (*Emboldened by his success*)   I feel that if I could find the words— Somewhere there must be the words that would say what I feel for you. And once you knew what I feel, I feel you would love me.

MONICA   (*Half-listening*)   I wonder—

AUSTIN   Yes. I feel that. What I say to you is banal, trite. I have no gift of speech. I know it. I—I'm dumb.

MONICA   (*Touched, patting his hand*)   You *are* a dear, Austin. I'm very fond of you.

AUSTIN   Last night you said—you never wanted to see me again.

MONICA   (*Rising, walking about the room*)   Last night? I was tired, upset—

AUSTIN   You said—

MONICA   Please, Austin, don't talk to me any more about last night.

AUSTIN   (*Meekly*)   All right, Monica. (*One of those pauses*) Would you—would you like to go to a theatre?

MONICA   No. Thank you.

AUSTIN   Storey says Gertrude Lawrence—

MONICA   I've seen her.

AUSTIN   We could go to the opera. My mother has a box—

MONICA   Not tonight, Austin, thanks. Storey said he'd telephone, didn't he?

AUSTIN   Did he?

MONICA   I think he did. (*A pause.* MONICA *lights a cigarette. Walks about restlessly*)

AUSTIN I believe Storey's dining with Mrs. Frayne.

MONICA Is he?

AUSTIN Yes.

MONICA Austin?

AUSTIN Yes?

MONICA Do you like Mrs. Frayne?

AUSTIN Yes. I think she's a lovely woman. Don't you?

MONICA She probably was.

AUSTIN I wonder—will Storey marry her?

MONICA I've no idea.

AUSTIN I think she's in love with him.

MONICA Why not?

AUSTIN I think it would be a good match. Don't you?

MONICA How can I tell?

AUSTIN Storey sees her every day.

MONICA Can't we really find anyone to talk about except Storey?

AUSTIN Well, you're so keen about him.

MONICA What makes you think that?

AUSTIN Aren't you?

MONICA I despise him.

AUSTIN But last night—

MONICA Last night doesn't matter. Today does.

AUSTIN (*Very happy*) Then you—!

MONICA I despise him. (*She slumps into the chair near the tabouret where* STOREY *has put the check* KENDALL *has given him*)

AUSTIN Then perhaps— (*He moves toward her uncertainly, pauses, does not know what to say. She is lost in a dream, does not hear him*) Then perhaps—

MONICA Perhaps what?

AUSTIN If there's no one else—I mean if you're not in love with Storey—or anyone else—perhaps—

MONICA (*Almost in tears*)   Please, Austin—be a darling and don't—don't make love to me.

AUSTIN   I can't help it. Isn't it awful? I can't make love to you—and I don't know what else to talk about.

MONICA   Talk to me—talk to me about evolution.

AUSTIN   But you said you preferred the Garden of Eden.

MONICA   To—primeval chaos. Yes. Don't you? Isn't a nice garden full of wild flowers better than a lot of—slime?

AUSTIN (*Distressed*)   But the Bible isn't true.

MONICA   What of it? Adam and Eve were such a *nice* couple.

AUSTIN   I can't see the use in talking about anything—that isn't true.

MONICA (*With a sigh*)   That shuts out so many subjects.

AUSTIN (*Hesitating*)   Did you—did you get the—my—the article I sent you?

MONICA   Oh, yes, thanks! How awfully clever you are!

AUSTIN (*Greatly flustered, blushing*)   Oh—it was just—that's what I've been working on a good deal lately—a new method of separating radium—

MONICA (*Gently*)   Of course I don't pretend to have understood it—

AUSTIN   That's the trouble—unless you know the vocabulary of science it doesn't mean much—like giving the score of a symphony to a person who can't read it.

MONICA   I know. I'm terribly ignorant, Austin.

AUSTIN   You think what I do is awfully dull, don't you? If you'd come with me sometimes to the laboratory—I'd like to show you—it's really awfully interesting—it's exciting.

MONICA   Oh, for you!

AUSTIN   No, for anybody—Monica, I wish you'd let me read you something—

MONICA   From your article?

AUSTIN   No. From a book I've brought you.

MONICA   Oh! Thank you, Austin. What's the book?

AUSTIN (*Producing it*)   It's by Bertrand Russell—

MONICA (*A bit let down*)   Oh!

AUSTIN   You know who he is, don't you?

MONICA (*Doubtfully*)   Well, I've heard of him.

AUSTIN   Well, he's just one of the greatest men alive, that's all.

MONICA (*Touched by his eagerness; she pats his arm*)   Is he, Austin?

AUSTIN   I came across this passage the other day—I marked it—I thought—the minute I read it—"I *must* get this for Monica!"

MONICA (*Peering over at book*)   "Mysticism and Logic." What a nice title! Ordinarily you'd never think of putting those two together, would you? (*But her thoughts wander off to* STOREY)

AUSTIN   They're a lot of essays—this one's about mathematics. (*Reading*) "Mathematics, rightly viewed, possesses not only truth but supreme beauty—a beauty cold and austere, like that of sculpture, without appeal to any part of our weaker nature, without the gorgeous trappings of painting or music, yet sublimely pure, and capable of a stern perfection such as only the greatest art can show. The true spirit of delight, the exultation, the sense of being more than man, which is the touchstone of the highest excellence is to be found in mathematics as surely as in poetry." (*The cadence of* AUSTIN'S *voice, his profound sincerity and the beauty of the passage itself affect* MONICA—*as a bit of sad music might. She is quite rapt. But* AUSTIN *feels suddenly unsure*) Interesting, isn't it?

MONICA   Oh, yes! Do go on!

AUSTIN   "Remote from human passions, remote even from the pitiful facts of nature, the generations have gradually created an ordered cosmos, where pure thought can dwell as in its natural home, and where one, at least, of our nobler impulses can escape from the dreary exile of the actual world." (*He stops a moment to look at her and finds her eyes full of tears*)

AUSTIN   Monica! You're crying!

MONICA   I wish *I* could do that!

AUSTIN   What?

MONICA   Escape from the dreary exile of the actual world.

AUSTIN   Aren't you happy, Monica?

MONICA   Not very. Why don't you marry somebody else, somebody worthy of you?

AUSTIN   Whom?

MONICA   That awfully clever girl. You know, that girl I met you with. You told me she was a research chemist. What's a research chemist?

AUSTIN   A person who engages in chemical research.

MONICA   Oh!—Well, why don't you marry *her,* Austin? She seemed awfully nice.

AUSTIN   She *is* nice.

MONICA   And I suppose she adores you.

AUSTIN   Yes. She does like me.

MONICA   There you are!

AUSTIN   (*Shaking his head*)   No.

MONICA   Why not?

AUSTIN   For one thing—she knows too much for me.

MONICA   Ho! Vain!

AUSTIN   She wears woollen stockings.

MONICA   Ah, Austin, *you are* a funny man. (*Looking at him closely*) I believe you're quite serious. You've no sense of humour, Austin. Sometimes—it's delicious.

AUSTIN   I prefer you, Monica.

MONICA   For a man who lives by his brain—you're awfully illogical, Austin.

AUSTIN   I know I am. I've tried to reason you—out of my—consciousness. I can't do it.

MONICA   Well, I'm as stupid as you are. Stupider.

AUSTIN   Why?

MONICA   For—loving him.

AUSTIN   Loving whom?

MONICA   Storey.

AUSTIN   Storey!

MONICA   Of course. Who else?

AUSTIN   (*Altogether bewildered*)   But—but you just said—you despised him.

MONICA   (*Helplessly*)   Oh, Austin— (*She covers her face with her hands*)

AUSTIN   I don't understand you at all, Monica.

MONICA   You really shouldn't try, Austin— (*She gets up, her dress catches in the tabouret, overturning it. He rights it, picking up the check and papers*)

AUSTIN   (*Picking up the things*)   How careless Storey is—leaving a check lying around like this.

MONICA   A check? Didn't know he had a check.

AUSTIN   Five hundred dollars for a story.

MONICA   Five hundred! Why, he didn't tell me. Let me see it. (*She takes check, looks at it and sees* MRS. FRAYNE'S *signature. Her fingers clutch over it. Casually*)   How do you know he got it for a story?

AUSTIN   He told me. I asked him whether he needed money.

MONICA   He did, of course!

AUSTIN   He said he didn't—because he'd just had this check.

MONICA   (*Bitterly, crumpling the check*)   The highest bidder!

AUSTIN   (*Alarmed*)   Here, what are you doing—?

MONICA   I'm sorry.
     (*She returns check to him, he straightens it, refolds it neatly. Can't help seeing the name, looks at* MONICA, *whose eyes do not meet his. Puts check back*)

AUSTIN   Well—why not?

MONICA   I think it's—beastly.

AUSTIN   As they'll probably marry soon—I don't see any harm in it.

MONICA   (*Passionately*)   They shan't marry!

AUSTIN   Monica—do you want to marry Storey yourself?

MONICA   Storey's in love with me.

AUSTIN   He isn't. He told me so.

MONICA   When?

AUSTIN   Just before you came.

MONICA   He lied.

AUSTIN   Why should he lie? I asked him to tell me the truth.

MONICA   He did lie. You wait. You'll see.

AUSTIN   He wouldn't take money from Mrs. Frayne—like this—if—

MONICA   You're naïve, Austin.

AUSTIN   I don't understand. I don't understand Storey. Why he should lie—

MONICA   She's trying to buy him.

AUSTIN   (*A little bitterly*)   He seems willing to sell.

MONICA   He has no character. Not an ounce. No backbone—

AUSTIN   And yet—you want him.

MONICA   Yes. Worse luck—

AUSTIN   I wish I'd never met you, Monica.

MONICA   (*Snapping up the check again*)   Money! Money, Austin! (*Abruptly*) I'm through with him.

AUSTIN   I should think you'd have more—pride.

MONICA   I'm off him for life. I swear it, Austin. Try me. Test me.

AUSTIN   How do you mean?

MONICA   Make love to me. Do something. You'll see.

AUSTIN   You know, Monica, I—I'm crazy about you. I don't have to tell you—

MONICA   Propose to me.

AUSTIN   You know how I feel.

MONICA   Are your intentions honourable?

AUSTIN   What do you mean?

MONICA   You still want to marry me, don't you?

AUSTIN   Of course. What else?

MONICA   I accept.

AUSTIN   Monica! Really?

MONICA   Yes.

AUSTIN   You'll—marry me?

MONICA (*Suddenly colourless*)   If you like, Austin.

AUSTIN (*Overjoyed, advancing toward her*)   Monica! Can I —can't I—?

MONICA (*Drawing away*)   No, Austin—!

AUSTIN   I mean—can I tell everybody?

MONICA   Oh! Of course. Why not?

AUSTIN   I'll try to make you happy, Monica.

MONICA (*With an impulse to cry*)   Thanks, Austin.
 (*The doorbell rings*)

AUSTIN   I wonder who that is.

MONICA   Must be Storey.

AUSTIN   And Mrs. Frayne.
 (*There is a knock on the inside door*)

STOREY (*Off*)   It's only me. (*He comes in*) Thought I'd warn you.

AUSTIN   Hello, Storey!

STOREY   Hello, Archimedes. Well, Miss Grey— (MONICA *turns her back on him and walks up-stage*) Nice dinner?

AUSTIN   Fine.

STOREY   Kendall and I dined at the Colony. (*Looking from one to the other*) What are you depressed about? Eh?

AUSTIN   We're not depressed. That is—I'm not.

STOREY   Well, you act like it. What's the matter, Monica?

AUSTIN (*As* MONICA *turns away*)   Monica's just accepted me.

STOREY   Really? No—really?

AUSTIN (*Doubtfully*)   That's what she said.

STOREY   Splendid. I congratulate you, Austin. I congratulate you both. Austin—mind if I kiss the bride? (*He turns to kiss her*)

MONICA (*Fiercely*)   Don't come near me!

STOREY   What's the matter?—Austin—

AUSTIN   She's a little upset—who wouldn't be?

STOREY   Well!

AUSTIN   Where's Mrs. Frayne?

STOREY   Gone home to dress. Too bad Monica's in such a singular mood. Kendall wants us to go on a party.

MONICA   I want to go home. Austin, take me home.

STOREY   Oh, come now, Monica, be a sport. Now you're finally engaged to Austin—that's all the more reason to celebrate. You both run along and dress and we'll all meet here at eleven o'clock. Go to that new coloured cabaret in Harlem. Kendall's sending champagne—

MONICA   I don't want her champagne.

STOREY   Because you haven't tasted it. I had some at dinner. Marvellous.

MONICA   I tell you I don't want to go.

STOREY   Austin, exert your new-found authority. Make her behave.

AUSTIN   If she wants to go home—

STOREY   That's a bad way to start, Austin. If you begin by giving her her own way she'll bully you all your life.

MONICA (*Bitterly*)   Yes, Austin, listen to him. Do what *he* tells you. The authority! The philosopher. Knows everything. Tells everybody what to do, how to behave—

STOREY   Of course. My own behaviour is so bad I can point the path of righteousness to other people. The drunkard lecturing on temperance—

(*There is a pause.* AUSTIN'S *conquest has not made him happy.* MONICA *stands still, undecided, trembling with anger.* STOREY *alone remains imperturbable. He rather enjoys the situation*)

AUSTIN   Guess we'll go home—

STOREY   The truth is, children, I'm a little tight. Ever get drunk, Austin?

AUSTIN   Once. Long time ago.

STOREY   Remember how it felt?

AUSTIN   Like *mal de mer*.

STOREY   Must have been bad stuff. Wait till you taste Kendall's champagne. It gives you ultimate sight, ultimate comprehension—

AUSTIN   And a head in the morning.

STOREY   But isn't it worth it? Wonderful illusions of grandeur—

AUSTIN   What's the good of illusions?

STOREY   Make reality bearable.

MONICA (*Suddenly*)   I think they make it more difficult.

AUSTIN   Well, Monica—

MONICA (*To* STOREY)   Pay our respects to Mrs. Frayne. Tell her we're grateful for her invitation but that we can't take advantage of her hospitality tonight.

STOREY   For pity's sake, Monica, stop talking like an etiquette-book.

AUSTIN   Monica's right. It *would* be better—

STOREY   Oh, come now. Have a heart, both of you.

MONICA   I don't see why you want *us* when you have Mrs. Frayne.

STOREY   Of course I want you. I feel gay tonight!

MONICA   Be gay with Mrs. Frayne!

STOREY   Be nice, now, Monica. I've a peculiar feeling about tonight—that it's a sort of valedictory, a sort of farewell. . . . After tonight, things won't be the same, life won't be the same.

AUSTIN (*Gloomily*)   I hope not.

STOREY   You know what I mean—you and Monica'll get married . . . and, I hope, Kendall and I. We'll be stolid, married people. We'll get old. We'll change. We'll drift apart —am I getting sentimental? Well, why not? Be nice, Monica, for once—

MONICA (*Defiantly*)   All right!

STOREY   You're a dear.

AUSTIN (*Worried*)   If you're tired, Monica—

MONICA   No, I've decided. I'm in great spirits now, Storey. All excited. Come on, Austin. (*She runs out*)

AUSTIN (*Shaking his head*)   I don't understand her.

STOREY   If you did—you'd disown her. . . . Come back soon. I'll be lonely.

(AUSTIN *goes out. In a moment* MONICA *thrusts her head inside the door and speaks in a loud whisper*)

MONICA   I'll be right back.

STOREY   Don't you dare. (*She makes a face at him and disappears. After a moment he goes to window in the left wall to watch for their departure. He feels a sense of loss for* MONICA. *Is worried by this mood. Goes to the telephone*) Regent 2772—please—yes—hello—Mrs. Frayne please—Mr. Storey—hello, Kendall?—what're you doing?—nearly finished?—I want you to come sooner, I'm lonely—want to see you—am I?—unusually what?—oh, ardent—I don't know—feel funny tonight—in the grip of a peculiar emotion —I don't know—when you come I'll describe it to you—by the way, Monica and Austin Lowe're engaged—they've just left—yes, I want consolation— (*The doorbell rings*) Excuse me—what did you say? (*The doorbell rings again*) There's someone at the door—I've no idea—do come as soon as you can, will you, Ken?—And don't forget the champagne. 'Bye, dear. (*He hangs up, rushes to door, disappears, returns, following* MONICA) What did you do this for? (*It is obvious that* STOREY *is a little frightened; he is very fond of her just now*)

MONICA   I persuaded Austin—as he lives uptown and I live down—to let me go home alone.

STOREY   You're crazy.

MONICA   I wanted to see you alone—to warn you—

STOREY   Suppose Austin saw you.

MONICA   It can't be helped.

STOREY   But it's cruel. You just told him you'd marry him.

MONICA   I had a moment of hating you, of utterly despising you.

STOREY   Go right away. I warn *you*.

MONICA   I saw that check.

STOREY   What check?

MONICA   Mrs. Frayne's for five hundred dollars. Is that your monthly stipend? Or is it weekly?

STOREY   Monica, go away. I've got to dress.

MONICA (*Aware of her hold on him*)   What's the matter, Storey? (*She stands very close to him*) What's the matter?

STOREY (*Seizing her in his arms*) Little darling . . . (*He kisses her passionately*)

MONICA   You do love me, don't you, Storey? It's me you love.

STOREY   This isn't very nice, Monica. It's not at all nice.

MONICA   But, Storey, there's no reason in the world why we shouldn't. We're neither of us married or anything—

STOREY   Austin!

MONICA   Oh, Austin!

STOREY   Kendall.

MONICA   Oh, Kendall!

STOREY   I feel funny about Austin. He's—so—helpless. He's so—in love with you.

MONICA   What about me?

STOREY   When you came in just now and told me you were engaged I felt a quick pain.

MONICA (*Delighted*) Did you?

STOREY   I felt suddenly as if nothing could ever make you up to me.

MONICA   You didn't look it. You seemed to take it—quite casually.

STOREY   I'm glad you came back. I want to tell you now. I *do* love you. . . .

MONICA   Tell me. . . .

STOREY   You're rare and exquisite, precious.

MONICA   You're always laughing at me.

STOREY   I know.

MONICA   Make love to me, Storey.

STOREY   I never really forget you. You're never out of my mind. Your gaiety, your sadness, your lovely youth. Your dear laughter—when you laugh it's like the beginning of the world, before sorrow and death came—

MONICA   Darling.

STOREY   I am old, dearest one.

MONICA   Old! You're not.

STOREY   I am. There's someone else inside me—a second man—a cynical, odious person, who keeps watching me, who keeps listening to what I say, grinning and sophisticated, horrid. . . . He never lets me be—this other man. . . .

MONICA   Kill him.

STOREY   I can't kill him. He'll outlive me.

MONICA (*Nestling to him*)   I'll kill him for you.

STOREY   You can't. Even now he's looking at me. He's mocking me. He's saying: "You damn fool, talking nonsense to this girl—pretending you want her above everything. You're making love to her because words come easily to you. But really you wouldn't get up early in the morning for her. You like to touch her because she's young and firm and lovely. . . ."

MONICA   Don't, Storey.

STOREY   "You wouldn't mind having her but after that—"

MONICA   Storey, listen, darling. I know you're fine and decent.

STOREY   He hears you say: "I'm fine and decent." And he says: "The illusion of an adolescent, of a love-struck girl. . . ."

MONICA   I'll beat him, Storey—I'll beat him.

STOREY   I wish you could, honey.

MONICA   I just needed to know that you love me—tell me it again. Let me hear you say it again.

STOREY   I love you.

MONICA   The way you said it before.

STOREY   I'm afraid I can't now.

MONICA   Storey. . . .

STOREY   You see how capricious I am.

MONICA   But you just said it. And when you did I knew it was true.

STOREY   It probably was—then.

MONICA   A minute ago!

STOREY (*Lightly*)   A minute, a year, a century—what's the difference?

MONICA   But, Storey, I must believe in your love for me.
I *must!*

STOREY   Why?

MONICA   Because I've got to believe in something. And if
you don't love me—what is there?

STOREY   My dear child. You—*baby!*

MONICA   Don't turn me down, Storey. (*There is a pause.
STOREY considers*)

STOREY   I want you to go away—and marry Austin—and
don't come back to see me alone again—ever.

MONICA   I won't. I tell you I won't.

STOREY   But don't you understand? I'm crazy about you.
Do you think I'm made of wood?

MONICA   Why don't you take me, Storey? (*A pause, he is
nonplussed*)

STOREY   My God, child. . . .

MONICA   I'd rather you married me but if you don't want to
—well—

STOREY   Won't you allow me one shred of decency? I want
to be loyal to Austin. I want to protect you—

MONICA   I don't want to be protected. Besides, it's all a pose.
You want to marry Kendall Frayne so you can have lots of
money.

STOREY   What's the use?

MONICA   It's true. You talk about decency. With that check
lying there. . . . You ought to be ashamed, Storey.

STOREY   I'm not in the least ashamed. . . .

MONICA   You're just one of those men who goes around
eating fine dinners and having a good time—a parasite,
Storey.

STOREY   That's what everybody's trying to be in one way or
another. Mine's as good as any.

MONICA   Instead of escaping from all this life and—and
fighting your own battles with me by your side to help you.

STOREY (*Accompanying himself on the piano*)   Sounds like
a popular song. (*Hums*) "With me by your side to help
you—"

MONICA   For pity's sake, Storey, how did you get this way? You couldn't have been always like this!

STOREY   Oh, no. I went through the idealistic stage. I used to sit in a garret and believe in Socialism. I used to commit realistic fiction and moonlit poetry. I dreamed—

MONICA   I want to bring back those dreams.

STOREY   Why? What for?

MONICA   You must have been lovely then, Storey. . . .

STOREY   Oh, I was! Lovely!

MONICA (*Hurt*)   Storey!

STOREY   Lovely. I dressed badly and followed the Cults. It didn't take me long to find out how easy it is to starve on Idealism. I had facility and there was a ready market for facility. I got five thousand dollars for writing a white-washed biography of a millionaire sweatshop owner. That started me. . . . I took the money and went to Italy—and I had a *very good* time.

MONICA   But, Storey—you *must* believe in *something*—don't you ever regret—don't you ever wish—?

STOREY   Regret? No. Not in the least. Why should I? I'd do it all over again.

MONICA   I can see that horrid second man in your eyes now laughing. . . .

STOREY (*Rather gently*)   You amuse him.

MONICA   You wait! I'm going to beat him—in spite of you.

STOREY (*Swayed for a moment, by the possibility*)   He's got a terrific start on you, Monica.

MONICA (*Very confident now*)   Trust me. Leave him to me. . . . (*Whispering*)   We'll be happy yet, sweetheart!

STOREY (*Taking her in his arms*)   God knows I've done my best . . . ! (*Their embrace lasts several seconds. The door-bell rings.* STOREY, *a bit grimly*)   Lucky for you, young lady—

MONICA   Don't go.

STOREY   Got to. Run home and dress—go upstairs and out through my bedroom.

MONICA (*To stairs*)   All right. But I'm not worried about Kendall now. I'm not worried about anything—

(*The doorbell rings insistently. She runs upstairs and disappears.* STOREY *exits to open the door. For a moment the stage is deserted*)

STOREY (*Off*) Oh, from Mrs. Frayne? Thank you! (*He returns, carrying a hamper of champagne. He puts it on the table. Lifts the cloth covering the bottles. There is a note addressed to him. He takes it out of the envelope. Reads*) For a good time for all . . .

(*For a moment this symbol of* KENDALL'S *generosity makes him hate himself. . . . The curtain slowly falls*)

CURTAIN

ACT TWO | Scene Two

SCENE: *A lapse of two hours. It is now eleven o'clock.*

AT RISE: MRS. FRAYNE *is discovered at the piano. She is play-*
ing the waltz from Strauss' "Rosenkavalier." After a mo-
ment she stops and then plays a few bars of a popular
sentimental song from music on the piano. The doorbell
rings. She rises and goes to open the door. A splendid
figure, "majestic" but graceful. She wears a black velvet
evening dress cut very low. Fine arms, columnar throat,
rather like Sargent's portrait of "Madame X." KENDALL
goes out into the hallway and returns in a moment fol-
lowed by AUSTIN. *He is in evening-dress. His manner with*
KENDALL *at first is embarrassed and hesitant. Gradually,*
however, she puts him at ease; she has that sort of manner.

KENDALL   Storey's dressing. I'm the first one here.

AUSTIN   Monica's not come yet?

KENDALL   No. Cigarette?

AUSTIN   Er—thanks. (*She lights it for him*) Thanks.

KENDALL   You and I are the only prompt ones.

AUSTIN   Yes. . . .

KENDALL   Do you know what time it is?

AUSTIN (*Looking*)   Ten minutes past eleven.

KENDALL   I was here promptly at eleven. Storey hadn't even
begun to dress.

AUSTIN   He hadn't!

KENDALL   I'm awfully glad you came. It was lonesome. (*She
smiles at him*)

52

AUSTIN I—I'm glad I found *you*.

KENDALL Why do I never see you?

AUSTIN Er—see me?

KENDALL Storey talks about you all the time. You're one of the few people he respects. I always ask him to bring you to my house but you never come.

AUSTIN I'm in the laboratory such a lot.

KENDALL I know. Still I do wish you'd come some time—and bring Miss Grey. . . . (*She notices him staring at* MONICA'S *coloured scarf which is lying across a chair*) What is it?

AUSTIN That scarf.

KENDALL You know it?

AUSTIN It's—it's Monica's.

KENDALL You dined here with her—didn't you?

AUSTIN Yes. I did.

KENDALL Well, then—

AUSTIN She wore it when I left with her.

KENDALL Didn't you take her home?

AUSTIN She told me to go home alone—to save time.

KENDALL Well, she probably ran back to tell Storey something.

AUSTIN (*Bitterly*) She probably did. It must have taken a long time because—when you came, Storey hadn't even begun to dress.

KENDALL (*After a moment*) I think you can trust Storey.

AUSTIN Can I?

KENDALL He told me over the phone—you and Miss Grey are engaged.

AUSTIN There's something funny about it.

KENDALL There's something funny about most things.

AUSTIN (*Warming to her*) Mrs. Frayne—

KENDALL Call me Kendall.

AUSTIN Thank you. I wonder—I wonder if Storey tells me everything. I mean—about Monica and himself.

KENDALL Perhaps he doesn't know everything.

AUSTIN You mean—perhaps he's in love with her and doesn't know it?

KENDALL Doesn't know it or won't admit it—even to himself. Perhaps.

(*There is a pause*)

AUSTIN (*Abruptly*) Are you going to marry Storey?

KENDALL I don't know.

AUSTIN (*Naïvely*) I wish you would.

KENDALL It would solve your problem, wouldn't it? It might complicate mine.

AUSTIN I'm not even sure it would solve mine. I wish I hadn't got into this.

KENDALL (*She stops playing*) It's comforting to know that even a scientific genius is not immune. It rather justifies a weak woman—like me.

AUSTIN It's rotten to be this way. Wondering about everything, suspecting everybody. Why should I care if Monica came back here or not? And yet—I do.

KENDALL (*Slowly*) I care too, Austin. Isn't it—stupid?

AUSTIN Do you think Monica's in love with Storey?

KENDALL You want me to tell you she isn't, don't you?

AUSTIN Sometimes she tells me she loathes him. . . .

KENDALL That's bad.

AUSTIN Do you think so?

KENDALL Wouldn't it be nice if people were like molecules or electrons or whatever you work with? It would be nice for you because you understand all about those things.

AUSTIN Molecules are mysterious but they're more predictable than Monica. They obey some sort of law.

KENDALL (*Amused and touched by his sincerity*) I think you're charming, Austin.

AUSTIN Don't say that. I know better.

KENDALL But you are!

AUSTIN I'm dull and thick-witted and I—I have no words. I can't talk.

KENDALL I think you do very well.

AUSTIN (*Emboldened*) Well, that's because it's you.

KENDALL (*She is still at piano. She plays "A Night in Granada" by Debussy*) I?

AUSTIN I find it easy to talk to you. Why is it?

KENDALL Perhaps it's because—we're sympathetic.

AUSTIN I feel I know where I am with you. With Monica I never know.

KENDALL But you don't want to be anywhere with me. With me—you don't have to make an effort. That's why you find me easy to be with.

AUSTIN I—I'd like you to be my friend.

KENDALL Gladly.

AUSTIN Won't you tell me—what to do?

KENDALL Aren't you assuming—I'm wiser than I really am?

AUSTIN But you *are* wise. You know all about the world and—you know—you're sophisticated. (KENDALL *is amused*) You've had all sorts of—experiences.

KENDALL I'm more experienced than you, I fancy. But no amount of experience can keep you from falling in love with the wrong man, or the wrong woman. . . .

AUSTIN I know that Storey isn't the right man for Monica. I know that he won't make her—happy.

KENDALL I think he's sufficiently honest to have told her that himself.

AUSTIN But he should *convince* her. What's the good of all his talk if he can't convince her?

KENDALL (*Still amused*) The more he talks the less convinced she probably is.

AUSTIN (*Fingering scarf*) I don't see why she should have returned here.

KENDALL (*Shrugging her shoulders*) Some trivial reason, most likely.

AUSTIN She must have been here quite a time—if Storey wasn't dressed—when you came.

KENDALL You know Storey. Never hurries. . . .

AUSTIN It's funny. . . .

KENDALL   I've said—I think you can trust Storey.

AUSTIN (*Bitterly*)   Can I?

KENDALL (*Surprised at his tone*)   Why, Austin . . . !
(*Enter* STOREY, *dressed.* KENDALL *moves to the piano.*
AUSTIN *remains fixed, makes no move toward* STOREY)

STOREY   Awfully sorry to keep you waiting. But, then,
Monica isn't here yet, either.

KENDALL (*From the piano*)   Two hours to dress. There's a
fop for you, Austin. (*She plays a sentimental song*)

STOREY (*To* AUSTIN)   Fact is I tried to write a little after
you and Monica left.

AUSTIN (*Stiffly*)   Did you?

STOREY   A few lines. . . .

KENDALL (*Continuing to play*)   You're getting industrious,
Storey. What's the matter?

STOREY   I've decided to marry, settle down, cultivate the
virtues.

AUSTIN   Marry?

STOREY   Don't you know I propose to Mrs. Frayne every
day? And if I'm to support her in the style to which she's
been accustomed I've got to work much harder.

KENDALL (*Leaving the piano*)   Don't you believe him,
Austin. I looked at your manuscript before Austin came and
there was only one sentence added to what I read this afternoon. (*She goes to the tabouret and picks up manuscript*)

STOREY   But that one sentence was born of a travail—last-
ing two hours.

KENDALL (*Picking up manuscript and reading*)   "She rose
and left him . . ." Did it take you two hours to write that?

STOREY   I did brilliantly to write that in two hours. The
exquisite simplicity of that sentence! The compactness of it!
Think of the million things I might have written. Think of
all the sentences in the world. And I picked that one. In two
hours! The tremendous—celerity of the choice astonishes me
now I think of it. How did I do it?

KENDALL (*To* AUSTIN)   Is he drunk?

STOREY   No, but it's a good idea. (*He pours champagne*)
Kendall . . .   (*He hands her a glass*) Austin . . .

AUSTIN   No, thanks.

STOREY   But you've got to. It's to celebrate your engagement
to Monica.

AUSTIN   I don't feel like it.

STOREY   But I want us all to be gay tonight. I can't get
comfortably drunk with a sober man in the party.

KENDALL   Don't make him drink if he doesn't want to,
Storey.

STOREY   Austin, have you ever been drunk in your life?

AUSTIN   Not really drunk, no.

STOREY   (*To* KENDALL)   Imagine that!

KENDALL   If you're gloomy when you begin, drink only
intensifies your mood.

STOREY   Nonsense.

KENDALL   Well, so I've heard.

STOREY   Here, Austin. It's glorious stuff. Drink it and in ten
minutes you'll feel imperial, omniscient. You'll know more
about physics than Einstein—the Universe'll stretch out below you like a plaid.

AUSTIN   What's the use of a sensation like that?

STOREY   What's the use of love?

AUSTIN   Well, I'll drink it anyway.
    (*They lift their glasses*)

KENDALL   Happy days. . . .

STOREY   Happy days. . . .   (*They drink. Quoting*) "The
true, the blushful Hippocrene."

KENDALL   Nothing blushful about Roget. You're colour-
blind, Storey.

STOREY   Just an excuse to quote Keats. "With beaded bub-
bles winking at the brim . . ."

AUSTIN   (*Truculently*)   Let's have another!

STOREY   That's the spirit. . . .
    (*The doorbell rings*)

KENDALL   Miss Grey. . . .

STOREY   I'll let her in. Pour the drinks, Austin. . . . (*He goes out.* AUSTIN *looks uncomfortable. He pours the champagne. Watches the door.* KENDALL *watches him.* MONICA *comes in. She looks charming in a simple evening frock, a picture of youthful loveliness.* STOREY *follows her*) May I present Miss Grey . . . ?

MONICA (*A bit self-conscious*)   Hello, Mrs. Frayne.

STOREY   I believe you've met Mr. Lowe. . . .

MONICA   Hello, Austin.

STOREY   Austin's on the loose tonight, Monica. Just guzzling champagne. . . .

KENDALL   Where would you like to go, Miss Grey? I haven't made a reservation anywhere. I wanted to know which dance-place you preferred.

MONICA   I am crazy about the music at the Trocadero.

KENDALL.   Storey, will you telephone?

MONICA   Although you can't dance there. It's too crowded.

KENDALL   They're all crowded.

STOREY   I've heard of a marvellous coloured place—

MONICA   Oh, where?

STOREY   In the heart of Harlem.

MONICA (*Excited*)   Oh, let's go!

STOREY   I'm told you have to be a good shot . . .

KENDALL   Is that the place where the man was killed?

STOREY   Yes.

MONICA   How exciting!

STOREY   Austin, you're marrying a savage.

AUSTIN   Am I?

MONICA   Are you jilting me, Austin?

KENDALL   If we're going anywhere—we'd better start.

AUSTIN (*A trifle desperately*)   One more drink. . . .

STOREY   Good! I always felt, Austin, if you ever got started — (*He pours*)

MONICA   A little one for me.

STOREY This is Rogε 15.

MONICA Is it? Well, then, a big one.

KENDALL None for me, Storey.

STOREY Oh, please—we'll drink a toast. (*He pours for himself*) To our married life . . . !

MONICA But I haven't got one.

STOREY But you will.

MONICA Proposing to me, Storey?

STOREY Don't flirt, Monica. Austin's jealous enough already. . . .

KENDALL What a prosaic toast!

STOREY Exactly. (*Lifting glass*) To our married life—may it be like the good prose of the English masters, solid, clear, sometimes hovering close to poetry—but in the main sensible and intelligent and—well-behaved.
  (*They drink*)

KENDALL Nice toast, Storey.

MONICA I don't think it's nice at all. I certainly don't want that sort of marriage.

STOREY Let's drink to your sort.

MONICA I'd like my marriage to be always like fine poetry—thrilling and exciting—and occasionally sensible and well-behaved—like prose.

STOREY A large order, Austin!

AUSTIN (*Bitterly*) I suppose you mean that only you could fill it.

MONICA (*Amazed*) Why, Austin. . . . !
  (*There is an embarrassed pause*)

KENDALL We'd better be starting.

STOREY No, wait a minute. (*To* AUSTIN) Are you angry with me?

KENDALL It's the wine . . .

AUSTIN (*Sullenly*) No, it's not the wine.

STOREY What is it then? Come on—out with it. In *vino veritas!*

MONICA What does that mean?

STOREY   It means that when you're tight you tell your right name.

MONICA   Oh, that's exciting! Everybody tell the truth—the absolute truth.

STOREY   We're not drunk enough for that.

AUSTIN   (*To* MONICA)   You might begin by telling me why you lied to me tonight.

KENDALL   Now, you see, Storey . . . !

STOREY   You *have* had too much, Austin.

AUSTIN   (*Defiant*)   I'll have as much as I like (*He pours himself another glassful and gulps it. He still addresses* MONICA) You told me you were going downtown. You came back here.

MONICA   Yes, I did!

AUSTIN   I found your scarf.

STOREY   (*Pouring himself a drink*)   What if she did?

AUSTIN   I suspected something. When she told me to go on alone—I came back and saw her go in. I hung around in the street—

KENDALL   Do let's get started.

STOREY   (*Drinking*)   Let's talk it out. You hung around in the street. *You,* Austin!

AUSTIN   Yes, I did. It was all I could do to keep from bursting in on you and—shouting. I hated you, Storey. I hate you now.

STOREY   Why?

AUSTIN   I resent you. I resent your fluency, your gift of words, your superficial . . . I resent you.

STOREY   (*Pours*)   Have another.

KENDALL   Please, Storey . . . !

STOREY   Why not? All of us. It's a rare moment. I feel we'll talk. We'll really talk—all of us. This sort of thing doesn't happen. It'll be—revealing. (*Lifting his glass*) I swear to tell the truth—and nothing but the truth—so help me—Horace!
    (*They all stand, glass in hand*)

KENDALL   Something tells me we'll all be sorry for this. You, Storey, more than the rest.

STOREY (*Recklessly*)   I'll risk it. (*Lifting his glass*) To the Truth. (*He drinks and* AUSTIN, MONICA *and* KENDALL *just sip their wine*) Think of it—here is Austin Lowe—standing in the street, eating his heart out, hating me. Why? Because Monica ran upstairs to prattle some nonsense that seemed to her important. The most promising young scientist in America—reduced to the level of an Apache. Did you hate me bitterly, Austin?

AUSTIN   I wanted you to die.

STOREY   What did you think was happening in here?

KENDALL   This is silly.

STOREY (*To* AUSTIN)   I'll reward your frankness. I'll be frank too.

AUSTIN   I pictured her coming in here—going to you—I pictured her looking up to you with love in her eyes—love that should have been meant for me. I pictured—I wanted you to die!

STOREY   Sex reduces everybody to a common denominator. Here's Austin . . . always telling me that all creation is the result of an accident . . .

AUSTIN   What's that got to do with it?

STOREY   You told me once that a slight change in the temperature a few thousand years ago would have put us all at the mercy of the ants. . . . You're more conscious than any of us of the insignificance of man, of the feebleness of his cry amid the vast solitudes of time and space. Your knowledge makes you one man in ten million. And yet you stand in the streets looking up at that window and wanting to kill me because I'm kissing a girl! Savage, Austin!

AUSTIN   I suppose you're so damn civilised.

STOREY   I? Not at all. When I came into this room before and you told me Monica was going to marry you I felt a pang of resentment too.

MONICA (*Delighted*)   It was true, then! ·

STOREY   Oh, it didn't spring from love for you. I felt: Why does *he* deserve her? I felt an impulse to take her away from you.

KENDALL   This is interesting, Storey.

STOREY (*To her*)   It's not that I'm in love with Monica.

MONICA (*Sipping her wine*)   Fib!

STOREY (*Ignoring her*)   It's that I resent Austin. I'm jealous of him. I envy him his scientific eminence, I envy him his money. . . .

KENDALL   You might envy his sincerity, his character.

STOREY   I wouldn't have his character for worlds. It would destroy my amusements. (*Interested in his own reaction*) I said to myself: "Why should this mole-like creature"— meaning Austin—"possess this radiant girl?"

AUSTIN   I know that's what you think—I'm a mole, a scientific mole.

STOREY   Did I say that?

KENDALL   You're a third-rate writer and Austin is a first-rate scientist.

MONICA   Storey's not third-rate.

STOREY   My dear child, it's true. Artistically I'm third-rate. My mind is not as superficial as my work. . . .

KENDALL   Or as your life.

STOREY   I can't take myself seriously—that's my tragedy.

MONICA   Well, I don't care *what* you are. . . . I love you, Storey!

STOREY   Really, Monica, you'll embarrass me.

KENDALL   We musn't give Miss Grey more champagne.

AUSTIN   I don't think I'll have a very good time at this party. I'm going home.

STOREY   You won't. I won't let you.

AUSTIN (*Like a child who feels he's not wanted by anybody*) I don't see why *I* should stay.

KENDALL   Nor I. It appears we ought to leave Monica and Storey alone.

STOREY   That would be a calamity.

KENDALL (*Feline*)   For Miss Grey?

STOREY   For both of us. It would tie us to each other for ever.

MONICA   I don't see where the calamity comes in . . .

STOREY   You're too young to see. You're too much in love to see. But I see—for both of us.

KENDALL   If Austin and I had any sense we'd leave you together.

MONICA   Why don't you?

KENDALL   Why don't I?

MONICA   (*Challengingly*)   Why don't you?

KENDALL   (*Slowly*)   Because—

MONICA   Because?

KENDALL   I'm afraid I should have a sleepless night.

STOREY   If I were a cad I should have an affair with Monica. But regrettably I am a Puritan. Can't help it. It's in my blood.

MONICA   Liar!

STOREY   You are right, Monica. It is not Puritanism. It's prudence. I'd have to marry you. That would be fatal.

MONICA   Why?

STOREY   You would be happy for a year and unhappy the rest of your life. If you marry Austin you'll be unhappy for a year and happy the rest of your life.

KENDALL   And if I marry you?

STOREY   (*Pouring champagne for her*)   Your life will have the excitement of a perilous risk.

KENDALL   But I don't want excitement. I want—tranquility, I want to be secure.

STOREY   Then you should marry Austin. Matrimonially he is a gilt-edged bond. I am a highly speculative stock.

KENDALL   What do you say, Austin?

AUSTIN   (*Who is befuddled now*)   What do I say to what?

KENDALL   Shall we be sensible? Shall we get married—you and I?

MONICA   Say yes, Austin.

AUSTIN   But I'm not in love with her. I'm in love with you.

KENDALL (*To* STOREY)   I'm out of luck, Storey.

STOREY   Don't weep over him. I'll take you on.

KENDALL   You're the only resource left me. I accept you—not because you're worthy—but because I can't help it.

STOREY   You hear, everybody—she accepts me.

KENDALL   I'll take a—flyer in you.

STOREY (*Touching his glass to hers*)   And I'll try not to fluctuate too much. (*After he drinks*) Now then, Austin. Your way is clear.

KENDALL   And now I really think we've talked enough nonsense. We'd better start.

STOREY   I'm just in the mood for a good jazz-band.

KENDALL   Who'll carry the champagne?

STOREY   Austin.

AUSTIN (*In better spirits*)   I'll take it. (*He lifts hamper*) Monica, I don't dance. Will you teach me?

MONICA (*Tensely*)   Before we go—there's something *I* want to say.

STOREY   You'll tell us in the taxi.

MONICA   No. Here.

KENDALL   Another revelation?

MONICA   Yes. (*Her voice and manner are very strained, like one keyed up to accomplish an impossible feat*)

STOREY   What's the matter, Monica? Aren't you well?

KENDALL   You would start this.

AUSTIN (*Very concerned*)   Monica . . . !

MONICA   Since everybody's telling the truth—why shouldn't I?

STOREY   Don't say anything you'll be sorry for.

MONICA   Even if I *am* sorry—I'm going to say it.

KENDALL   I really think we ought to go out.

AUSTIN   The fresh air'll do her good.

MONICA   I'll say it if it—kills me.

AUSTIN (*Anxious*)   What *is* it, Monica?

STOREY (*Suspicious*) Watch your step, child.

MONICA I think you ought to know it, Mrs. Frayne. Austin, I think you ought to know it.

AUSTIN I know more than I want to now. (*Picking up her wraps*) There's been too much confession. Let's start.

MONICA No, stop. All of you. I want you to know—that Storey—Storey is the father of my child—my unborn child.

STOREY (*Amazed*) Monica!

MONICA There now, I've said it. I feel better.
  (*She takes a quick gulp of champagne.* KENDALL *and* AUSTIN *stare accusingly at* STOREY. *They are speechless*)

STOREY She's ill. She's had too much champagne.

MONICA I haven't. I've had less than any of you.

STOREY Monica—you're— (*Turning to the others*) Surely, you don't believe—

MONICA If I had the courage to tell it. . . . (*She turns away. She cannot finish. The strain has really made her faint*)

KENDALL I did think, Storey, that you observed *some* code.

STOREY But I tell you, the child is—she's irresponsible. She's doing this—

AUSTIN (*Almost screaming*) You cad! You damn, dirty cad!

KENDALL We'd better go. Austin, will you take me home?

STOREY She doesn't know what she's saying, I tell you.

MONICA I do, too.

STOREY Kendall, for pity's sake, listen.

KENDALL I never want to see you again. Are you coming, Austin? (*She is at the door*)

AUSTIN (*Broken*) Monica, is it—true?

MONICA Yes, Austin.
  (KENDALL *goes out*)

AUSTIN True. . . .

STOREY Austin, I swear to you it's not true. She's crazy.

AUSTIN (*Laughing a bit wildly*) Well—of course. Why not? (*He picks up* MONICA'S *scarf lying on the chair, drops it and goes out. Between* STOREY *and* MONICA *there is a long silence. He simply stares at her*)

MONICA (*At last*)   Gee, what've I done? (STOREY *still stares at her*) I had no idea they'd raise such a fuss. . . . But once I got started I couldn't back out, could I? (*As he does not speak*) You're angry? After all it was harder for me than it was for you. (*He still says nothing*) Please say something, Storey. If you don't—I'll cry.

STOREY   You think you're smart, don't you?

MONICA   I think I'm brave. Storey, it's for you I did it too.

STOREY   Oh, for me.

MONICA   Storey—don't you want me?

STOREY   No.

MONICA   Tonight—when I came back here—you made me feel you did. I was sure you did.

STOREY   That will pass and what will be left?

MONICA   Isn't there more to it than that, Storey?

STOREY   No.

MONICA   I won't let you go, Storey. I'm going to fight for you—I'm going to bring you back—to what you were—to that youth you've let go. . . . It's your one chance now, Storey—your last desperate chance—don't you see, Storey?

STOREY   But I don't want to go back. I can't go back.

MONICA   It's such a little distance, Storey.

STOREY   Is it?

MONICA   These things you're selling yourself for—what good are they? Is *this* (*She includes the room in a gesture*) what you *really* want? I can't believe it. Storey, dearest, I can see such a fine way we might live. . . .

STOREY   I tell you it wouldn't work, Monica—even if I did try to be what you think I could be—it would be no use.

MONICA   I can't think of arguments the way you can—I can't put things the way you can—I just know that if you had any bravery—if you had any courage . . . all these things you say are lies you've made up—lies to justify yourself, to prop you up—you're a pampered, weak thing dawdling away your life on a sofa when you might be standing up straight on your own feet. . . .

STOREY Perhaps. Only I can see us now—five years from now—in a cheap flat—you looking blowsy—with little wrinkles under your eyes—and I in cheap shirts and cracked shoes—brooding in a room over the corpse of my genius. . . . (*He gets up and goes to the piano and fills her glass*) Well, I'll marry you—but the joke's on you. . . . You can't have life on your own terms, Monica. I can't. Nobody can.

MONICA (*Watching him, trembling—she is seeing him as if for the first time*) I see I can't. . . . !

STOREY I'll marry you, Monica—but the joke's on you. . . . (*He sits at the piano and plays, singing rather savagely the improvised catch*) "With me by your side to help you."
(*She falters to the chair, weeping piteously*)

MONICA Storey—stop—
(*But he plays on, cruelly, in an ecstasy of self-revealment —she huddles in the chair to escape the flagellation of sound, as the curtain falls*)

CURTAIN

ACT THREE

SCENE: *The same.*
TIME: *The next morning.*

AT RISE: STOREY *is discovered, immured within his writing
board, trying to work. Puts down a sentence. Regards it.
Isn't pleased. Gets up. Lights a cigarette. Takes a turn
about the room, returns, picks up his Ms. and, with an
impulse of disgust crumples it in his hand and throws it
into the empty fireplace. Picks up the magazine* KENDALL
*had been reading in the first act, looks at that and flings
the magazine, too, into the fireplace.*

STOREY (*Savagely*) Trash . . . trash . . . trash . . . !
(*Catches sight of himself in the mirror above fireplace, regards himself in it*) Trash . . . ! (*Nevertheless he straightens
his tie, and settles his dressing gown, an instinct of foppish-
ness not to be denied. The doorbell rings*) Damn . . . ! (*It
rings again . . . Shouting*) I'm not at home . . . (*He
starts across the room to see who it is.* AUSTIN *appears in
the doorway*)

AUSTIN Hall door was open.

STOREY (*Really glad to see him*) Hello! I say—you look
done in. What's the matter? (AUSTIN *does, in fact, look terrible. He has evidently been walking in the rain, his clothes
are bedraggled. He hasn't slept. The champagne has made
him ill all night. He is unshaved. His hands tremble. He is
feverish and on the verge of being really ill*) What's the
matter? Here—sit down. (AUSTIN *shakes his head as* STOREY
proffers a chair) You've been out in the rain.

AUSTIN Yes.

STOREY What doing?

AUSTIN   Walking.

STOREY   But, my dear fellow. You shouldn't be doing that. You're obviously ill.

AUSTIN   (*Deadly serious*)   This isn't a friendly visit.

STOREY   No?

AUSTIN   I've come to kill you.

STOREY   My dear Austin. You *are* ill!

AUSTIN   That's why I've come.

STOREY   I tell you there isn't a reason on earth why you should hate me.

AUSTIN   No reason!

STOREY   Last night was as illusory as a nightmare.

AUSTIN   Don't deny anything. It only makes you more— hateful.

STOREY   Today Monica will probably tell you herself—it was a lie.

AUSTIN   Nothing can save you, Storey.

STOREY   My dear chap, let me get you a cup of tea. . . .

AUSTIN   (*Flaring*)   Don't you laugh at me! (*He whips out a gun and points it at him*)

STOREY   Is it loaded? Am I facing death? The situation is novel but not as thrilling as I might have expected. Do you really mean to kill me, Austin?

AUSTIN   Why do you think I bought it?

STOREY   Did you buy that thing? You needn't have. I have one upstairs. I'd have lent it to you.

AUSTIN   You don't believe I'll do it. That's why you're so gay. . . .

STOREY   Ah, I suppose you will. I suppose—at the Threshold of the Great Unknown as they call it—I should be solemn. . . .

AUSTIN   Epigrams!

STOREY   Force of habit, sorry. You press that thing—and no more epigrams. Death is probably very commonplace. Disintegration. Resolution into original elements. Your province, Austin.

AUSTIN   Talker!

STOREY   Can't help it, old dear. It will wag.

AUSTIN   Not a real emotion, not a real feeling—even in the face of death.

STOREY   Real emotions and real feelings are destructive. I've learned to do without them. That's civilisation.

AUSTIN   The old boast . . . !

STOREY   It's true. *You're* in the grip of a real emotion, a real feeling. What's it doin' to you? Never mind what it wants to do to me. Listen a second. If you could empty your heart of its burden as easily as you can empty that cylinder there'd be some sense in curving your little finger. But after I am lying there, silent for once, will you be happier? The world will be emptier for I shall no longer be there—for you to hate.

AUSTIN   The world will be better off without you.

STOREY   Please be honest. Don't pretend this is a crusade. You want to shoot me because you think Monica's belonged to me. You want to shoot me because you're eaten by jealousy. You're not doing it to raise the general level of morality. Don't be a hypocrite, Austin. (*He lights a cigarette*)

AUSTIN   No matter what the reason—I can't endure your living. . . .

STOREY   That I can understand. (*There is a pause.* AUSTIN *backs off from him as if to take better aim*) Er—have you made any plans for the future?

AUSTIN   What is it to you?

STOREY   (*Shrugging his shoulders*) Curious. . . .

AUSTIN   First you—then myself.

STOREY   Oh, both of us? Teutonic efficiency. You *are* German, aren't you, Austin? Lowe. Löwe. (*He pronounces it with the umlaut*)

AUSTIN   (*In a knot of anger*)   Be quiet. . . .

STOREY   It's rather a pity. Loss to the community. You, I mean. First-rate men are too rare to be permitted the luxury of suicide. I shan't matter. But *you*. It's a shame, really.

AUSTIN   Don't worry about me.

STOREY   But I do. Think of it. You've—let's say thirty years left to make your discoveries in. Science is an endless chain, isn't it? I suppose, really, there is only one science as there is only one art. You might discover a little trifling thing that'll help some other fellow discover another trifling thing and that might lead to—well, anything, mightn't it? (AUSTIN backs *off a little farther. Pursuing his vein*) Something perfectly tremendous—a cure for cancer or an escalator to Mars or anything, mightn't it? (AUSTIN *backs off more*) Austin, do you mind not moving away from me? I admit—it makes me nervous.

AUSTIN   Have you nothing else to say?

STOREY   Do you want a last speech? Dear me! I can't think of a thing. Isn't it funny? Now that I'd like to say something brilliant I can't. I've often wondered how all those great men in history pulled their death-bed speeches. Made 'em up in advance, I bet.

AUSTIN   All right then. . . .   (*He levels his gun*)

STOREY   Wait! I've thought of something. . . .

AUSTIN   Say it quick. . . .

STOREY   His last words were: "Give my love to Monica. . . ."

AUSTIN (*Wildly*)   Damn you. . . . !
    (*He fires.* STOREY *has dropped to the ground, the bullet goes three feet over his head.* AUSTIN *thinks he has killed him; he staggers, almost fainting, into a chair*)

STOREY   God! Austin. You nearly frightened the life out of me. God! (*He pours a drink of Scotch and gulps it. Pours another for* AUSTIN) Here. (AUSTIN *shakes his head*) Do you good.

AUSTIN   Let me alone.

STOREY (*Drinking it himself*)   I saved your life, Austin, as well as my own. I give you back to Science. If you'd hit me they'd have sent you to jail for life. A valuable man like you. The jury system is one of the prime stupidities of democracy, don't you think? (AUSTIN *rises to his feet. He is pitiful*) Where you going?

AUSTIN   Home.

STOREY   You're in no condition to go home. . . . You're ill, trembling.

AUSTIN   Sorry. Made a fool of myself.

STOREY   (*Supporting him*)   What did you do when you left here last night?

AUSTIN   Last night?

STOREY   Yes.

AUSTIN   Went home. Ill. Not used to drinking. That champagne.

STOREY   Eaten anything today? (AUSTIN *shakes his head*) And you've been walking in all that rain? Look here—you've got to drink this. (*He forces some whiskey between his lips*)

AUSTIN   Guess I'll go on.

STOREY   Wait till it stops raining.

AUSTIN   Sorry to have . . . (*He sways*)

STOREY   Shan't let you go out in this condition.

AUSTIN   Feel wobbly.

STOREY   Tell you what—you'll go in my room and lie down.

AUSTIN   Too much trouble.

STOREY   You've got to. A little nap'll make you as right as— unfortunate simile for a day like this. This way. . . . (*He partly supports him and leads him up the stairs. The doorbell rings*) Must be Kendall. (*Shouts through door*) Come in. . . .

AUSTIN   I'll just lie down a minute. . . .

STOREY   A good sleep and a hot bath. . . . (*They exit upstairs.* KENDALL *comes in. She looks around the room.* STOREY *sticks his head in at bedroom door*) Be with you in a minute, Kendall. Austin. . . .

(*His sign mystifies* KENDALL, *except that she gathers that* AUSTIN *is inside.* STOREY *disappears into the bedroom.* KENDALL *catches sight of the pistol which* STOREY *has picked up and put on the table. She sniffs the powder. Goes to fireplace, picks up* STOREY'S *crumpled manuscript. Lets it fall again. She is full of thoughts.* STOREY *returns, and, after a moment*)

He came to kill me and remained—to take a nap.

KENDALL   Poor fellow.

STOREY   Poor fellow! I like that. What about *me?*

KENDALL   You deserve it, Storey.

STOREY   What for?

KENDALL   We don't need to discuss it.

STOREY   You mean—last night. It's too silly. Even if it were true . . .

KENDALL   Don't deny it, Storey. Spare me that!

STOREY   Even if it *were* true—about Monica and me—one doesn't deserve death for that sort of thing.

KENDALL   I'm afraid I'm a very conventional person, Storey. By your standards at any rate.

STOREY   I leave standards to the moralists. I do the best I can. That's what everybody does—in the long run.

KENDALL   I didn't come here to reproach you, Storey.

STOREY   It's a mess, I know. It all comes—from trying to be intelligent.

KENDALL   (*After a moment*)   I came to say good-bye. . . .

STOREY   Good-bye?

KENDALL   I'm going abroad.

STOREY   When?

KENDALL   Probably on the *Olympic*. Sailing on the tenth. That will give me time to get my passports.

STOREY   You hate me, don't you?

KENDALL   I don't think so. I feel—dead about you. Just now. . . .

STOREY   I tell you solemnly—that what Monica said last night—isn't true.

KENDALL   Don't stoop to that, Storey. (*She crosses him to fireplace. There is a pause.* STOREY *gives it up*) I see you've been throwing away your manuscripts.

STOREY   Yes.

KENDALL   A good sign. I believe you might do good work— if you'd settle down.

STOREY   (*Ironically*)   Monica's idea.

KENDALL   She must love you very much—to confess before everybody—the way she did last night.

STOREY (*Wearily*)   You don't know the half of it.

KENDALL   It's Monica—Miss Grey—I came to speak to you about—really.

STOREY   Yes?

KENDALL   At first I suppose it'll be a little hard for you—economically. Especially if you mean to do serious work. . . . I thought perhaps . . .

STOREY   You want to give us money—to start the new life on?

KENDALL   I have so much—and I'm alone.

STOREY   It's an excellent idea. But I'm afraid Monica—wouldn't see it.

KENDALL   She needn't know.

STOREY (*Ironically*)   Would you have us start the new life —with a lie?

KENDALL   Always laughing. . . .

STOREY   Why not? Life is amusing.

KENDALL   You ought to turn over a new leaf, really, Storey.

STOREY (*Pointing to fireplace*)   Look at that manuscript.

KENDALL   That *is* a good sign.

STOREY   Nonsense. An impulse of irritation. The day after I marry I shall be regretting I tore it up. I shall be writing it again—from memory. I shall have to redouble my output because I shall have Monica to support and—you will be in Europe. In time Monica will come to see that I haven't in me the great works which she suspects are secreted in my brain like bonds in a vault. She'll begin to despise me a little bit. And I'll begin—to deceive her a little bit. And there we'll be—a typical married couple.

KENDALL   Poor Monica!

STOREY   It's too bad for both of us, really. You and I might have lived a civilised life. You have the two great requirements for the wife of a poor but intelligent man: money and tolerance.

KENDALL   Unfortunately my tolerance doesn't extend—to this.

STOREY   This—as you call it—is a lie. It doesn't exist.

KENDALL   Good-bye, Storey.

STOREY   I tell you it simply isn't true.

KENDALL   Cheat!

STOREY   I should think Monica's—device—would be transparent to you.

KENDALL   Cad! Good-bye forever.

STOREY   In the end everything is reduced to cliché.

KENDALL   I never want to see you again. . . . (*She sweeps to the door*)

AUSTIN   (*Off*)   Storey. Storey. . . .

STOREY   Coming. . . . Wait a second, will you, Kendall?

KENDALL   I'm going.
   (*The doorbell rings*)

STOREY   (*On the stairs*)   See who that is. And don't go. Have a heart.
   (*He disappears.* KENDALL *is at the door when it opens. It is* MONICA)

MONICA   Oh! I'm sorry. I rang.

KENDALL   I'm just leaving.

MONICA   Is Storey home?

KENDALL   (*Uncertain how much to tell her*)   He's—inside.

MONICA   I wanted to see him just for a minute. Please don't go.

KENDALL   I must. I only dropped in—to say good-bye to Storey.

MONICA   Good-bye?

KENDALL   I'm going abroad. I shall be gone a long time.

MONICA   Oh! But you needn't go. . . .

KENDALL   My dear child. . . .

MONICA   And you needn't call me a child. I'm old—now.

KENDALL   All of a sudden?

MONICA   Yes.

KENDALL   What's—aged you?

MONICA   Never mind. But I tell you—sincerely—you needn't go—on my account.

KENDALL   What inspires this mood—of renunciation?

MONICA   It's not renunciation. It's indifference.

KENDALL   I'm afraid—you're deceiving yourself.

MONICA   I'm not. Honestly. You'll see. I came—to tell that —to Storey.

KENDALL   I came once—to tell him that. I stayed, though.

MONICA   This is different.

KENDALL   Oh, you're angry with him. That will pass.

MONICA   But I'm *not* angry with him. This is something else I tell you—something else altogether.

KENDALL   I think you'll be as happy as most people. Good luck. . . . (*She reaches out her hand to* MONICA)

MONICA   (*Taking it*)   You're very much in love with him, aren't you?

KENDALL   I'm used to it. It's only uncomfortable—when I see him. But I'm going away now. I enjoy travelling and alto-gether I have a pretty good time.

MONICA   But I tell you if it's on account of me—you needn't go.

KENDALL   You're worse off than I am, really. You're in love with a man who doesn't exist. I'm in love with one who does. That's why this sort of thing is less of a shock. . . . If it ever happens to you . . .

MONICA   Mrs. Frayne, I must tell you—what I said last night—wasn't true.

KENDALL   Thanks. But one doesn't invent that sort of lie. . . .

MONICA   But I swear to you I—
    (*Enter* STOREY)

STOREY   Hello, Monica.

MONICA   Hello, Storey.

KENDALL   Good-bye.

STOREY Oh, don't go. . . .

KENDALL I really must. . . . (*To* MONICA) Good luck. (*She grips her hand, smiles at her and goes*)

MONICA She's—awfully nice.

STOREY Oh, Kendall's one of the best. Understands everything.

MONICA It hasn't done her much good, has it?

STOREY How do you mean?

MONICA She's not very happy.

STOREY When it comes to that—who is?

MONICA You manage to have a pleasant time.

STOREY I manage to behave as if I were having a pleasant time. One owes that to one's friends, I believe—just as one owes it to them to be decently shaved and to wear clean linen.

MONICA That's bunk. You have a good time because you're built that way. You're too selfish to worry about anything.

STOREY I've reformed. I'm a better man, now, Monica.

MONICA Are you?

STOREY Yes.

MONICA How can you tell?

STOREY Well, for one thing, I've thrown away the story I was working on. It's in the grate.

MONICA What made you do that?

STOREY Last night after you left I had several hours of heroic introspection. Henceforth I shall devote myself to the sincerities, the eternal verities, that sort of thing.

MONICA I wonder. . . .

STOREY The trouble is the masses bore me, democracy bores me. I'd like to be Henry James and live with you in England on a private income.

MONICA Poor Storey! I've robbed you of your subsidy.

STOREY What do you mean?

MONICA Mrs. Frayne. I just told her the truth about—last night.

STOREY   Did you?

MONICA   She said: "One doesn't invent that sort of lie."

STOREY   Well, it doesn't matter.

MONICA (*Sarcastic*)   How generous you are!

STOREY   I dare say it'll be the finest possible thing for me to buckle down to hard work. I'll do hack-work to make a living and the rest of the time—

MONICA   The rest of the time?

STOREY   The rest of the time I'll write sombre masterpieces, blood and tears—I'll anatomise suffering. . . .

MONICA   But, Storey, you don't know anything about suffering.

STOREY   Most suffering *is* the bunk, you know, Monica. Unintelligent people who want things beyond their limitations.

MONICA (*Stamping her foot*)   How *can* you be so complacent?

STOREY   You're a victim of the popular prejudice in favour of agony. Why is a book about unhappy, dirty people better than one about gay and comfortable ones?

MONICA   But life *isn't* gay—or comfortable.

STOREY (*Seriously*)   Dear darling, life is sad. I know it's sad. But I think it's gallant—to pretend that it isn't.

MONICA   Poor Austin. . . .

STOREY   What makes you think of him?

MONICA   I've been thinking a lot of him—since last night. I'll never forget his face—the way he looked. And *you* think life is gay—and comfortable! (*There is a pause*)

STOREY (*Sincerely*)   Monica . . .

MONICA (*Out of a brown study*)   Yes.

STOREY   If you take me on—I'll do my best. (*She stares at him with curiosity, fixedly*)

MONICA   Will you?

STOREY   I'll try to be—what you think me.

MONICA   Thank you, Storey.

STOREY   Don't you believe me?

MONICA (*Abstractedly*) What?

STOREY Don't you believe me? That I'll try. What's the matter? Why are you staring at me?

MONICA I'm trying to discover what it is.

STOREY What *what* is? Why is everyone so cryptic today?

MONICA I'm trying to discover what it is—that's changed everything. You *look* the same as you did yesterday.

STOREY The same face. . . .

MONICA But I can't remember the time when I loved you. Is it only yesterday—that I loved you?

STOREY This morning—one A.M.

MONICA Can't recall what it was like.

STOREY What's this? Don't tell me you're fickle, too.

MONICA It's not—fickle. It's that—you seem to be another person. Your voice is different.

STOREY Slight cold.

MONICA The things you say—sound hollow to me. I don't love you today, Storey.

STOREY One can't have everything.

MONICA I'll never be in love with you again, Storey. I'm sure. It's over. It's dead.

STOREY How do you know? Tell me. I'm interested.

MONICA I just—know it.

STOREY The things I said to you last night?

MONICA I suppose so. I feel—old now, Storey. I see myself —all this time I've loved you—like a person looking from outside, a very old person. I see a little girl, a rather stupid little girl, reading a fairy-tale and believing it true—long after the other children knew it to be a lie.

STOREY I always told you your idea of me was an idealisation.

MONICA But I never believed it—till last night. Last night I saw you as you really are—mercenary and unadventurous and—practical. I saw your soul.

STOREY *Must* we drag the soul into it?

MONICA   I saw it—a rather fat thing lying in an armchair—with a brain ticking, inside, like a clock. . . .

STOREY   But I'm not fat, Monica.

MONICA   Your body isn't and your brain isn't, but your soul *is*, Storey. You know it is.

STOREY   Why *will* women talk about the soul?

MONICA   All night I saw you like that. I said to myself: "When you see him, when he stands in front of you—you'll forget all that, you'll feel as you did before." But I do see you. You do stand in front of me. And it doesn't matter.

STOREY   Don't talk like that. I'll fall in love with you.

MONICA   You're too clever for me, Storey. Your emotions are too complicated.

STOREY   I wish I were like Austin. *His* emotions are as simple as those—

MONICA   (*Tenderly*)   As simple as those of a child.

STOREY   (*Rather bitterly*)   No second man peering over *his* shoulder.

MONICA   He's a darling.

STOREY   (*Abruptly*)   The darling almost shot me this morning.

MONICA   Shot you!
     (STOREY *points to the revolver lying on the table. She looks at it, horrified*)

STOREY   He came here in a simple, uncomplicated mood. He's a rotten shot.

MONICA   Where'd he go?

STOREY   He's upstairs, taking a nap.

MONICA   How is he?

STOREY   Feverish. He'd been up all night, walking in the rain.

MONICA   We ought to have a doctor.

STOREY   I don't think so. Champagne and jealousy.

MONICA   What did he say?

STOREY   He was incoherent. Had an idea he ought to avenge

your honour, I suppose. Acted like a moving-picture hero and talked like a commuter. Really, he was ridiculous.

MONICA   Didn't you tell him—that what I said last night—?

STOREY   Of course I told him. But he wouldn't believe me. Nobody'll ever believe the truth now. Really, Monica . . .

MONICA (*Thinking only of* AUSTIN)   Think what he must have gone through—to want to do that.

STOREY   Can you imagine the trial if he'd succeeded! (*Tracing imaginary headline*) "Scientist Kills Writer Over Woman. Following an all-night champagne party in Clark Storey's luxurious West Side apartment . . ." The note of licentiousness—and you on the witness-stand—the story of your confession—everybody'd say I got my deserts and Austin would come out a vindicated Saint George. . . .

MONICA   Don't, Storey.

STOREY   But it's so *pretty,* Monica. It's almost a shame he didn't hit me. Can't you see the humour of it, the lovely irony of it? What would you say on the witness-stand? Would you tell them the truth? That I never ruined you at all, that you lied, to save me from myself, as you call it, to prevent me from making a mercenary marriage. But if you did that you'd deprive the defence of a case. You'd send Austin to the chair. . . .

MONICA   You're dreadful, Storey.

STOREY   And even if you said it was true—there must be difficulties. The prosecution would try to undermine you. They'd want proof beyond your statement. I believe you said you were the mother of my child. Well, they'd want the child. Monica, you'd have to produce a child. . . .

(MONICA *snatches up her wrap to go. She is outraged by his facetiousness.* AUSTIN *appears on the landing*)

AUSTIN (*A bit wildly*)   Monica! (*He comes downstairs*)

STOREY   I thought you were asleep.

MONICA   He *is* ill!

AUSTIN   I'm going now.

MONICA   Why, he's trembling, feverish. . . .

STOREY   Wait. I'll get him something hot to drink. (*He goes out*)

AUSTIN   Did Storey tell you why I—what I—

MONICA   Yes. He told me.

AUSTIN   Think if I had killed him!—the man you love—I'll never forgive myself, Monica.

MONICA   Whatever has happened is my fault.

AUSTIN   I've found out things about myself—what I really am. Look what I tried to do.

MONICA   Don't blame yourself. I can't bear it. It's I . . .

AUSTIN   No. You must know everything. I must tell you everything. You've got to know. I made up my mind to kill him. And do you know why? It wasn't alone because I hated him—but because I wanted to hurt you. I hated you, Monica.

MONICA   I know.

AUSTIN   But all the time—it's hard for me to explain it—I loved you. You were inside of me. I was desperate—to tear you out. I see now I can't do it. I'll never do it. I have no existence apart from you.

MONICA   Wait—Austin—listen to me. You're trying to explain yourself to me. You needn't. I understand you. I understand you very well. You are clear to me. My trouble is—how will I make myself clear to you? How can I make you understand what happened last night? How I could have said what I did? Because it isn't true, Austin.

AUSTIN   (*Repeating mechanically*)   Isn't true. . . .

MONICA   It seemed to me—I thought—that by saying it—I could change everything—make everything over—all in a second. It was so childish. I thought . . .

AUSTIN   You needn't tell me, Monica.

MONICA   How can I make you understand—that all that's over now—that last night—yesterday—I loved Storey? That today I don't?

AUSTIN   (*Simply*)   You don't owe me—explanations, Monica.

MONICA   No, but I must. I want you to know everything that's in my thoughts. I mustn't hold anything back from you. I feel pain still about Storey, even now. But it isn't for *him*, do you understand, Austin? It isn't for losing *him!* It's for the feeling I had for him—that it should have been wasted—

that feeling that will never come again—that can't come again. . . .

AUSTIN   Mine—remains.

(*There is a pause*)

MONICA   Are you sorry?

AUSTIN   No.

MONICA   Austin—if you want me—I'll love, honour and obey you. And I'll try to make it up to you—for the bad time I've given you.

AUSTIN   You're here. You're close to me. It's like being alive —for the first time.

(STOREY *comes back; carries glass of punch*)

STOREY   I had this finished five minutes ago. I drank it and made another. Here, Austin. . . .

AUSTIN   No, thank you, Storey.

MONICA   We're just leaving.

STOREY   Oh! (*A pause*) Bless you, my children!

AUSTIN   (*Embarrassed*)   Er—thanks. Coming, Monica?

MONICA   Yes. Good-bye, Storey.

(AUSTIN *goes out*)

STOREY   I'm awfully glad, Monica. It's what I always told you to do, isn't it? (*She says nothing. They look at each other. She is affected and he is, too. To break the moment he reverts to flippancy*) Life does occasionally imitate fiction. A happy ending, eh, Monica?

MONICA   I think so, Storey. Good-bye. (*She goes out*)

STOREY   (*After a moment*)   That's that. . . . (*He ponders; he is serious. He takes another drink. Walks across the room, sits down, entrenches himself behind the sewing board, is about to write, looks toward the fireplace, goes to it, picks up the torn script and looks at it ruefully*) Damn fool. . . . ! (*Goes back, begins writing, can't concentrate, gets up again, "snaps out of it" and goes to phone*) Regent 2772 please—is Mrs. Frayne there—hello—Kendall?—Storey—I'm fright-fully low, Kendall—you've got to come and cheer me up —oh, now, are *you* going to drop me too?—she's gone— certainly, with Austin—we'll dance at their wedding, Kendall—what about dinner?—you're busy—what?—oh, packing —oh, don't go abroad—if you do let's go together—that *is* an idea—but why?—now please be reasonable—don't tell me you still believe that silly story of Monica's—God, Ken, I've never known you so stubborn—in common justice you ought to take me back on probation until Austin and Monica— that's the very least you can do—and, Kendall, I promise you —I absolutely promise you—that if their baby—if their baby bears the *slightest* resemblance to me—thank God, Kendall, you're laughing—what?—no, why should you?—keep your passport and I'll get another—of course—I can write as well in Europe as I can here—even better—no, I've got a better idea—you cancel your passage and we'll go the Southern route—oh, yes, lovely this time of the year—land at Naples and motor to Nice—certainly—along the Riviera—beautiful trip . . .

(*The descending curtain cuts short his itinerary*)

CURTAIN

☆

Biography

★

☆ *for*
Sonya and Carl

Biography *was first produced by the Theatre Guild, Inc., at the Guild Theatre, on Monday evening, December 12, 1932, with the following cast:*

(IN THE ORDER IN WHICH THEY SPEAK)

RICHARD KURT 25   Earle Larimore
MINNIE, Marion Froude's maid 50   Helen Salinger
MELCHIOR FEYDAK, a Viennese composer 45   Arnold Korff
MARION FROUDE 35   Ina Claire
LEANDER NOLAN 45   Jay Fassett
WARWICK WILSON 25-30   Alexander Clark
ORRIN KINNICOTT 55   Charles Richman
SLADE KINNICOTT, his daughter   Mary Arbenz

PRODUCTION DIRECTED BY Philip Moeller
SETTING DESIGNED BY Jo Mielziner

Scenes

ACT ONE	About five o'clock of an afternoon in November.
ACT TWO	Afternoon, three weeks later.
ACT THREE	Late afternoon, two weeks later.

The curtain will be lowered during the act to denote a lapse of time.

The entire action takes place in Marion Froude's studio in New York City. The time is now.

ACT ONE

SCENE: *The studio-apartment of* MARION FROUDE *in an old fashioned studio building in West 57th St., New York. A great, cavernous room expressing in its polyglot furnishings the artistic patois of the various landlords who have sublet this apartment to wandering tenants like* MARION FROUDE. *The styles range from medieval Florence to contemporary Grand Rapids; on a movable raised platform in the center is a papal throne chair in red velvet and gold fringes. Not far from it is an ordinary American kitchen chair. The hanging lamp which sheds a mellow light over a French Empire sofa is filigreed copper Byzantine. Another and longer sofa across the room against the grand piano is in soft green velvet and has the gentility of a polite Park Avenue drawing room. Under the stairs, rear, which go up to* MARION'S *bedroom, are stacks of her canvases. There is a quite fine wood carving of a Madonna which seems to be centuries old and in the wall spaces looking at audience are great, dim canvases—copies by some former tenant left probably in lieu of rent—of Sargent's Lord Ribblesdale and Mme. X.*

Whether it is due to the amenable spirit of the present incumbent or because they are relaxed in the democracy of art, these oddments of the creative spirit do not suggest disharmony. The room is warm, musty, with restful shadows and limpid lights. The enormous leaded window on the right, though some of its members are patched and cracked, gleams in the descending twilight with an opalescent light; even the copper cylinder of the fire extinguisher and its attendant axe, visible in the hall, seem to be not so much implements against calamity, as amusing museumbits cherished from an earlier time. Every school is represented here except the modern. The studio has the mellowness of anachronism.

There is a door up-stage left leading to the kitchen and

89

MINNIE'S *bedroom door, center, under the stairs leads into hall-way. A door on the stair landing, center, leads to* MINNIE'S *bedroom.*

TIME: *About five o'clock of an afternoon in November.*

AT RISE: RICHARD KURT *is finishing a nervous cigarette. He has the essential audacity which comes from having seen the worst happen, from having endured the keenest pain. He has the hardness of one who knows that he can be devastated by pity, the bitterness which comes from having seen, in early youth, justice thwarted and tears unavailing, the self reliance which comes from having seen everything go in a disordered world save one, stubborn, unyielding core of belief—at everything else he laughs, in this alone he trusts. He has the intensity of the fanatic and the carelessness of the vagabond. He goes to the door from the hall and calls.*

KURT   Say, you, hello there—what's your name?
(MINNIE, *Marion Froude's inseparable maid, a German woman of about fifty, comes in. She is indignant at being thus summarily summoned, and by a stranger*)

MINNIE (*With dignity*)   My name iss Minnie if you please.

KURT   What time did Miss Froude go out?

MINNIE   About two o'clock.

KURT   It's nearly five now. She should be home shouldn't she?

MINNIE   She said she vas coming home to tea and that iss all I know.

KURT (*Grimly*)   I know. She invited me to tea. . . . Where did she go to lunch?

MINNIE (*Acidly*)   That I do not know.

KURT   Did someone call for her or did she go out alone? I have a reason for asking.

MINNIE   She went out alone. Any more questions?

KURT   No. I see there's no point in asking you questions.

MINNIE   Denn vy do you ask dem?
(*The doorbell rings.* MINNIE *throws up her hands in de-*

spair. She goes out muttering: "Ach Gott." KURT *is rather
amused at her. He lights another cigarette)*
*(Sounds of vociferous greeting outside. "Ach mein lieber
Herr Feydak. . . ."* MELCHIOR FEYDAK, *the Austrian composer, comes in. He is forty-five, tall, hook-nosed, thin-
faced, a humorist with a rather sad face)*

FEYDAK Nun, Minnie, und wo ist die Schlechte. . . . ?
(MINNIE *makes a sign to him not to disclose their free-
masonry in the presence of strangers. She is cautious. . . .)*
Not home yet, eh Minnie? Where is she? Well—well. How
do they say—gallivanting—I love that word—gallivanting as
usual. Well, I'll wait. It's humiliating—but I'll wait. Chilly!
Brr! I don't mind so much being cold in London or Vienna.
I expect it. But I can't stand it in New York. (*He warms
himself before fire*) And who is this young man?

MINNIE (*Shortly*) Ich weiss nicht! . . . Er hat alle fünf
Minuten gefragt, wo sie ist—
(*She goes out*)

FEYDAK You've offended Minnie I can see that.

KURT That's just too bad!

FEYDAK We all tremble before Minnie. . . . Been waiting
long?

KURT Over half an hour!

FEYDAK Extraordinary thing—ever since I've known Marion
there's always been someone waiting for her. There are two
kinds of people in one's life—people whom one keeps waiting—and the people for whom one waits. . . .

KURT Is that an epigram?

FEYDAK Do you object to epigrams?

KURT (*With some pride*) I despise epigrams.

FEYDAK (*Tolerantly sizing* KURT *up*) Hm! Friend of Miss
Froude's?

KURT Not at all.

FEYDAK That at least is no cause for pride.

KURT I just don't happen to be that's all.

FEYDAK I commiserate you.

KURT I despise gallantry also.

FEYDAK (*Lightly*)   And I thought Americans were so senti-mental. . . .

KURT   And, together with other forms of glibness, I loathe generalization. . . .

FEYDAK (*Drily*)   Young man, we have a great deal in com-mon.

KURT   Also, there is a faint flavor of condescension in the way you say "young man" for which I don't really care. . . .

FEYDAK (*Delighted and encouraging him to go on*)   What about me do you like? There must be something.

KURT   If I were that kind your question would embarrass me.

FEYDAK (*Very pleased*)   Good for Marion!

KURT   Why do you say that?

FEYDAK   She always had a knack for picking up originals!

KURT   You are under a misapprehension. Miss Froude did not pick me up. I picked her up. (FEYDAK *stares at him. This does shock him*) I wrote Miss Froude a letter—a business-letter. She answered and gave me an appointment for four-thirty. It is now after five. She has taken a half-hour out of my life. . . .

FEYDAK   I gather that fragment of time has great value. . . .

KURT   She has shortened my life by thirty minutes. God, how I hate Bohemians!

FEYDAK (*Innocently*)   Are you by any chance—an Evangel-ist?

KURT   I am—for the moment—a business-man. I'm not here to hold hands or drink tea. I'm here on business. My presence here is a favor to Miss Froude and likely to bring her a handsome profit. . . .

FEYDAK   Profit! Ah! That accounts for her being late. . . .

KURT (*Sceptically*)   You despise profit I suppose! Are you—by any chance—old-world?

FEYDAK   Young man, your technique is entirely wasted on me. . . .

KURT   Technique! What are you talking about?

FEYDAK   When I was a young man—before I achieved any sort of success—I was rude on principle. Deliberately rude and extravagantly bitter in order to make impression. When it is no longer necessary for you to wait around for people in order to do them favors you'll mellow down I assure you.

KURT (*Fiercely, he has been touched*)   You think so, do you! That's where you're mistaken! I'm rude now. When I'm successful I'll be murderous!

FEYDAK (*Genially*)   More power to you! But I've never seen it happen yet. Success is the great muffler! Not an epigram I hope. If it is—forgive me.
   (*A moment's pause.* KURT *studies him while* FEYDAK *crosses to stove and warms his hands*)

KURT   I know you from somewhere. It's very tantalising.

FEYDAK   I don't think so. I have only just arrived in this country. . . .

KURT   Still I know you—I'm sure—I've seen you somewhere. . . .

FEYDAK (*Understanding the familiarity*)   Maybe you know Miss Froude's portrait of me. . . .

KURT (*Doubtfully*)   Yes—maybe that's it . . . may I ask. . . . ?

FEYDAK   Certainly. My name is Feydak.

KURT   The composer?

FEYDAK (*Drily*)   Yes. . . .

KURT   I thought he was dead. . . .

FEYDAK   That is true. But I hope you won't tell anyone—for I am his ghost. . . .

KURT (*Putting this down for Continental humor and genuinely contrite*)   Forgive me. . . .

FEYDAK   But why?

KURT   If you really are Feydak the composer—I have the most enormous admiration for you. I worship music above everything.

FEYDAK (*Slightly bored*)   Go on. . . .

KURT   I read in the paper—you're on your way to Hollywood. . . .

FEYDAK   Yes. I am on my way to Hollywood. . . .

KURT   In the new state men like you won't have to prostitute themselves in Hollywood. . . .

FEYDAK   Ah! A Utopian!

KURT   Yes. You use the word as a term of contempt. Why?
Every artist is a Utopian. You must be very tired or you
wouldn't be so contemptuous of Utopians.

FEYDAK (*With a charming smile*)   I am rather tired. Old-
world you would call it.

KURT   You can be anything you like. . . .

FEYDAK (*Satirically*)   Thank you. . . .

KURT   You've written lovely music—I have a friend who
plays every note of it. I didn't see your operetta when it
was done here. . . . I didn't have the price . . . it was very
badly done though, I heard. . . .

FEYDAK   I must explain to you—you are under a misapprehension. . . .

KURT   It was done here, wasn't it?

FEYDAK   Not about the operetta. You are under a misapprehension—about me. I am a composer—but I didn't write
"Danubia." That was my brother, Victor Feydak. You are
right. He is dead. You are the first person I have met in New
York who even suspected it.

KURT   I'm sorry.

FEYDAK   Not at all. I am flattered. At home our identities
were never confused. Is this the well-known American hospitality? It is, in some sort, compensation for his death. . . .
   (KURT *is embarrassed and uncomfortable. It is part of his
   essential insecurity; he is only really at home in protest.
   He wants to get out*)

KURT   I'm sorry—I . . .

FEYDAK (*Easily*)   But why?

KURT   I think I'll leave a note for Miss Froude—get that
girl in here, will you?

FEYDAK   Let's have some tea—she's sure to be in any minute. . . .

KURT   No, thanks. And you might tell her for me that if she wants to see me about the matter I wrote her about she can come to my office. . . .

(MARION FROUDE *comes in. She is one of those women, the sight of whom on Fifth Ave. where she has just been walking, causes foreigners to exclaim enthusiastically that American women are the most radiant in the world. She is tall, lithe, indomitably alive. Unlike* KURT, *the tears in things have warmed without scalding her; she floats life like a dancer's scarf in perpetual enjoyment of its colors and contours*)

MARION   (*To* KURT)   I'm *so* sorry!

FEYDAK   (*Coming toward her*)   I don't believe a word of it! (*She is overjoyed at seeing* FEYDAK. *She can't believe for a second that it is he. Then she flies into his arms*)

MARION   Feydie! Oh Feydie I've been trying everywhere to reach you—I can't believe it. . . . Feydie darling!

FEYDAK   (*Severely*)   Is this how you keep a business appointment, Miss Froude?

MARION   How long have you waited? If I'd only known. . . . (*Suddenly conscious that* KURT *had waited too*) Oh, I'm so sorry, Mr. —— Mr. —— . . . ?

KURT   Kurt. Richard Kurt.

MARION   Oh, of course, Mr. Kurt. I say—could you possibly —would it be too much trouble—could you come back?

FEYDAK   (*Same tone*)   This young man is here on business. It is more important. I can wait. I'll come back.

MARION   No, no, Feydie—no, no. I can't wait for that. I'm sure Mr. Kurt will understand. Mr. Feydak is an old friend whom I haven't seen in ever so long. It isn't as if Mr. Kurt were a regular business-man. . . .

FEYDAK   (*Amused*)   How do you know he isn't?

MARION   (*Breathless with excitement*)   I can tell. He's not a bit like his letter. When I got your letter I was sure you were jowley and you know— (*She makes a gesture*) convex. I'm sure, Feydie—whatever the business is— (*To* KURT) you did say you had some, didn't you?—I'm sure it can wait. A half hour anyway. Can't it wait a half hour? You see Feydie and I haven't seen each other since. . . .

KURT Vienna!

MARION (*Astonished*) Yes. How did you know?

KURT It's always since Vienna that Bohemians haven't seen each other, isn't it? I'll be back in thirty minutes.
(*He goes*)

MARION What a singular young man!

FEYDAK I've been having a very amusing talk with him. Professional rebel I think. Well, my dear—you look marvelous!
(*They take each other in*)

MARION Isn't it wonderful. . . .

FEYDAK It *is* nice!
(*They sit on sofa,* MARION *left of* FEYDAK)

MARION How long is it?

FEYDAK Well, it's since. . . .

MARION (*Firmly*) Since Vicki died.

FEYDAK That's right. I haven't seen you since.

MARION Since that day—we walked behind him.

FEYDAK Yes.

MARION I felt I couldn't bear to stay on. I left for London that night.

FEYDAK Yes.

MARION It's six years isn't it?

FEYDAK Yes. Six years last June.
(*A pause*)

MARION What's happened since then? Nothing. . . .

FEYDAK How long have you been here?

MARION Two weeks.

FEYDAK Busy?

MARION Not professionally, I'm afraid. People are charming —they ask me to lunch and dinner and they're—"oh, so interested"—but no commissions so far. And God, how I need it. . . .

FEYDAK I'm surprised. I gathered you'd been very successful.

MARION   It's always sounded like it, hasn't it? The impression, I believe, is due to the extreme notoriety of some of my sitters. Oh, I've managed well enough up to now—if I'd been more provident I dare say I could have put a tidy bit by—but at the moment people don't seem in a mood to have their portraits done. Are they less vain than they used to be? Or just poorer?

FEYDAK   Both, I think. . . .

MARION   Last time I came here I was awfully busy. Had great réclame because I'd been in Russia doing leading Communists. Obeying some subtle paradox the big financiers flocked to me. Pittsburgh manufacturers wanted to be done by the same brush that had tackled Lenin. Now they seem less eager. Must be some reason, Feydie. But what about you? Let me hear about you. How's Kathie?

FEYDAK   Well. She's here with me.

MARION   And Sadye?

FEYDAK   Splendid.

MARION   She must be a big girl now.

FEYDAK   As tall as you are.

MARION   Kathie used to hate me, didn't she? Frightened to death of me. Was afraid I was after Vicki's money. . . .

FEYDAK   Yes. She was afraid you'd marry him and that we should have less from him. When we knew he was dying she was in a panic.

MARION   Poor dear—I could have spared her all that worry if she'd been half-way civil to me.

FEYDAK   Kathie is practical. And she is a good mother. Those are attributes which make women avaricious. . . .

MARION   Did Vicki leave you very much?

FEYDAK   Not very much. Half to you.

MARION   Really? How sweet of him! How dear of him!

FEYDAK   We've spent it. . . .

MARION   Of course you should.

FEYDAK   But I'll soon be in position to repay you your share. I'm on my way to Hollywood.

MARION   Are you really? How wonderful for you, Feydie! I'm so glad. . . .

FEYDAK   You've been there, haven't you?

MARION   Yes. Last time I was in America.

FEYDAK   Did you like it?

MARION   Well, it's the new Eldorado—art on the gold-rush.

FEYDAK (*With a kind of ironic bitterness*)   Vicki left me an inheritance subject, it appears, to perpetual renewal.

MARION   How do you mean?

FEYDAK   Things have been going from bad to worse in Vienna—you haven't been there since '25 so you don't know. The theatre's pretty well dead—even the first-rate fellows have had a hard time making their way. I managed to get several scores to do—but they were not—except that they were failures—up to my usual standard. . . .

MARION (*Laughing, reproachful*)   Oh, Feydie . . . !

FEYDAK   If it weren't for the money Vicki left me—and you!—I don't know how we should have got through at all these six years. About a month ago we reached the end of our rope—we were hopelessly in debt—no means of getting out—when the miracle happened. . . .

(MARION *is excited, touches his knee with her hand*)

MARION (*Murmuring*)   I can't bear it. . . .

FEYDAK   It was my dramatic agent on the phone. A great American film magnate was in town and wanted to see me. Ausgerechnet me and no other. Even my agent couldn't keep the surprise out of his voice. Why me? I asked. God knows, says the agent. Well, we went around to the Bristol to see the magnate. And, as we talked to him, it gradually became apparent. He thought I was Vicki. He didn't know Vicki was dead! He thought I had written "Danubia."

MARION   Did he say so?

FEYDAK   No—not at all. But as we shook hands at the end he said to me: "Any man that can write a tune like this is the kind of man we want." And he whistled, so out of tune that I could hardly recognize it myself, the waltz from Danubia. Do you remember it? (*He starts to hum the waltz and* MARION *joins him. They hum together, then* FEYDAK *continues to talk as* MARION *continues to hum a few more measures*) He was so innocent, so affable that I had an impulse to say to him: "Look here, old fellow, you don't want me, you want my brother and, in order to get him you'll have to resurrect him!" But noble impulses are luxury impulses. You have to be well off to gratify them. I kept quiet. We shook hands and here I am. Tonight they're giving me a dinner at the Waldorf Astoria for the press to meet my brother! Irony if you like, eh, Marion?

(*There is a pause*)

MARION   Feydie . . . (*A moment. He does not answer*) Feydie—do you mind if I say something to you—very frankly?

FEYDAK   I doubt whether you can say anything to me more penetrating than the remarks I habitually address to myself.

MARION   You know Vicki was very fond of you. He used to say you put too high a valuation on genius.

FEYDAK   Because he had it he could afford to deprecate it.

MARION   Over and over agian he used to say to me: "You know Marion," he would say, "as a human being Feydie's far superior to me, more amiable, more witty, more talented, more patient. . . ."

FEYDAK   (*Shakes his head*)   Not true. I simply give the impression of these things. . . .

MARION   You under-rate yourself, Feydie. . . . How this would have amused him—this incident with the Hollywood man!

FEYDAK   (*Smiling bitterly*)   It would rather. . . .

MARION   Why do you grudge giving him a laugh somewhere? I never had a chance to tell you in Vienna—things were so—so close and terrible—at the end—but he had the greatest tenderness for you. He used to speak of you—I can't tell you how much. "Because of this sixth sense for making tunes which I have and he hasn't," he said to me one day—not a week before he died—"he thinks himself less than me." He used to tell me that everything he had he owed to you—to the sacrifices you made to send him to the Conservatory when he was a boy. . . . The extent to which he had outstripped you hurt him—hurt him. I felt he would have given anything to dip into the golden bowl of his genius and pour it over you. And do you know what was the terror of his life, the obsessing terror of his life—his fear of your resenting him. . . .

FEYDAK (*Moved, deeply ashamed*) Marion. . . .

MARION Don't resent him now, Feydie. . . . Why, it's such fun—don't you see? It's such a curious, marginal survival for him—that a badly-remembered waltz-tune, five years after his death, should be the means of helping you at a moment when you need it so badly. . . . It's delicious, Feydie. It's such fun! The only awful thing is the possibility that he is unaware of it. It would have pleased him so, Feydie. Must you grudge him it?

FEYDAK You make me horribly ashamed. . . .

MARION (*Brightly*) Nonsense. . . .

FEYDAK Because I did grudge him it—yes—I won't, though —I see now that it never occurred to me how . . . (*Bursts out laughing suddenly*) God, it is funny, isn't it. . . .

MARION (*Joining in his laughter*) Of course—it's delight-ful. . . .

(*They both laugh heartily and long*)

MARION And the funny thing is—you'll be much better for them out there than he would have been.

FEYDAK Surely! They'll be able to whistle *my* tunes!

MARION Don't you see!

FEYDAK Oh, Lieber Schatzel, come out there with me.

MARION Can't!

FEYDAK I wish, Marion, you would come. I never feel life so warm and good as when you are in the neighborhood.

MARION Dear Feydie, you're very comforting.

FEYDAK Is there someone that keeps you here?

MARION No, there's no one. I'm quite alone.

FEYDAK Well then . . . !

MARION No, this isn't the moment for me, Feydie. Besides, I can't afford the journey. I'm frightfully hard up at the moment.

FEYDAK Well, look here, I . . .

MARION No, that's sweet of you but I couldn't.

FEYDAK   I don't see why—it's too silly. . . .

MARION   Vanity. A kind of vanity.

FEYDAK   But I owe it to you!

MARION   I suppose it is foolish in a way—but I've a kind of pride in maneuvering on my own. I always have done it—in that way at least I've been genuinely independent. I'm a little proud of my ingenuity. And do you know, Feydie, no matter how hard up I've been at different times something's always turned up for me. I have a kind of curiosity to know what it will be this time. It would spoil the fun for me to take money from my friends. Nothing—so much as that would make me doubtful of my own—shall we say—marketability?

FEYDAK   Paradoxical, isn't it?

MARION   Why not? Anyway it's a pet idée fixe of mine, so be a darling and let me indulge it, will you, Feydie, and don't offer me money. Anyway, I've a business proposition on. . . .

FEYDAK   Have you?

MARION   That young man who was just here. Do you suppose he'll come back? Now I think of it we were a bit short with him, weren't we? I was so glad to see you I couldn't be bothered with him! (*Sound of door-bell*) Ah! You see! (*Calls outside*) Show him in, Minnie!

(MINNIE *comes in and exits hall-door to admit the visitor*)

FEYDAK   What are you doing for dinner?

MARION   There's a young man who attached himself to me on the boat. . . .

FEYDAK   Oh, Marion!

MARION   I seem to attract youth, Feydie. What shall I do about it?

FEYDAK   Where are you dining?

MARION   I don't know. . . . Which speakeasy? Tell me which one and I'll . . .

(MINNIE *ushers in* MR. LEANDER NOLAN. *He is middle-aged, ample, handsome. Looks like the late Warren Gamaliel Harding. Soberly dressed and wears a waistcoat with white piping on it. The façade is impeccable but in* NOLAN'S *eye you may discern, at odd moments, an uncertainty, an almost boyish anxiety to please, to be right, that is rather engaging)*

(MARION, *who expected the young man, is rather startled.* MR. NOLAN *regards her with satisfaction)*

NOLAN   Hello, Marion.

MARION (*Doubtfully, feels she should remember him*)   How do you do? Er—will you excuse me—just a second . . . ?

NOLAN (*Genially*)   Certainly.

(*He moves right.* MARION *walks* FEYDIE *to the hall-door*)

FEYDAK (*Under his breath to her*)   Looks like a commission. . . .

(*She makes a gesture of silent prayer*)

MARION (*Out loud*)   Telephone me in an hour will you Feydie, and let me know which speakeasy. . . .

FEYDAK (*Once he has her in the hall-way out of* NOLAN'S *hearing*)   Also, Du kommst ganz sicher?

MARION   Vielleicht später. Bye, Feydie dear.

(FEYDIE *goes out.* MARION *turns to face* NOLAN *who is standing with his arms behind his back rather enjoying the surprise he is about to give her*)

NOLAN   How are you, Marion?

MARION (*Delicately*)   Er—do I know you?

NOLAN   Yes. You know me.

MARION   Oh yes—of course!

NOLAN   About time!

MARION (*Brightly insecure*)   Lady Winchester's garden-party at Ascot—two summers ago. . . .

NOLAN   Guess again!

MARION   No—I know you perfectly well—it's just that—no, don't tell me. . . .

(*She covers her eyes with her hand, trying to conjure him out of the past*)

NOLAN   This is astonishing. If someone had said to me that I could walk into a room in front of Marion Froude and she not know me I'd have told 'em they were crazy . . . !

MARION (*Desperate*) I do know you. I know you perfectly well—it's just that . . .

NOLAN You'll be awful sore at yourself—I warn you . . .

MARION I can't forgive myself now—I know!

NOLAN I don't believe it!

MARION The American Embassy dinner in Rome on the Fourth of July—last year—you sat on my right. . . .

NOLAN I did not!

MARION (*Miserably*) Well, you sat somewhere. Where did you sit?

NOLAN I wasn't there.

MARION Well, I think it's very unkind of you to keep me in suspense like this. I can't bear it another second!

NOLAN I wouldn't have believed it!

MARION Well, give me some hint, will you?

NOLAN Think of home—think of Tennessee!

MARION Oh . . . !

NOLAN Little Mary Froude. . . .

MARION (*A light breaking in on her*) No! Oh, no!

NOLAN Well, it's about time. . . .

MARION But . . . ! You were . . .

NOLAN Well, so were you!

MARION But—Bunny—you aren't Bunny Nolan, are you? You're his brother!

NOLAN I have no brother.

MARION But Bunny—Bunny dear—how important you've become!

NOLAN I haven't done badly—no. . . .

MARION Here, give me your coat and hat— (MARION, *taking his coat and hat, crosses up-stage to piano, and leaves them there*) (*Laughing, a little hysterical*) You should have warned me. It's not fair of you. Bunny! Of all people— I can scarcely believe it. . . . (*A moment's pause. He doesn't quite like her calling him Bunny but he doesn't know how to stop it. She sits on model-stand looking up at him as she says:*) You look wonderful. You look like a—like a—Senator or something monumental like that.

NOLAN (*Sits on sofa below piano*)   That's a good omen. I'll have to tell Orrin.

MARION   What's a good omen? And who is Orrin?

NOLAN   Your saying I look like a Senator. Because—I don't want to be premature—but in a few months I may be one.

MARION   A Senator!

NOLAN (*Smiling*)   Senator. Washington. Not Nashville.

MARION   Do you want to be a Senator or can't you help it?

NOLAN (*To whom this point of view is incomprehensible*) What do you mean?

MARION   I'll paint you, Bunny. Toga. Ferrule. Tribune of the people.

NOLAN   Not a bad idea. Not a bad idea at all. I remember now—you were always sketching me. Sketching everything. Say, you've done pretty well yourself, haven't you?

MARION   Not as well as you have, Bunny. Imagine. Bunny Nolan—a Senator at Washington. Well, well! And tell me—how do I seem to you? You knew me at once, didn't you?

NOLAN   Sure I did. You haven't changed so much—a little perhaps. . . .

MARION (*Delicately*)   Ampler?

NOLAN (*Inspecting her*)   No . . . not that I can notice. . . .

MARION (*With a sigh of relief*)   That's wonderful. . . .

NOLAN   You look just the same. You are just the same.

MARION   Oh, you don't know, Bunny. I'm artful. How long is it since we've seen each other? Twelve years anyway. More than that—fifteen . . .

NOLAN   Just about—hadn't even begun to practice law yet. . . .

MARION   We were just kids . . . children. . . . And now look at you! I can see how successful you are, Bunny.

NOLAN   How?

MARION   White piping on your vest. That suggests directo-
rates to me. Multiple control. Vertical corporations. Are you
vertical or horizontal, Bunny?

NOLAN   I'm both.

MARION   Good for you! Married?

NOLAN   Not yet . . .

MARION   How did you escape? You're going to be, though.

NOLAN   I'm engaged.

MARION   Who's the lucky girl?

NOLAN   Slade Kinnicott. Daughter of Orrin Kinnicott.

MARION   Orrin Kinnicott. The newspaper publisher?

NOLAN   Yes. He's backing me for the Senate.

MARION   Well, if he's backing you you ought to get in. All
that circulation—not very good circulation is it? Still, one
vote's as good as another, I suppose. . . .

NOLAN   (*Hurt*)   In my own state the Kinnicott papers are
as good as any . . .

MARION   Well, I wish you luck. I'm sure you'll have it. My!
Senator Nolan!

NOLAN   If I get in I'll be the youngest Senator . . .

MARION   And the best-looking too, Bunny . . .

NOLAN   (*Embarrassed*)   Well . . .

MARION   You're fussed! How charming of you! (*She sits
beside him*)   Oh, Bunny, I'm very proud of you, really.

NOLAN   You see, Marion, I've been pretty successful in the
law. Tremendously successful I may say. I've organized some
of the biggest mergers of recent years. I've made a fortune—
a sizeable fortune. Well, one day I woke up and I said to
myself: Look here, Nolan, you've got to take stock. You've
got to ask yourself where you're heading. I'd been so busy I'd
never had a chance to ask myself these fundamental questions before. And I decided to call a halt. You've got enough,
more than enough for life, I said to myself. It's time you
quit piling up money for yourself and began thinking about
your fellow-man. I've always been ambitious, Marion. You
know that. You shared all my early dreams . . .

MARION   Of course I did. . . .

NOLAN   Remember I always told you I didn't want money and power for their own sakes—I always wanted to be a big man in a real sense—to do something for my country and my time . . .

MARION   Yes. Sometimes you sounded like Daniel Webster, darling. I'm not a bit surprised you're going in the Senate.

NOLAN   I never thought—even in my wildest dreams. . . .

MARION   Well, you see you under-estimated yourself. You may go even higher—the White House—why not?

NOLAN   I never let myself think of that.

MARION   Why not? It's no more wonderful than what's happened already, is it?

NOLAN   (*Napoleon at Saint Helena*)   Destiny!

MARION   Exactly. Destiny!

NOLAN   (*Kind, richly human, patronizing*)   And you, my dear . . . ?

MARION   As you see. Obscure. Uncertain. Alone. Nowhere at all. Not the remotest chance of my getting into the Senate —unless I marry into it. Oh, Bunny, after you get to Washington will you introduce me to some Senators?

NOLAN   Well, that's premature . . . Naturally if the people should favor me I'd do what I could. I never forget a friend. Whatever faults I may have, disloyalty, I hope, is not one of them.

MARION   Of course it isn't. You're a dear. You always were.
   (*A moment's pause*)

NOLAN   Who was that fellow I found you with when I came in?

MARION   An old friend of mine from Vienna—a composer.

NOLAN   You've been a lot with foreigners, haven't you?

MARION   A good deal . . .

NOLAN   Funny, I don't understand that.

MARION   Foreigners are people, you know, Bunny. Some of 'em are rather nice.

NOLAN   When I'm abroad a few weeks home begins to look pretty good to me.

MARION   I love New York but I can't say I feel an acute nostalgia for Tennessee.
(*Another pause. He stares at her suddenly—still incredulous that he should be seeing her at all, and that, after all these years and quite without him, she should be radiant still*)

NOLAN   Little Marion Froude! I can't believe it somehow. . . .

MARION   Oh, Bunny! You're sweet! You're so—ingenuous. That's what I always liked about you.

NOLAN   What do you mean?

MARION   The way you look at me, the incredulity, the surprise. What did you expect to see? A hulk, a remnant, a whitened sepulchre . . . what?

NOLAN   (*Uncomfortable at being caught*) Not—not at all. . . .

MARION   Tell me, Bunny, what . . . ? I won't be hurt . . .

NOLAN   (*Miserably, stumbling*) Well, naturally, after what I'd heard . . .

MARION   What have you heard? Oh, do tell me Bunny.

NOLAN   Well, I mean—about your life. . . .

MARION   Racy, Bunny? Racy?

NOLAN   No use going into that. You chose your own way. Everybody has a right to live their own life I guess.

MARION   (*Pats his arm*) That's very handsome of you Bunny. I hope you take that liberal point of view when you reach the Senate.

NOLAN   I came here, Marion, in a perfectly sincere mood to say something to you, something that's been on my mind ever since we parted but if you're going to be flippant I suppose there's no use my saying anything—I might as well go, in fact.
(*But he makes no attempt to do so*)

MARION   (*Seriously*) Do forgive me, Bunny. One gets into an idiom that passes for banter but really I'm not so changed.

I'm not flippant. I'm awfully glad to see you, Bunny. (*An undertone of sadness creeps into her voice*) After all, one makes very few real friends in life—and you are part of my youth—we are part of each other's youth . . .

NOLAN   You didn't even know me!

MARION   Complete surprise! After all I've been in New York many times during these years and never once—never once have you come near me. You've dropped me all these years. (*With a sigh*) I'm afraid Bunny, your career has been too much with you.

NOLAN (*Grimly*)   So has yours!

MARION   I detect an overtone—faint but unmistakable—of moral censure.

NOLAN (*Same tone*)   Well, I suppose it's impossible to live one's life in art without being sexually promiscuous!
    (*He looks at her accusingly*)

MARION   Oh, dear me, Bunny! What shall I do? Shall I blush? Shall I hang my head in shame? What shall I do? How does one react in the face of an appalling accusation of this sort? I didn't know the news had got around so widely . . .

NOLAN   Well, so many of your lovers have been famous men. . . .

MARION   Well, you were obscure . . . But you're famous now, aren't you? I seem to be stimulating if nothing else . . .

NOLAN   If I had then some of the fame I have now you probably wouldn't have walked out on me at the last minute the way you did . . .

MARION   Dear, dear Bunny, that's not quite—

NOLAN (*Irritated beyond control*)   I wish you wouldn't call me Bunny. . . .

MARION   Well, I always did. What is your real name?

NOLAN   You know perfectly well . . .

MARION   I swear I don't. . . .

NOLAN   My name is Leander. . . .

MARION   Bunny, really. . . .

NOLAN   That is my name.

MARION   Really I'd forgotten that. Leander! Who was he—he did something in the Hellespont, didn't he? What did he do in the Hellespont?

NOLAN (*Sharply*)   Beside the point. . . .

MARION   Sorry! You say you wanted to tell me something—

NOLAN (*Grimly*)   Yes!

MARION   I love to be told things.

NOLAN   That night you left me—

MARION   We'd quarreled about something, hadn't we?

NOLAN   I realized after you left me how much I'd grown to depend on you—

MARION   Dear Bunny!

NOLAN   I plunged into work. I worked fiercely to forget you. I did forget you— (*He looks away from her*) And yet—

MARION   And yet—?

NOLAN   The way we'd separated and I never heard from you —it left something bitter in my mind—something—
    (*He hesitates for a word*)

MARION (*Supplying it*)   Unresolved?

NOLAN (*Quickly—relieved that she understands so exactly*) Yes. All these years I've wanted to see you, to get it off my mind—

MARION   Did you want the last word, Bunny dear?

NOLAN (*Fiercely*)   I wanted to see you, to stand before you, to tell myself—"Here she is and—and what of it!"

MARION   Well, can you?

NOLAN (*Heatedly, with transparent over-emphasis*)   Yes! Yes!

MARION   Good for you, Bunny. I know just how you feel—like having a tooth out, isn't it? (*Sincerely*) In justice to myself—I must tell you this—that the reason I walked out on you in the summary way I did was not as you've just suggested because I doubted your future—it was obvious to me, even then, that you were destined for mighty things—but the reason was that I felt a disparity in our characters not conducive to matrimonial contentment. You see how right I was. I suspected in myself a—a tendency to explore, a spiritual and physical wanderlust—that I knew would horrify you once you found it out. It horrifies you now when we are no longer anything to each other. Imagine, Leander dear, if we were married how much more difficult it would be— If there is any one thing you have to be grateful to me for it is that instant's clear vision I had which made me see, which made me look ahead, which made me tear myself away from you. Why, everything you have now—your future, your prospects,—even your fiancée, Leander dear—you owe to me—no, I won't say to me—to that instinct—to that premonition. . . .

NOLAN (*Nostalgic*) We might have done it together. . . .

MARION I wouldn't have stood for a fiancée, Bunny dear—not even *I* am as promiscuous as that. . . .

NOLAN Don't use that word!

MARION But, Leander! It's your own!

NOLAN Do you think it hasn't been on my conscience ever since, do you think it hasn't tortured me . . . !

MARION What, dear?

NOLAN That thought!

MARION Which thought?

NOLAN Every time I heard about you—all the notoriety that's attended you in the American papers . . . painting pictures of Communist statesmen, running around California with movie comedians!

MARION I have to practice my profession, Bunny. One must live, you know. Besides, I've done Capitalist statesmen too. And at Geneva. . . .

NOLAN (*Darkly*) You know what I mean . . . !

MARION You mean . . . (*She whispers through her cupped hand*) you mean promiscuous? Has that gotten around, Bunny? Is it whispered in the sewing-circles of Nashville? Will I be burned for a witch if I go back home? Will they have a trial over me? Will you defend me?

NOLAN (*Quite literally, with sincere and disarming simplicity*) I should be forced, as an honest man, to stand before the multitude and say: In condemning this woman you are condemning me who am asking your suffrages to represent you.

For it was I with whom this woman first sinned before God. As an honorable man that is what I should have to do.

MARION   And has this worried you—actually . . . !

NOLAN   It's tortured me . . . !

MARION   You're the holy man and I'm Thais! That gives me an idea for the portrait which I hope you will commission me to do. I'll do you in a hair-shirt. Savonarola. He was a Senator too, wasn't he? Or was he?

NOLAN (*Gloomily contemplating her*)   I can't forget that it was I who . . .

MARION   Did you think you were the first, Bunny? Was I so unscrupulously coquettish as to lead you to believe that I—oh, I couldn't have been. It's not like me.
   (*She crosses to right of model stand*)

NOLAN (*Fiercely*)   Don't lie to me!

MARION (*Sitting on stand*)   Bunny, you frighten me!

NOLAN (*Stands over her almost threateningly*)   You're lying to me to salve my conscience but I won't have it! I know my guilt and I'm going to bear it!

MARION   Well, I don't want to deprive you of your little pleasures but . . .

NOLAN   You're evil, Marion. You haven't the face of evil but you're evil—evil!

MARION   Oh, Bunny darling, now you can't mean that surely. What's come over you? You never were like that—or were you? You know perfectly well I'm not evil. Casual—maybe—but not evil. Good Heavens, Bunny, I might as well say you're evil because you're intolerant. These are differences in temperament, that's all—charming differences in temperament.

NOLAN (*Shakes his head, unconvinced*)   Sophistry!

MARION   All right, Dean Inge. Sophistry. By the way I've met the Gloomy Dean and he's not gloomy at all—he's very jolly. (*Gets up from stand*) Let's have a cup of tea, shall we? Will your constituents care if you have a cup of tea with a promiscuous woman? Will they have to know?

NOLAN   I'm afraid I can't, Marion. I have to be getting on. . . .

MARION Oh, stay and have some tea— (*Makes him sit down*) what do you have to do that can't wait for a cup of tea? . . . (*Calls off*) Minnie—Minnie. . . .

MINNIE (*Appears in doorway*) Ja, Fräulein. . . .

MARION Bitte—Tee. . . .

MINNIE Ja, Fräulein. . . .
  (*She goes out*) (MARION *smiles at* NOLAN *and sits beside him. He is quite uncomfortable*)

NOLAN (*Slightly embarrassed*) About the painting, Marion. . . .

MARION Oh, I was only joking . . . don't let yourself be bullied into it . . .

NOLAN I've never been painted in oils. It might do for campaign purposes. And, if I should be elected, it would be very helpful to you in Washington.

MARION You're awfully kind, Bunny. I must tell you frankly though that the dignified Senatorial style isn't exactly my forte. However, I might try. Yes—I'll try . . . (*She gives him a long look*) I'll go the limit on you, Bunny— when I get through with you you'll be a symbol of Dignity. Solid man. No nonsense. Safe and sane. Holds the middle course—a slogan in a frock-coat. I'll make you look like Warren G. Harding—even handsomer— Get you the women's votes.

NOLAN Well, that'll be very nice of you. . . .
  (MARION *suddenly kisses him*)

MARION Thank you, darling!
  (*He is very uncomfortable, embarrassed and thrilled*)

NOLAN Marion . . . !

MARION Just a rush of feeling, dear!

NOLAN You understand that this—this commission . . .

MARION Of course. Strictly business. Don't worry. I shan't kiss you again till it's finished.

NOLAN I don't know whether I told you—I'm going to be married in a month.

MARION I'll have the portrait ready for your wedding-day.

NOLAN   And I am devoted to Slade with every fibre of my being. . . .

MARION   Every fibre—how thorough!

NOLAN   I'm not a Bohemian, you know, Marion.

MARION   Don't tell me! You're a gypsy! (*She continues to study him, poses him, poses his hand.* MINNIE *enters from left with tea-tray containing tea-pot, cups and saucers, spoons, sugar and cream, and a plate of cakes. She puts tray on model stand and exits left*) Oh, Bunny, what fun it'll be to do you. Thank you, Minnie. Tell me—how do you see yourself?

NOLAN   What do you mean?

MARION   In your heart of hearts—how do you see yourself? Napoleon, Scipio, Mussolini . . . ?

NOLAN   Nonsense! Do you think I'm an actor?

MARION   Of course. Everybody is. Everybody has some secret vision of himself. Do you know what mine is? Do you know how I see myself?
     (*The doorbell rings*)

NOLAN (*Ironically*)   More visitors!

MARION (*Calls to* MINNIE)   See who it is, will you, Minnie? . . . Probably the young man I met on the boat coming to take me to dinner.

NOLAN   What's his name?

MARION   I've forgotten. He's just a boy I met on the boat.

NOLAN   How can anybody live the way you live!

MARION   It's a special talent, dear. (*Doorbell rings again*) Minnie, go to the door. (MINNIE *comes in and exits hall-way*) This is my lucky day, Bunny.

NOLAN   Would you mind, in front of strangers, not to call me Bunny?

MARION   Oh, of course, what is it?

NOLAN (*Irritated*)   Leander.

MARION (*Mnemonic*)   Leander—Hellespont—Leander. . . .
     (MINNIE *comes down-stage a few feet from the door*)

MINNIE (*Just inside the room*)   It's the Junge who was here before—er sagt er ist ausgeschifft da—

MARION   Oh, show him in, Minnie, and bring a cup for him too.

MINNIE (*As she goes*)   Ja.

NOLAN   And don't use these extravagant terms of endearment—anybody who didn't know you would misunderstand it. . . .

MARION (*Very happy*)   All right, darling. (MINNIE *ushers in* RICHARD KURT, *goes out, comes back again with more tea.* MARION *comes forward to greet him*) I'm so glad to see you again, Mr. ——. . . .

KURT   Kurt.

MARION   Oh. . . .

KURT   With a K.

MARION (*Reassured*)   Oh—I'll try to remember. This is Senator Nolan—Mr. Kurt. . . .

NOLAN (*Glowering*)   I am not Senator Nolan.

MARION   But you will be. (*She offers him a cup of tea, he takes it*) Can't I just call you that—between ourselves? It gives me such a sense of quiet power. And maybe it'll impress my visitor. Do have a cup of tea, Mr. Kurt.
(*She gives him one*)

KURT (*Puts his hat on sofa left*)   I am not impressed by politicians. And I didn't come to drink tea. I am here on business.
(*Nevertheless he takes a hearty sip*)

MARION   Well, you can do both. They do in England. American business-men are so tense.

KURT   I'm not a business-man.

NOLAN   Well, whatever you are, you are very ill-mannered.

KURT (*Pleased*)   That's true!

MARION (*Delighted*)   Isn't it nice you agree. For a moment I thought you weren't going to hit it off. . . .

NOLAN   In my day if a boy came in and behaved like this before a lady he'd be horsewhipped.

KURT   Well, when you get into the Senate you can introduce a horsewhipping bill. Probably bring you great kudos.

NOLAN   You talk like a Bolshevik.

KURT   Thank you! You talk like a Senator!
(MARION *wants to laugh but thinks better of it. She looks at* KURT *with a new eye*)

MARION (*Quickly offering him more tea*)   Another cup, Mr. Kurt. . . .

KURT (*Taking it*)   Thank you.

MARION   And one of these cakes—they're very nice . . . Minnie made them—almost as good as Lebkuchen. Minnie spoils me.

KURT (*Taking it*)   Thank you. (*Eats cake*) Having said, from our respective points of view, the worst thing we could say about each other, having uttered the ultimate insult, there's no reason we can't be friends, Senator. Damn good cake. No lunch as a matter of fact.

MARION   That's what's the matter with him—he was hungry —hungry boy. . . .

NOLAN (*Puts tea-cup on piano*)   He probably wants to sell you some insurance. . . .

KURT   Not at all. I'm not here to sell. I'm here to buy.

MARION   A picture!

KURT   Do I look like a picture-buyer!

MARION   As a matter of fact you don't . . . but I haven't anything to sell except pictures.

KURT (*Confidently*)   I think you have!

MARION (*To* NOLAN)   This young man is very tantalizing.

NOLAN   Well, why don't you ask him to state his proposition and have done with it?

MARION (*Turns to* KURT *and repeats mechanically*)   State your proposition and have done with it.

KURT (*Puts his cup down on table rear of sofa left*)   What a nuisance women are!

NOLAN (*Starting toward him*)   Why, you insolent young whelp—I've half a mind to . . .

KURT (*Pleasantly*) That's an impulse you'd better control. I wrote to this lady a business letter asking for an appointment. She granted it to me at four o'clock. It is now six. In that interval I've climbed these five flights of stairs three times. I've lost over an hour of my life going away and coming back. An hour in which I might have read a first-class book or made love to a girl or had an idea—an irreparable hour. That's rudeness if you like. It's unbusinesslike. It's sloppy. (*To* MARION) Now will you see me alone or will you keep me here fencing with this inadequate antagonist?

MARION You are unquestionably the most impossible young man I've ever met. Go away!

KURT Right! (*He turns to go and means it and she knows that he means it. And she is consumed with curiosity*) (*As he goes*) So long, Senator! Yours for the Revolution!

MARION (*As he reaches door, goes after him—pleads pitifully*) Young man! Mr. Nolan is an old friend of mine. I should consult him in any case about whatever business you may suggest. Can't you speak in front of him.
(*At the same time she shakes her head to him not to go away*)

KURT I cannot!

MARION Please wait a minute. . . .

KURT All right—one.
(*He picks up a magazine and leafs through it negligently*)

MARION (*To* LEANDER) After all, Leander, I can't afford—it may be something. . . . (*She takes his arm and starts walking him to the door, whispering*) I'm just curious to hear what he's got to say for himself. . . .

NOLAN I'm not sure it's safe to leave you alone with a character like that. . . .

MARION Minnie's in her room . . . with a bow and arrow!

NOLAN (*Going up to hall-door*) I have to go in any case —I'm late now.

MARION When will I see you, Bunny?
(*She is at door with him*)

NOLAN (*Taking up his hat and coat*) I don't know. I'm very busy. I'll telephone you.

MARION Do. Telephone me tonight. I'll tell you what he said. It'll probably be funny.

NOLAN (*Out loud at* KURT) It pains me, Marion, that you are so unprotected that any hooligan— (KURT *turns page of magazine*) can write you and come to see you in your apartment. However, that is the way you have chosen. Good night.

MARION Good night, dear. Are you in the book? I'll telephone you . . .

NOLAN (*Hastily*) No—no—you'd better not. I shall communicate with you. Good-bye.

KURT Good-bye, Sir Galahad.
(NOLAN *starts to retort, changes his mind and, in a very choleric mood, he goes out. There is a pause*)

MARION Well, I'm afraid you didn't make a very good impression on him!

KURT (*Putting magazine away*) That's just too bad!

MARION That's no way for a young man to get on in the world—he's a very important person.

KURT That's what passes for importance. You're not taken in by him, are you? Stuffed shirt—flatulent and pompous— perfect legislator!

MARION As a matter of fact he's a very nice man—simple and kindly.
(*Gets cigarettes and offers one to* KURT *who takes it and lights it. She takes one too but he forgets to light hers*)

KURT I bet he isn't simple and he isn't kindly. I bet he's greedy and vicious. Anyway he's a hypocrite. When a man starts worrying out loud about unprotected women you may know he's a hypocritical sensualist.

MARION You're a violent young man, aren't you?
(*Not getting light from* KURT *she lights her own*) (*Throwing match to floor*)

KURT Yes. The world is full of things and people that make me see red. . . . Why do you keep calling me youth and young man? I'm twenty-five.

MARION Well, you seem to have the lurid and uncorrected imagination of the adolescent.

KURT   Imagination! That's where you're wrong. I may tell you, Miss Froude, that I'm as realistic as anybody you've ever met.

MARION   (*Sitting on up-stage arm of sofa, right*)   Anybody who'd be so unreasonable over a nice fellow like Bunny Nolan . . . if you only knew—if only you'd been present at the interview I had with him just before you came. You'd have seen how wrong you are about him. Why, he was—he was awfully funny—but he was also touching.

KURT   You're one of those tolerant people, aren't you—see the best in people?

MARION   You say that as if tolerance were a crime.

KURT   Your kind is. It's criminal because it encourages dishonesty, incompetence, weakness and all kinds of knavery. What you call tolerance I call sloppy laziness. You're like those book-reviewers who find something to praise in every mediocre book.

MARION   You are a fanatical young man.

KURT   Having said that you think you dispose of me. Well, so be it. I'm disposed of. Now, let's get down to business.
(*His manner plainly says: "Well, why should I bother to convince you? What importance can it possibly have what you think of me?" It is not wasted on* MARION)

MARION   You are also a little patronizing . . .

KURT   (*Pleased*)   Am I?

MARION   However, I don't mind being patronized. That's where my tolerance comes in. It even amuses me a little bit. (*Crossing to piano-seat*) But as I have to change for dinner perhaps you'd better . . .

KURT   Exactly.

MARION   Please sit down . . .
(*A moment . . . She sits on piano-bench facing him*)

KURT   (*Goes to piano and talks to her across it*)   I am the editor of a magazine called Every Week. Do you know it?

MARION   It seems to me I've seen it on news-stands. . . .

KURT   You've never read it?

MARION   I'm afraid I haven't.

KURT   That is a tribute to your discrimination. We have an immense circulation. Three millions, I believe. With a circulation of that size you may imagine that the average of our readers' intelligence cannot be very high. Yet occasionally we flatter them by printing the highbrows—in discreet doses we give them, at intervals, Shaw and Wells and Chesterton. So you'll be in good company anyway. . . .

MARION (*Amazed*)   I will?

KURT   Yes. I want you to write your biography to run serially in Every Week. Later of course you can bring it out as a book.

MARION   My biography!

KURT   Yes. The story of your life.

MARION (*With dignity*)   I know the meaning of the word.

KURT   The money is pretty good. I am prepared to give you an advance of two thousand dollars.

MARION   Good Heavens, am I as old as that—that people want my biography!

KURT   We proceed on the theory that nothing exciting happens to people after they are forty. . . .

MARION   What a cruel idea!

KURT   Why wait till you're eighty. Your impressions will be dimmed by time. Most autobiographies are written by corpses. Why not do yours while you are still young, vital, in the thick of life?

MARION   But I'm not a writer. I shouldn't know how to begin.

KURT   You were born, weren't you? Begin with that.

MARION   I write pleasant letters, my friends tell me. . . . But look here, why should you want this story from me— why should anybody be interested?—I'm not a first-rate artist you know—not by far—I'm just clever. . . .

KURT (*Bluntly*)   It's not you—it's the celebrity of your subjects. . . .

MARION (*Amused*)   You're a brutal young man—I rather like you . . .

KURT   Well, you've been courageous. You've been forthright. For an American woman you've had a rather extraordinary career—you've done pretty well what you wanted. . . .

MARION   The Woman Who Dared sort-of-thing. . . . Isn't that passé?

KURT   I think your life will make good copy. You might have stayed here and settled down and done Pictorial Review covers of mothers hovering fondly over babies. Instead you went to Europe and managed to get the most inaccessible people to sit for you. How did you do it?

MARION   You'd be surprised how accessible some of these inaccessible people are!

KURT   Well, that's just what I want to get from your story. Just that. Tell what happened to you, that's all. The impulse that made you leave home, that made you go, for instance, to Russia, before the popular emigration set in, that's made you wander ever since, that's kept you from settling down in any of the places where you had a chance to get established.

MARION   (*Quite seriously*)   But supposing I don't know that. . . .

KURT   Well, that's interesting. That enigma is interesting. Maybe, while writing, you can solve it. It's a form of clarification. The more I talk to you the more I feel there's a great story in you and that you'll have great fun telling it.

MARION   Young man, you make me feel like an institution!

KURT   Should do you a lot of good in your professional career too—we'll reprint the portraits you've made of Lenin, Mussolini, Shaw—anything you like. . . .

(*She begins to laugh, quietly at first, then heartily*)

MARION   Forgive me. . . .

KURT   (*Unperturbed*)   What's the matter?

MARION   Something I remembered—the funniest thing—isn't it funny how the oddest things pop into your mind?

KURT   What was it?

MARION   Something that happened years ago. . . .

KURT   What?

MARION   Oh, I couldn't possibly tell you. It wouldn't be fair!

KURT   In that case it'll probably be great for the magazine. Save it!

MARION   (*Frightened*)   You won't do anything lurid, will you?

KURT   Just print the story—just as you write it—practically as you write it.

MARION   I'm scared!
  (*She puts out her cigarette in ash-tray on the piano*)

KURT   Nonsense. Here's your first check. Two thousand dollars.
  (*He puts the check down on the table in front of her*)

MARION   (*Wretched suddenly, picks up check, rises, looks at check*)   I can't tell you how old this makes me feel!

KURT   Suppose I asked you to write a novel! That wouldn't make you feel old, would it? Well, I'm simply asking you to write a novel of your life. The only lively reading these days is biography. People are bored with fiction. It's too tame. The fiction-writers haven't the audacity to put down what actually happens to people.

MARION   You may be disappointed, you know. You probably see headlines in your mind. The Woman of a Hundred Affairs, The Last of the Great Adventuresses, The Magda Who Wouldn't Go Home. I promise you—it won't be a bit like that.

KURT   We'll announce it next month—first installment the following month. O.K.?

MARION   (*Puts down check, paces down right*)   Oh dear! I can't promise a thing like that—I really can't. . . .

KURT   Why not?

MARION   It'll worry me too much.

KURT   Well, don't promise. Just get to work.

MARION   (*Faces him*)   But what'll I do first?

KURT   (*Getting up*)   Well, if I were you I'd sit down. (*She does so helplessly on piano-bench.* KURT *then gives her paper, one of his own pencils*)   There now! You're all set!

MARION   (*Wailing*)   How can I go out to dinner—how can I ever do anything—with a chapter to write?

KURT   After all you don't have to make up anything. Just tell what happened to you.

(*He lights a fresh cigarette*)

MARION   Can I use names?

KURT   When they're prominent, yes. The obscure ones you can fake if you want to. Nobody'll know 'em anyway.

MARION (*Looks at him*)   Oh . . . what's your name?

KURT (*Looks at her*)   I told you—my name's Kurt.

MARION   I know—with a K—I can't call you Kurt! What's your *name?*

KURT (*Sulkily*)   Richard.

MARION   That's better. I tell you, Dickie, when I think—when I think—of the funny men I've known . . . they're pretty nearly all brothers under the skin you know, Dickie.

KURT   Well, that, as they say in the office, is an angle.

(*Suddenly her fear vanishes and she is overcome with the marvelous possibilities*)

MARION (*Jumps up and leans toward him as if to kiss him, but quickly thinks better of it*)   Dickie, I think it'll be marvelous! It'll be a knockout. And imagine— (*Picking up check*) I'm going to be paid for it! Dickie, you're an angel!

KURT (*Sardonically*)   That's me! Angel Kurt! Well, so long. I'll be seeing you.

(*Starts up-stage toward hall-door*)

MARION (*Suddenly panicky*)   Oh, don't go!

KURT   You don't think I'm going to sit here and hold your hand while you're remembering your conquests, do you?

MARION   Well, you can't go away and leave me like this—alone with my life. . . .

KURT   Perhaps it's time you got a good, straight, clear-eyed look at it—alone by yourself, without anybody around to hold your hand. . . .

MARION (*Suddenly*)   No. I don't want to. (*Shrugs her shoulders as if she were cold*) I think it would worry me. Besides, I feel superstitious about it.

KURT (*Following her down-stage*)   Superstitious!

MARION   Yes. A kind of—ultimate act. After you've written your biography, what else could there possibly be left for you to do?

KURT   Collect material for another!

MARION   What could you do over again—that wouldn't be repetitious?
(*Sits right arm of sofa right*)

KURT   It's repetitious to eat or to make love, isn't it? You keep on doing it.

MARION   You're cynical!

KURT (*Almost spits it out*)   You're sentimental.

MARION   I am—Sentimental Journey—no, that's been used, hasn't it?

KURT   Don't worry about a title—I'll get that from the story after you've finished it.

MARION   There's something about it—I don't know—

KURT   What?

MARION   Vulgar. *Everybody* spouting memoirs. Who cares?

KURT   Well, wrong hunch! Sorry to have taken your valuable time. Good-bye.

MARION (*The finality frightens her*)   What do you mean?

KURT (*He is withering—crosses to her*)   I'm prepared to admit I was mistaken—that's all. In your desire to escape vulgarity you would probably be—thin. You might even achieve refinement. I'm not interested. Padded episodes hovering on the edge of amour—

MARION (*Turns on him*)   Young man, you're insufferable!

KURT   And you're a false alarm!

MARION (*After a moment*)   I congratulate you! You've brought me to the verge of losing my temper! But I tell you this—you're quite mistaken about the character of my life— and about my relations with my friends. My story won't be thin and episodic because my life hasn't been thin and episodic. And I won't have to pad—the problem will be to select. I'm going to write the damn thing just to show you. Come in tomorrow afternoon for a cocktail.

KURT   Whose memoirs are these going to be, yours or mine?

MARION Well, you're an editor, aren't you? (*She smiles at him*) Come in and edit.

KURT All right, I'll come. But if you aren't here I'll go away. I won't wait a minute.

(*He goes out quickly.* MARION *stands looking after him, inclined to laugh, and yet affected. This is a new type even for her*)

MARION (*She speaks to herself*) What an extraordinary young man! (*In a moment* KURT *comes back in.* MARION *is very glad to see him, greets him as if there had been a long separation*) Oh, hello!

KURT (*Embarrassed*)   I forgot my hat!

(*He can't see it at once*)

MARION (*Without moving nor looking away from him, she indicates the hat on the sofa left*)   There it is! Right next to mine.

KURT (*Crosses for it*)   Oh yes. (*Picks up the hat*) Thanks. (*For a moment he stands uncertainly, hat in hand, looking at* MARION *who has not taken her eyes off him. He is embarrassed*) Well, so long!

MARION So long. (KURT *leaves again. She stands as before looking after him. She turns toward the piano—sees the check —picks it up and reads it to make sure it's true. The whole thing has a slightly fantastic quality to her. She is very happy and excited. She waves the check in her hand like a pennant and humming she crosses to the piano seat and sits and plays the waltz from "Danubia." She sees the pad and pencil on the piano and stops playing and picking up the pencil and the pad she crosses to the small arm chair in the up-stage end of the window and sits with her feet on the window seat. She repeats the first words of the first chapter aloud to herself as she writes them down*) I am born . . . (MINNIE *enters from door left to get the tea things she had left on the model stand.* MARION *taps the pencil on the pad as she repeats the words:*) I am born . . . (*The time seems remote to her*) I am born—I meet Richard Kurt—Well, Minnie, here's the outline—I am born . . . I meet Richard Kurt—now all I have to do is to fill in. . . . (MINNIE, *used to having irrelevancies addressed to her, takes this program rather stolidly*)

MINNIE Was, Marion?

MARION (*Trying to get rid of her*)   Fix something light, will you, Minnie . . . I'm not going out.

MINNIE   Aber der Junge kommt!

MARION   What Junge?

MINNIE   Der Junge, den Sie . . .

MARION   Oh, yes! The Junge I met on the boat. You'll have to send him away. I can't go out tonight. From now on, Minnie, no more frivolous engagements!

MINNIE (*Astonished*)   Sie bleiben den ganzen Abend zu Hause!

MARION   Yes, Minnie. I'm spending the evening alone with my life . . . (*She remembers* KURT'S *words and repeats them as if, after all, they have made a profound impression on her*) . . . get a good, straight, clear-eyed look at it . . .

MINNIE (*Picks up the tea-tray and bustling toward the kitchen, promising delights*)   Eine Fleischbrühe und Pfann-kuchen! . . .
   (MINNIE *exits door left*)

MARION (*Already brooding over her past*)   I am born. . . .
   (*Slowly the* CURTAIN *falls*)

ACT TWO

SCENE: *The same. About three weeks later. Afternoon.*

AT RISE: MARION *is putting some touches on the full length portrait of* LEANDER NOLAN *which stands away from the audience. She is wearing her working costume, baggy red corduroy trousers, a sash and a worn blue smock over a kind of sweater-jacket. She is very happy. . . . On the piano nearby are her writing things. While touching up* LEANDER *she is struck by an idea for her book. Puts down her brush and palette and goes to the piano to jot down some notes. The idea pleases her. She giggles to herself. Then she returns to her easel.* MINNIE *comes in and stands watching her a moment before* MARION *sees her.*

MARION (*Sees* MINNIE *at last*)   Oh yes, Minnie—do you want anything?

MINNIE   You asked me to come right away, Marion.

MARION   Did I?

MINNIE   Ja. (*Sitting on sofa right*)   So! You have left a note on the kitchen I should come in right away I am back from the market.

MARION (*Studying the portrait*)   Of course I did. That's right, Minnie.

MINNIE   Well, what did you want, Marion?

MARION (*Washing paint brush in turpentine jar*)   Did I tell you there'd be two for dinner?

MINNIE   Ja. Gewiss! Das ist vy I vent to the market.

MARION   Well, I've changed my plans. I'm dining out with Feydie after all.

126

MINNIE (*Rising and looking at picture*)   Ach, Gott!
(*She studies the portrait*)

MARION (*Looks humorously at* MINNIE *and puts her arm
about* MINNIE'S *shoulders*)   Gut?

MINNIE   Ziemlich gut—

MARION   Do you know who it is?

MINNIE   Oh, das sieht man ja gleich. Das ist Herr Nolan!

MARION (*Shaking her hand in gratitude*)   Thank you,
Minnie! (*Doorbell rings*) See who that is, will you, Minnie?

MINNIE   Fräulein ist zu Hause?

MARION   Ich erwarte Herrn Feydak. Für ihn bin ich immer
zu Hause.

MINNIE (*Agreeing heartily as she crosses to the door*)   Ja,
ja, der Herr Feydak. . . .
(MINNIE *goes out.* MARION *jots down a note on the pad
which is on the piano.* FEYDAK *enters.* MINNIE *closes the
door and exits left*)

MARION (*At piano*)   Hello Feydie! Sit down!

FEYDAK   Well, my dear, which career do I interrupt?

MARION (*Laughing*)   I don't know!

FEYDAK   One comes to see you with diffidence nowadays.
(FEYDAK *removes coat and hat and places them on the up-
stage end of the sofa right, and sits on the left side of the
sofa*)

MARION   While I'm painting I think of funny things to say,
funny phrases. It won't be a serious biography, thank God.
I'm dedicating it to Vicki: "To Vicki—the gayest person I
have ever known!" By the way, have you got any little snap-
shots of Vicki—all I've got are formal photographs with his
orders. I'd like to get something a little more intimate.

FEYDAK   I'll hunt some up for you.

MARION   Have you heard from the Powers yet, when you are
to leave?

FEYDAK   Tomorrow.

MARION (*Stricken—sits right of him*)   Feydie!

FEYDAK (*Fatalistically*)   Tomorrow. (*They sit*)   I shall
leave you with sorrow, Marion.

MARION   I'll have no one to laugh with.

FEYDAK   For me it's an exile.

MARION   You'll have a wonderful time. I shall miss you terribly.

FEYDAK   Perhaps you'll come out.

MARION   Perhaps I will. I've always wanted to go to China. If I have enough money left from all my labors I'll stop in on you—en route to China.

FEYDAK   That would be marvelous.

MARION   You know writing one's life has a sobering effect on one—you get it together and you think: "Well! look at the damn thing . . ."

FEYDAK   Do you want to be impressive?

MARION   Well, I don't want to be trivial . . .

FEYDAK   I think *you* escape that.

MARION   My friendships haven't been trivial. . . .
    (*She gives his hand a squeeze*)

FEYDAK   Have you seen that bombastic young man?

MARION   Oh, yes. He comes in every once in a while to see how I'm getting on. He's quite insulting. Underneath his arrogance I suspect he's very uncertain.

FEYDAK   Oh, now, don't tell me he has an inferiority complex!

MARION   Well, I think he has!

FEYDAK   The new psychology is very confusing. In my simple day you said: "That young man is bumptious and insufferable" and you dismissed him. Now you say: "He has an inferiority complex" and you encourage him to be more bumptious and more insufferable. It's very confusing.

MARION   There's a kind of honesty about him that I like.

FEYDAK   (*Instantly putting two and two together*)   Oh!

MARION   Nothing like that, Feydie! As a matter of fact—I don't mind telling you . . . I like him very much—

FEYDAK   I think he is destined . . .

MARION   He's not interested. He's some kind of fanatic. Social, I think. I've met that kind in Russia—quite unassailable. But I'm optimistic. . . . (*They laugh*) Well, one must never despair, must one. Life is so much more resourceful and resilient than one is oneself. Three weeks ago when you came to see me I felt quite at the end of my rope. I didn't tell you quite but I actually didn't know which way to turn. I felt tired too—which troubled me. Well, now I find myself, quite suddenly, (*She indicates portrait*) doing Leander and — (*She indicates manuscript on piano*) doing myself. New Vista. Very exciting.

FEYDAK   All this enthusiasm for art alone?

MARION   (*Laughing*)   Of course!—Feydie, what did you think?

FEYDAK   I don't believe it.

MARION   Come here and have a look at Leander!

FEYDAK (*He rises—walks to the canvas on the easel*)   Hm! Formal!

MARION   It's to hang in the White House.
(*She winks at him, he laughs, puts his arm around her shoulder*)

FEYDAK   Marion, you're adorable!
(*They walk down-stage together, their arms around each other's shoulders, very affectionately*)

MARION   Oh, Feydie, I'm having a wonderful time. Quiet too. Writing *enforces* silence and solitude on one. I've always lived in such a rush—a kind of interminable scherzo. . . .

FEYDAK   Good title! . . .

MARION   Think so? I'll put it down. . . . (*Writes on pad on piano.* FEYDAK *sits on Right arm of sofa Left facing her*) Interminable scherzo. . . . How do you spell it? A little affected. Might do for a chapter heading maybe. . . . (*Returns to him—sitting on model stand—facing him*) But I realize now I haven't in years had time to stop and think. I sit here for hours, Feydie, and nothing comes to me. Then, suddenly, the past will come in on me with a rush—odd, remote, semi-forgotten things of the past. Are they true? How much is true? One can never be sure, can one? I remember certain griefs and fears. I remember their existence without recalling at all their intensity—their special anguish. Why? What was the matter with me? What made them so acute? It

is like recalling a landscape without color, a kind of color-blindness of the memory. (*Doorbell rings. She calls out to her factotum*) Minnie! (MINNIE *enters left and crosses rapidly to hall-door.* MARION *arranges the model stand on which stands the papal arm-chair in red and gold*) This is probably the Hon. Nolan. He's due for a sitting. He pretends he doesn't like to have his picture painted, but I know he does.
(MINNIE *enters from hall-way. She is flustered and giggly*)

MINNIE (*Very high-pitched voice*)   Herr Varvick Vilson!

MARION   Tympi Wilson!

MINNIE (*To* FEYDAK)   Der *film star!*

FEYDAK   So?

MINNIE (*Radiant*)   Ja! Ja!

MARION   Oh, Feydie, you'll adore this. Ask him in, Minnie.

MINNIE (*As she goes out to admit* WILSON)   Gott, ist er schön!

MARION   Warwick's public.

FEYDAK   And mine!

MARION (*In a quick whisper*)   What ever you do—outstay him!
(MINNIE *has opened the door and* WARWICK WILSON *enters. He is very handsome, explosively emotional, and given to cosmic generalization. He is in evening clothes*)

WILSON (*With a red carnation in his buttonhole, crossing to* MARION *and kissing her hand*)   Marion!

MARION   Warwick!

WILSON   Darling! How are you?

MARION   I'm splendid. Been up all night?

WILSON   No, no! This is business.
(MINNIE *has crossed to kitchen door upper-left, never taking her eyes from* WILSON)

MARION   This is Mr. Feydak. Mr. Warwick Wilson, the famous film star.

WILSON (*Crosses to sofa and shakes hands with* FEYDAK—*dramatically*)   Feydak! *The* Mr. Feydak?

FEYDAK (*Again mistaken for his brother*)   Ja.

WILSON   I've heard of you indeed!

FEYDAK   Have you? Thanks.

MARION   Mr. Feydak is on his way to Hollywood. He is to write the music for . . .

WILSON   (*Sits on the model stand—facing front*)   Of course! I am honored, Mr. Feydak—deeply honored. That unforgettable waltz—how does it go? . . . (*He starts to hum with a swaying gesture the waltz from the "Merry Widow"*) Music's my one passion!

MARION   Once you said it was me.

WILSON   A lot of good it did me!

MARION   (*To* WILSON)   Well, tell me . . . (*She sees* MINNIE *who is still staring at* WILSON) Look at Minnie. The mere sight of you has upset her so that she's speechless.

MINNIE   Aber, Fräulein! (WILSON *rises graciously and gives* MINNIE *a friendly wave of the hand. He's no snob.* MINNIE, *speechless with delight, exits left*) (WILSON *returns to his position on the model stand*)

MARION   All right, Minnie! Warwick, Warwick! You mustn't do things like that to Minnie, at her age!

WILSON   (*Tragically*)   There you are! This face! This cursed face! I should go masked really. One has no private life!

MARION   (*Sits in throne chair on model stand*)   What would you do with it if you had it, eh, Tympi?

WILSON   (*Delighted*)   That nickname!

MARION   It just rolled off my tongue. Did I call you that?

WILSON   You did! You invented it. No one's called me that since you left Hollywood. And you promised to explain the significance to me, but you ever did.

MARION   Did it have a significance?

FEYDAK   Marion has a knack for nicknames.

MARION   I love 'em. I'd like to do a chapter on nicknames.

WILSON   (*Highly pleased*)   Tympi! Tympi! (*Very patronizing to* FEYDAK) You are an intuitive person, Mr. Feydak. I can see that. (FEYDAK *ad libs: "Danke schön"*) Can you imagine what she meant?

FEYDAK   Her vagaries are beyond me, Mr. Wilson.

WILSON (*Leaning back toward* MARION)   Speak, Oracle! No! Don't tell me now. Put it into that book you're writing.

MARION (MARION *and* FEYDAK *exchange glances*)   How things get around.

WILSON   It's been in the back of my mind for years, Marion . . . to have you paint me. Now that we're both in town together . . .

MARION   Well, I'd *love* to . . .

WILSON   In the costume of the Dane. (MARION *and* FEYDAK *exchange a look*) (*Strikes a pose*) I'd like to be done in *his* costume. I hope, Mr. Feydak, that they won't break your spirit in Hollywood as they've almost broken mine!

FEYDAK (*With a smile*)   My spirit is indestructible!

WILSON (*Rises and crosses to rear of sofa and pats* FEYDAK *on the back*)   I'm glad to hear it. (*Returns to left of model stand and stands with his right foot on it*) You know, for years I've been begging them to do Shakespeare.
  (*Gesticulates*)

MARION (*Interrupting him*)   Sit down and be comfortable.

WILSON   They simply won't listen. But I'm going to give up acting and produce!

MARION   Oh, good God! Don't do that!

WILSON   Why not?

MARION   What would Minnie do with her night off?

WILSON (*Smiles*)   My public, eh?

MARION   Yes!

WILSON   Quite so! (*Patronizingly*) You artists who work in media like painting or literature— (*To* FEYDAK) Or music, that too is a beautiful art, Mr. Feydak—transcends speech— transcends everything, by saying nothing it says all.

FEYDAK   Ja!
  (*The doorbell rings*)

WILSON   You are certainly lucky compared to us poor actors. We— (MINNIE *enters and crosses to hall-door upper center*) Wouldn't it be ironic if all that remained of me after I am gone were your painting of me. That is why I want it perhaps—my poor grasp on immortality.

FEYDAK   You see, Marion, you confer immortality!

MARION   I think immortality is an over-rated commodity. But tell me, Tympi, what are you doing away from Hollywood?

MINNIE (*Comes in announcing*)   Der Herr Nolan!
(MINNIE *then looks at* WILSON. WILSON *stands—looks at* MINNIE)

MARION   Show him in. Show him in. (*With a lingering look at* WILSON, MINNIE *goes back*) (*To others, after watching* MINNIE *exit*) You see!

FEYDAK   The effect is instantaneous—like music . . .
(NOLAN *enters.* MINNIE *follows* NOLAN *in and exits into kitchen, murmuring ecstatically,* "Gott! Ist er schön!" *looking at* WILSON)

MARION   Hello Bunny! (*Introducing* NOLAN) You know Mr. Feydak. Mr. Nolan, this is Warwick Wilson, you've heard of him.
(FEYDAK *bows to* NOLAN, *who returns the bow*)

WILSON   It's a pleasure, Mr. Nolan. I've heard of *you* indeed!
(*They shake hands*)

MARION   You're late for your sitting, Bunny. Will the presence of these gentlemen embarrass you? I don't mind if you don't.

NOLAN (*Has entered rather worried and angry. He has a magazine rolled in his hand. He now speaks very irritatedly*) As a matter of fact, Marion . . .

MARION (*Putting him in throne chair on model stand*)   Oh, sit down like a good fellow. The light is getting bad. (NOLAN *sits.* WILSON *sits on the right arm of the sofa left on which* FEYDAK *is sitting.* MARION *gets to work on* BUNNY) How did you find me, Tympi?

WILSON   I read in a magazine that you were barging into literature . . .

NOLAN (*Half rising, showing magazine*)   This is true then!

MARION   Don't get up, Bunny . . . (*Nevertheless she takes the magazine and looks at it*) Well, Dickie has gone and spread himself, hasn't he? (*She sits on sofa left between* WILSON *and* FEYDAK) Look here, Feydie!

(*Shows him the full-page announcement of her book in magazine*)

FEYDAK (*Looking*)   Do you think you can live up to this?

MARION   Why will they write this sort of thing! (*Rises and goes back*) Makes me out a kind of female Casanova. (*She drops the magazine on the stand at* NOLAN'S *feet*) Well, they'll be disappointed.

NOLAN (*Bitterly*)   Will they?

MARION   Bunny!

(*But she thinks nothing of it—merely pushes him into a better light*)

FEYDAK (*Tactfully—he senses danger*)   May I ask, Mr. Wilson—are you making a picture at the moment?

WILSON   No, I'm in New York making some personal appearances.

MARION   Personal appearances. I love that phrase. Has such an air of magnanimity about it.

(*Crosses to painting*)

WILSON   Pretty boring, I can tell you! I've got writer's cramp signing autograph books. It's a perfect martyrdom I assure you. It's no fun at all.

(WILSON *crosses to stand—puts his right foot on it, leans on his knee with his right arm and studies* NOLAN, *his face not six inches away from* NOLAN'S. NOLAN *fidgets*)

MARION   I can imagine! What's the matter, Bunny? You seem under a strain today . . . not relaxed.

NOLAN (*Bursting out and glaring at all of them*)   It's like being watched while you're taking a bath!

MARION   Oh, I'm so sorry, Bunny!

FEYDAK (*Rising*)   I quite sympathize with Mr. Nolan.

WILSON (*Moves away*)   Supposing I were so shy, eh, Mr. Nolan?

FEYDAK (*Crosses to* MARION *who is above her easel, right*) I'm off, Marion. (*Kisses her hand*) Auf Wiedersehen!

MARION (*Meaningfully*)   You'll have to go— (WILSON *sits again on arm of sofa left*) both of you . . .

WILSON (*Rises*) I was just going myself. My next appearance is at 6:45.
(*Speaks to others*)

FEYDAK (*To help her*) Perhaps I can drop you, Mr. Wilson.

WILSON (*Faces* FEYDAK) No, I'll drop you . . . (*Turns to* MARION) I say, Marion . . .
(FEYDAK, *helpless, goes up-stage putting on coat*)

MARION Yes, Tympi?

WILSON If you started my portrait right away and it turns out—I am sure it will turn out—you might put it in your book, mightn't you? I'm frankly sick of just appearing in fan-magazines.

MARION We'll see. Why not?

WILSON Splendid! *Don't fail to come tonight.* Good-bye dearest Marion. Good-bye again, Mr. Nolan.
(*He starts to shake* NOLAN'S *hand but is interrupted by* MARION, *almost screaming*)

MARION No, no, no! Don't do *that*—don't touch him.

WILSON Most happy! See you later. . . .
(*He waves himself off at last—*MARION *returns to her easel*)

MARION (*To* FEYDAK) Don't forget—I'm dining with you.

FEYDAK (*Like the player in Hamlet who burlesques Polonius*) Most happy—see you later.
(FEYDAK *leaves*)

MARION (*With relief*) Now then . . .

NOLAN (*Muttering to himself*) Silly ass!

MARION (*Working on painting*) That young man is one of the most famous people in the world, do you realize that, Bunny? His profile follows you all over Europe—*and* Asia. Ubiquitous profile. Have you ever seen him?

NOLAN (*Unswerved*) He's a silly ass!

MARION I admit he's somewhat on that side—but that other one—that Feydie—he's the darling of the world!

NOLAN (*Very short—bitterly*) Evidently!

MARION (*Surprised*) Bunny!

NOLAN (*Savage now*) Who isn't a darling! Everyone's a darling as far as I can see! The world's full of darlings. Your world at any rate.

MARION But, darling .   (*She suddenly stops—sits right end of sofa right*) Oh, Bunny, I remember now!

NOLAN You remember what!

MARION Tympi! Why I nicknamed him Tympi. Don't you see?

NOLAN No, I don't see . . .

MARION For tympanum—a large instrument in the orchestra producing a hollow sound. (*She beats an imaginary drum with her paint brush*) Boom! (*Suddenly* NOLAN *quits the pose*) What is it?

NOLAN I can't sit today. I'm not in the mood.

MARION I could tell there was something worrying you.

NOLAN There is something worrying me!

MARION Well, what is it?

NOLAN This confounded story! Are you really writing it?

MARION Well, yes—I am.

NOLAN What do you intend to tell?

MARION Well, that's a rather difficult question to answer—it's like asking me what I've been doing all my life.

NOLAN When does this biography start?

MARION (*Beginning to wonder about this questioning*) With my birth—coincidence, isn't it?

NOLAN All the time back home—when you were a girl in Knoxville?

MARION Yes, of course. I've had a wonderful time going back over it all.

NOLAN Everything?

MARION Everything I can remember.

NOLAN Do I come into it?

MARION (*Smiling to herself*) You do! You certainly do!

NOLAN You must leave me out of that story!

MARION But Bunny, how can I possibly leave you out?

NOLAN   You must, that's all.

MARION   But how can I? You were too important—think of the rôle you played in my life. By your own confession, Bunny darling, you—you started me. That's a good idea for a chapter-heading, isn't it? "Bunny Starts Me." I must put that down.

NOLAN   This is no joke, Marion. (*With menace*) I warn you . . .

MARION   Warn me! Let me understand you. Are you seriously asking me to give up an opportunity like this just because . . .

NOLAN   (*Rises and gets down from the model stand. Speaks with brutal command*)   Opporunity! Cheap exhibitionism! A chance to flaunt your affairs in a rag like this. (*Indicating magazine on piano*) I won't be drawn into it. I can tell you that!
   (*He is in a towering rage*)

MARION   (*After a pause*)   I know that by your standards, Bunny, I'm a loose character. But there are other standards, there just are.

NOLAN   (*Crosses to center—drops magazine on model stand*) Not in Tennessee!

MARION   (*Rises*)   I'm afraid you're provincial, Bunny.

NOLAN   I'm sorry.

MARION   (*Takes off her smock, crosses to small table down right, gets her notes, then crosses to desk upper right*)   I don't care what the advertisements say about my story—I know what I'm writing . . .

NOLAN   I'm sorry.

MARION   That's all right.
   (*But this has gone pretty deep*)

NOLAN   (*After a pause*)   If you're doing this for money— (*She turns and watches him*) I know you've been pretty hard up—I promise you I'll get you commissions enough to more than make up for this story. I was talking about you only the other day to my prospective father-in-law. He's a big man, you know. I am sure I can get him to sit for you . . .

MARION   The tip isn't big enough.

NOLAN (*Scared now that he sees the extent to which he has hurt her*)   Marion! . . .

MARION   It amuses me to write my life. I am pleasure-loving —you know that—I will therefore pass up the opportunity of painting your big father-in-law. I will even give up the pleasure of painting you. And we can part friends, then, can't we? (*She reaches out her hand to him*)   Good-bye, Bunny.

NOLAN (*Devastated*)   Marion—you can't do this to me— you can't send me away like this . . .

MARION   I don't think ever in my life that I've had a vulgar quarrel with anyone. This is the nearest I've come to it. I'm a little annoyed with you for that. I think it's better we part now while we can still do so with some—dignity. Shall we?

NOLAN   You don't realize what's involved—or you wouldn't talk like that . . .

MARION   What *is* involved?

NOLAN   My entire career. That's what's involved.

MARION   Oh!

NOLAN   This is the most critical moment of my life. My fiancée's father is the most powerful leader of opinion in my state. Frankly, I depend on him for support. To have this kind of thing bandied about now might cause a permanent rift between him and me—might seriously interfere not only with my candidacy for the Senate, but, with my marriage.

MARION   They are interlocking—I quite understand.

NOLAN   A revelation of this kind—coming at this moment— might be fatal . . .

MARION   Revelation! You make me feel like—I can't tell you what you make me feel like . . .
   (*She laughs—semi-hysterically*)

NOLAN (*Sepulchral*)   You must give this up, Marion.

MARION   I've met distinguished men abroad—politicians, statesmen—a Prime Minister even—and this kind of "revelation"—as you so luridly call it, is no more to them than a theme for after-dinner banter. They take it in their stride. My God, Bunny, you take it so big!

NOLAN These people I'm depending on to elect me aren't sophisticated like you or me. (MARION *looks at* NOLAN *with some surprise*) What I mean is—they're country people essentially—my future father-in-law is sympathetic to their point of view.

MARION Tell me—your father-in-law, is he the man with the chest-expansion?

NOLAN He's a fine sturdy man—as you perhaps know, he makes a fetish of exercise.

MARION (*Bubbling again*) You see his pictures in shorts in Health Magazines.

NOLAN There's no disgrace in that.

MARION (*Sits right arm of sofa left*) It doesn't shock me, Bunny. I was just identifying him, that's all.

NOLAN I owe everything to Kinnicott—I wouldn't be running for the Senate right now if not for him. I can't risk offending him.

MARION What the devil's happened to you anyway? You used to be quite a nice boy—even fun occasionally . . .

NOLAN (*Wistful—turns away*) Maybe—if you had stuck to me . . .

MARION Ts! Ts! Ts! Poor Bunny. I'm sorry for you. Really I am!
  (*She strokes his arm*)

NOLAN (*Suddenly passionate—faces her*) Don't touch me!

MARION (*Amazed*) Bunny!

NOLAN Do you think I'm not human!

MARION Well, if you aren't the most contradictory . . .

NOLAN I realized the moment I came in here the other day —the moment I saw you . . .

MARION (*Interrupting*) But Bunny! You're engaged and you're going to be a Senator.

NOLAN (*Walks away from her*) Forget it! Forget I ever said it. . . .

MARION You bewilder me . . .

NOLAN (*Bitterly*) I'm not surprised I bewilder you. You've spent your life among a lot of foreign counts. It's well known that foreigners are more immoral than we are.

MARION I'm very touched. I am really.
(*She kisses him in a friendly way*)

NOLAN Don't do that! I forbid you!

MARION All right. I'll never attack you again, I promise.

NOLAN I wish I had never come back into your life—it was a terrible mistake—you'd forgotten me.

MARION (*Seriously*) Oh, you're wrong. First love—one doesn't forget that.

NOLAN (*Passionately*) But you did! You forgot me! And if you got the chance again, you'd humiliate me again.

MARION Humiliate! What queer notions you have— Is it a question of pride or vanity between us? We're old friends—friends.

NOLAN (*Moves a step right*) Please forget this—I don't know what came over me—I . . .

MARION Of course. There's nothing to forget. (*Moves a step toward him*) It's quite all right, dear . . . (*She pats him on his hand*) . . . Oh, excuse me . . .

NOLAN I warn you, Marion—I solemnly warn you—if you persist in this—

MARION Never in my life have I seen a man vacillate so between passion and threat . . .

NOLAN I shall find ways to stop you. Mr. Kinnicott, my future father-in-law is a powerful man.

MARION I know. Extraordinary biceps.

NOLAN I warn you, Marion. This matter is beyond flippancy.

MARION (*Sits*) There'll be some very distinguished people in my biography. You needn't be ashamed.

NOLAN That movie-actor!

MARION Tympi in Hamlet costume—you in a toga. I'll print your portraits on opposite pages—my two men!

NOLAN You are malicious!

MARION I must admit, Bunny, that you provoke in me all my malicious impulses. You come here suddenly and you convey to me what I've missed in not marrying you. (*The back doorbell rings.* MINNIE *crosses to answer it during* MARION'S *speech*) You dangle before me the inventory of your felicities—a career, a fortune, a fabulous bride—and then, because I get a chance to chronicle my own adventures —you object—you tell me I mustn't! I have a nice nature, Bunny, or I should be angry—I should be indignant.

(KURT *enters*)

NOLAN (*Sharply and with threat*)   Now, Marion, I've warned you . . . You'll regret this.

MARION   Hello, Dickie, do talk to Bunny for a minute, will you? (*Crosses to the stairs and starts up them to her bedroom*) I've simply got to change. (MINNIE *enters up center and exits left*) Feydie's coming to take me out to dinner.

NOLAN   But, Marion . . .

MARION   I couldn't do anything about this in any case, Bunny dear, because I've promised Dickie. In fact, I signed something, didn't I, Dickie? Don't go away either of you. . . .
(MARION *blows them a kiss and exits into her bedroom. A pause between the two men.* KURT *crosses down-stage to above the model stand. Suddenly,* NOLAN *goes to* KURT *and reaches out his hand to him*)

NOLAN   How do you do, young man?

KURT (*Very much surprised*)   How do *you* do?
(*He looks at him narrowly, his head a little on one side, a terrier appraising a mastiff*)

NOLAN   I am very glad to see you.

KURT   Isn't that nice . . . ?

NOLAN   You may be surprised to learn that on the one occasion when we met you made quite an impression on me.

KURT   Did I?

NOLAN (*Sits sofa right*)   You did. Sit down. In fact—I hope you don't mind—if you will allow me as a prerogative of seniority—to ask you a few questions. I have a purpose in mind and not—I trust—an idle purpose.

KURT   Shoot! (*Sits*) Anything to enlighten the professor!
(*He knows he is going to be pumped and has decided to be casual, naïve and even respectful*)

NOLAN (*Clearing his throat*) Now then—your present position on the magazine you represent—have you been on it long?

KURT About two years.

NOLAN And before that?

KURT Newspaper work.

NOLAN And before that?

KURT Tramping around the world. Odd jobs. Quite a variety.

NOLAN College?

KURT Believe it or not—Yale—two years . . . worked my way through—washed dishes.

NOLAN Very interesting preparation . . . very interesting . . . Tell me now—your present work—do you find it interesting? Is the remuneration satisfactory?

KURT Two hundred smackers a week. That's twice what I've ever earned in my life before.

NOLAN Now then—to come to the point—no doubt you've heard of my prospective father-in-law, Mr. Orrin Kinnicott?

KURT Heard of him! We pay him the compliment of imitation. He is our model, our criterion, our guiding star!

NOLAN As you know, Mr. Kinnicott's interests are varied. He owns some powerful newspapers in my state. The other day I heard him say that he wanted a new man in Washington.

KURT (*Playing naïvely excited*) Now that's something to give one's eye-teeth for!

NOLAN (*Pleased at the result*) I think it might be possible to swing it—very possible.

KURT God, what a break!

NOLAN As it happens Mr. Kinnicott is at present in town. I shall arrange an appointment for you in the next few days. Naturally, I expect you to keep the matter entirely confidential.

KURT Naturally! You needn't worry on that score, Senator, I assure you.

NOLAN   Thank you, Mr. Kurt. That is all I ask.
(A pause)

KURT   Mr. Nolan—do you mind if I ask *you* something?

NOLAN   Certainly not . . .

KURT   You won't consider me impertinent?

NOLAN   *(With a smile)*   I don't object to impertinence, Mr. Kurt. I was often considered impertinent myself when I was your age.

KURT   Why are you making me this offer?

NOLAN   I am not making you an offer. I shall merely attempt to expedite . . .

KURT   Why? The first time we met we didn't exactly hit it off, now, did we? Why then are you going to all this trouble?

NOLAN   I have discussed you with Miss Froude who is an old friend of mine and whose opinion I greatly respect. She thinks very highly of you, Mr. Kurt. My own impression . . .

KURT   *(Inexorably)*   Why? What, as they say, is the pay-off?

NOLAN   I'll tell you. I'll tell you quite frankly. I don't want Miss Froude's autobiography, which you have persuaded her to write, to appear in your magazine. I want it killed!

KURT   Oh! You want it killed?

NOLAN   Exactly.

KURT   Why?

NOLAN   Marion knows why. We needn't go into that.

KURT   *(Wounded by a sudden and devastating jealousy)* Good God! You! You too!
   (MARION enters from balcony. She is wearing a dove-colored evening-dress—the gamine transformed into lady-of-the-world)

MARION   Well! How have you two boys been getting on? What do you think?

KURT   *(Seething. Crosses to foot of stairs)*   I'll tell you what I think. . . .

MARION   About the dress I mean . . .
   (She does a turn for them)

NOLAN   *(Without looking up at her or the dress. He is watching KURT)*   It's charming.

MARION   Thank you, Bunny. With all his faults Bunny is much more satisfactory than you are, Dickie.

KURT (*At boiling point*)   He's chivalrous he is! His chivalry is so exquisite that he has just been attempting to bribe me to keep your story from being published. His gallantry is so delicate that he's terrified about being mentioned in it.

MARION (*Comes down stairs during* KURT'S *speech*)   Don't be so worked up about it, Dickie. You're another one who takes it big. It's catching!

KURT (*Flaring at her*)   You're not very sensitive. . . .

MARION   Why should I be? You misapprehend Bunny. If he doesn't want to be in the same story with me that's his business. And it's nothing to do with chivalry or gallantry or nonsense like that.

NOLAN   Marion—this young man . . .

KURT (*Taunting him*)   What about Washington, Mr. Nolan? Mr. Nolan, a prospective Senator offers to bribe me with a post in Washington controlled by his prospective father-in-law. . . .

MARION   If it's a good job take it, Dickie, by all means. . . .

KURT   I am afraid, Marion, that your code is more relaxed than mine . . .

MARION   Code, nonsense! I gave up codes long ago. I'm a big laissez-faire girl!

NOLAN   If this young man is an example of the distinguished company you've come to associate with, Marion . . .

MARION   Don't quarrel children—please. It distresses me.

NOLAN   He's extremely objectionable.

KURT   What about Washington, now, *Senator?* Are you still willing to expedite . . . !
   (KURT *and* NOLAN *stand glaring at each other.* MARION *tries to calm the troubled waters. Crosses to* NOLAN)

MARION   Really, Dickie, you're very naughty. Don't mind him, Bunny. He's very young.

KURT   And incorruptible!

NOLAN   Marion, I claim the privilege of a friendship that antedates Mr. Kurt's by some years, to beg you, very solemnly, not to prostitute your talents to his contemptible, sensation-mongering rag.

KURT (*Faces them*)   There's a Senatorial sentence!

MARION   Hush, Dickie, hush! Bunny darling, it's true that Dickie's magazine isn't the Edinburgh Review. On the other hand your assumption that my story will be vulgar and sensational is a little gratuitous, isn't it?

NOLAN   You *refuse* then?

MARION (*Gently but with a serious overtone*)   Yes. This—censorship before publication seems to me, shall we say, unfair. It is—even in an old friend—dictatorial.

NOLAN (*With an air of finality*)   You leave me then no alternative. I am very sorry.

KURT   Don't let him frighten you, Marion, he can't do anything.

NOLAN   I can forgive you anything, Marion, but the fact that you value my wishes below those of this insolent young man.

MARION   But this insolent young man hasn't anything to do with it! Can't you see, Bunny—it's my own wish that is involved.

NOLAN   I have explained to you the special circumstances. If you would consent to delay publication till after election. . . .
    (*She turns to* KURT *to ask him to make this concession but can't get a word in. She is wedged between both of them*)

KURT   She has nothing to do with the publication-date. That's my province. Gosh, what a chance for the circulation-manager in Tennessee!
    (*He rubs his palms together in mock anticipation of profits*)

NOLAN (*Losing his temper at last*)   You are tampering with more than you bargain for Mr.—Mr. . . .

KURT   Kurt.

MARION   With a "K."

NOLAN   There are ways of dealing with a young man like this and you'll soon find out what they are!

KURT   Them's harsh words, Senator!

NOLAN   You wait and see.

MARION   Bunny!

NOLAN   Don't speak to me! I never want to see you again!
(*He goes out*)

MARION (*Really distressed*)   This is awful!

KURT (*Highly elated*)   It's wonderful!

MARION   But I'm very fond of Bunny. Oh dear! I'll telephone
him tonight . . .

KURT (*Grimly*)   Over my dead body!

MARION   Can it be, Dickie, that I control the election of
Senators from Tennessee?
(*Sits right end of sofa left*)

KURT (*After a moment*)   How could you ever have loved a
stuffed-shirt like that!

MARION   He wasn't a stuffed-shirt. That's the funny part. He
was charming. He was a charming boy. Rather thin. Rather
reticent. He was much nicer than you as a matter of fact. . . .

KURT   I'm sure he was!

MARION   He was much less violent!

KURT (*Sits*)   Hypocritical old buccaneer!

MARION   He used to work hard all day and at night he
studied law. We used to walk the country lanes and dream
about the future. He was scared—he was wistful. How did
he emerge into this successful, ambitious, over-cautious—
mediocrity? How do we all emerge into what we are? How
did I emerge into what I am? I've dug up some of my old
diaries. I was a tremulous young girl. I was eager. I believe
I was naive. Look at me now! Time, Dickie . . . What will
you be at forty? A bond-holder and a commuter . . . Oh,
Dickie!

KURT (*Tensely*)   I'll never be forty!

MARION (*Laughing*)   How will you avoid it?

KURT (*Same tone*)   I'll use myself up before I'm forty.

MARION   Do you think so? I don't think so. (*Rises*) I sometimes wake up on certain mornings feeling absolutely—immortal! Indestructible! One is perpetually reborn I think,
Dickie. Everyone should write one's life I think—but not for
publication. For oneself. A kind of spiritual Spring-cleaning!

KURT The Ego preening . . . !

MARION (*Sitting right arm of sofa left*) Well, why not? After all, one's ego is all one really has.

KURT Reminiscence is easy. So is anticipation. It's the *present* that's difficult and most people are too lazy or too indifferent to cope with it.

MARION It's natural for you to say that—at your age one has no past and no future either because the intimation of the future comes only with the sense of the past . . .

KURT (*With sudden bitterness*) *I* see the past as an *evil thing*—to be extirpated.

MARION How awful! (*Pause*) Why?

KURT That's not important.

MARION (*Rises*) You freeze up so whenever I try to find out anything about you. I'm not used to that. Usually people open up to me—I'm a born confidante. But not you. . . . I'm interested too, because in an odd way I've become very fond of you.

KURT My life's very dull, I assure you. *My* past lacks completely what you would call *glamour*.

MARION No, Dickie. I don't believe that. I don't believe that's true of anybody's life.

KURT Well, it's true. Moreover it's true of most peoples' lives. It's easy for anyone, who's lived as you have to make romantic generalizations. It's very pleasant for you to believe them. Well, I shan't disillusion you. (*Turns away from her*) Why should I? It's not important.
   (*She is sitting down, smoking a cigarette in a holder, watching him. He becomes conscious that she is studying him*)

MARION I had no idea you felt this way about me—you despise me, don't you? (*He doesn't answer*) Don't you?

KURT Yes.

MARION Why?

KURT (*Rises. Walks away*) Why did we start this?

MARION You're annoyed at having even momentarily revealed yourself, aren't you? I'll have your secret, Dickie—I'll pluck out the heart of your mystery.

KURT   Secret! Mystery! More romantic nonsense. I have no secret. Nobody has a secret. There are different kinds of greed, different kinds of ambition—that's all!

MARION   Oh, you simplify too much—really I'm afraid you do. Tell me—why do you disapprove of me? Is it—as Bunny does—on moral grounds?

KURT   (*Right end of sofa left—angrily*)   You're superficial and casual and irresponsible. You take life, which is a tragic thing, as though it were a trivial, bedroom farce. You're a second-rate artist who's acquired a reputation through vamping celebrities to sit for you.

MARION   (*Quietly, she continues smoking*)   Go on . . .

KURT   As an unglamorous upstart who has been forced to make my way I resent parasitism, that's all!

MARION   Isn't there in biology something about benevolent parasites, Dickie? Many great men, I believe, owe a debt of gratitude to their parasites, as many plants do . . . there are varieties. Again, Dickie, you simplify unduly. It is a defect of the radical and the young.

KURT   To return to the Honorable Nolan . . .

MARION   I return to him with relief . . .

KURT   He may exert pressure on us, you know . . .

MARION   How? I'm very interested. . . .

KURT   Well, for one thing, his future father-in-law might get me fired.

MARION   Could he do that?

KURT   He might. He might easily. (MARION *sits upright and looks at him*) Some form of bribery. He might go to my chief and offer him a bigger job—anything.

MARION   All on account of my poor little biography—it seems incredible that anyone would take all this trouble. . . .

KURT   I'd just like to see them try—I'd just like to, that's all . . .

MARION   What would you do?

KURT   Do?! I'd make the Honorable Nolan the laughing stock of the country and his athletic father-in-law too. I'd just plaster them, that's what I'd do.

MARION   You sound vindictive.

KURT   Baby, I am vindictive!

MARION   Funny, I'm just amused. . . .

KURT   Well, everything's a spectacle to you! (*Turns away from her*) God, how I hate detachment!

MARION   Your desire to break up Bunny is quite impersonal then.

KURT   Surgical. Just as impersonal as that.

MARION   You're a funny boy, Dickie.

KURT (*Turns away from her*)   I'm not funny and I'm not a boy. You've been around with dilettantes so long you don't recognize seriousness when you see it.

MARION   But it's the serious people who are funny, Dickie! Look at Bunny.

KURT (*Faces her*)   Yes, look at him! An epitome of the brainless muddle of contemporary life, of all the self-seeking, second-raters who rise to power and wield power. That's why I'm going to do him in. (*The phone rings—for a moment they pay no attention to it*) It's the most beautiful chance anybody ever had and I'd just like to see them try and stop me.
    (*Phone keeps ringing.* MARION *answers it*)

MARION   Yes . . . yes . . . certainly. (*To* KURT—*a bit surprised*) It's for you . . .
    (*She hands him hand-receiver*)

KURT (*Takes phone and talks from rear of sofa*)   Yes. Hello . . . sure. Well, what about it? . . . Oh, you want to talk to me about it, do you? . . . I thought you would . . . I'll be around . . . sure . . . so long. (*He hangs up*) They've begun!
    (*He is almost gay with the heady scent of battle*)

MARION   What do you mean?

KURT   That was my chief. He wants to talk to me about your story. Kinnicott's begun to put the screws on him. He's going to ask me to kill it. All right—I'll kill it!

MARION (*Faintly*)   I can't believe it. . . .

KURT   Neff's had a call from the father-in-law . . .

MARION Did he say so?

KURT No, but you can bet he has!

MARION I must say this puts my back up . . .

KURT I'll make a fight for it to keep my job. But if he's stubborn I'll tell him to go to Hell—and go to a publisher with your manuscript. And if I don't get quick action that way I'll publish it myself—I'll put every penny I've saved into it . . .

MARION But why should you? Why does it mean so much to you?

KURT Do you think I'd miss a chance like this?— It'll test the calibre of our magazines, of our press, our Senators, our morality . . .

MARION All on account of my poor little story—how Vicki would have laughed!

KURT (*A spasm of jealousy again*) Who's Vicki?

MARION (*Aware of it*) An old friend to whom I'm dedicating the biography.

KURT Yeah! (*Sits beside her then speaks*) Where is he now?

MARION He's dead. (*A pause. She gets up and crosses to center*) I've always rather despised these contemporary women who publicize their emotions. (*Another moment. She walks up-stage. She is thinking aloud*) And here I am doing it myself. Too much self-revelation these days. Loud speakers in the confessional. Why should I add to the noise? I think, as far as this story is concerned, I'll call it a day, Dickie.

KURT What!

MARION Let's forget all about it, shall we?

KURT If you let me down now, I'll hate you.

MARION Will you? Why won't you take me into your confidence then? Why won't you tell me about yourself? What are you after?

KURT (*After a moment of inhibition decides to reveal his secret dream*) My ambition is to be critic-at-large of things-as-they-are. I want to find out everything there is to know about the intimate structure of things. I want to reduce the whole system to absurdity. I want to laugh the powers that be out of existence in a great winnowing gale of laughter.

MARION That's an interesting research. Of course it strikes me it's vitiated by one thing—you have a preconceived idea of what you will find. In a research biased like that from the start you are apt to overlook much that is noble and generous and gentle.

KURT (*Challenging and bitter*) Have you found generosity and gentleness and nobility?

MARION A good deal—yes.

KURT Well, I haven't!

MARION I'm sorry for you.

KURT You needn't be. Reserve your pity for weaklings. I don't need it!

MARION Are you so strong? (*A pause.* KURT *doesn't answer*) How old are you, Dickie?

KURT (*Turns away*) What difference does that make?

MARION Who do you live with?

KURT I live alone.

MARION Are you in love with anybody?

KURT No.

MARION Where are your parents?

KURT They're dead.

MARION Long?

KURT My mother is. I hardly remember her. Just barely remember her.

MARION Your father? (*He doesn't answer*) Do you remember your father?

KURT (*In a strange voice*) Yes. I remember him all right.

MARION What did your father do?

KURT He was a coal miner.

MARION Oh! Won't you tell me about him? I'd like to know.

KURT I was a kid of fourteen. There was a strike. One day my father took me out for a walk. Sunny Spring morning. We stopped to listen to an organizer. My father was a mild little man with kind of faded, tired blue eyes. We stood on the outskirts of the crowd. My father was holding me by the hand. Suddenly somebody shouted: The militia! There was a shot. Everybody scattered. My father was bewildered—he didn't know which way to turn. A second later he crumpled down beside me. He was bleeding. He was still holding my hand. He died like that. . . . (*A moment. He concludes harshly—coldly—like steel*) Are there any other glamorous facts of my existence you would like to know?

MARION (*Stirred to her heart*)   You poor boy . . . I knew there was something . . . I knew. . . . !

KURT (*Hard and ironic*)   It's trivial really. People exaggerate the importance of human life. One has to die. (*Turns to her*) The point is to have fun while you're alive, isn't it? Well, you've managed. I congratulate you!

MARION (*Her heart full*)   Dickie darling—why are you so bitter against me? Why against me . . . ?

KURT   Do you want to know that too? Well, it's because . . .
    (*His voice rises. She suddenly doesn't want him to speak*)

MARION   Hush dearest—hush—don't say any more—I understand—not any more . . .
    (*His defenses vanish suddenly. He sinks to his knees beside her, his arms around her*)

KURT   Marion my angel!

MARION (*Infinitely compassionate, stroking his hair*)   Dickie—Dickie—Dickie . . . Why have you been afraid to love me?

THE CURTAIN FALLS

ACT THREE

SCENE: *The same.*
TIME: *Late afternoon. Two weeks later.*

The telephone is ringing as the curtain rises. There is a moment and MINNIE *enters and crosses to rear of the table rear of the sofa left. She picks up the receiver.*

MINNIE (*Speaking into the phone*)   Hello.—No, Mr. Kurt, she's not yet back. Vot. You're not coming home to dinner?! —But I've made the Pfannkuchen you like— Vot?— You're tired of my damn Pfannkuchen— (*She shouts angrily*) Every night I make dinner and you and Marion go out!— I'm *not* yelling— Vot? Vot shall I tell Marion?— Vot— (*Doorbell rings*) Wait—wait a minute.— Someone's ringing.

(*She puts the receiver on the table and goes to the door.* MINNIE *shows in* LEANDER NOLAN *who is followed by* ORRIN KINNICOTT, *who is a big, well-developed Southerner, about fifty-five, with a high-pitched voice. He is a superbly built man with a magnificent chest development. He is aware that he is a fine figure of a man, impeccably dressed in formal afternoon clothes*)

NOLAN (*To* MINNIE, *who has preceded him into the room*) Did Miss Froude say she was expecting us for tea, Minnie?

MINNIE   No, Mr. Nolan. She didn't say nothing to me.

NOLAN   Not even when she'd be back?

MINNIE (*Hangs up coats*)   No. She just went out.

NOLAN   All right, Minnie. We'll wait.

MINNIE   Yes, Mr. Nolan. (*She is about to go out into kitchen when she remembers that* KURT *is on the telephone. She picks*

153

up the receiver and says:) Hello—Mr. Kurt—you dere?—
Good-bye!

(*She then hangs up the receiver and exits left*)

KINNICOTT (*Querulously. Sits sofa right*)   Did you tell her
four o'clock?

NOLAN   Yes. I told her.

(NOLAN'S *manner with his father-in-law-to-be in this scene
conveys the beginnings of a secret irritation, an inner re-
bellion*)

KINNICOTT   Does she know I'm a busy man?

NOLAN (*Gloomily*)   She's not impressed much by busy men.

KINNICOTT   I know these fly-by-night characters. I've dealt
with 'em before . . . Bad— (*He sniffs the air of the room*)
bad air. (*Rises—tries to open window, fails, sits window
seat*) Bet she's under-exercised.

NOLAN   On the contrary—she's radiantly healthy!

KINNICOTT   Cosmetics, I bet! These fly-by-night characters. . . .

NOLAN (*Very irritated*)   Why do you keep calling her a fly-
by-night character? She's nothing of the sort!

KINNICOTT (*Crosses to* NOLAN)   Look here, Leander. . . .

NOLAN   Well?

KINNICOTT   Have you been entirely frank with me, in this
matter?

NOLAN   Of course I have. . . .

KINNICOTT (*Cryptic*)   About the past—yes. But I refer to
the present.

NOLAN   I don't know what you mean.

KINNICOTT   I think you do know what I mean. Sometimes
the way you talk I suspect—I suspect, Leander—that you are
still in love with this woman.

NOLAN   Nonsense! I simply tell you that she's not a fly-by-
night character. That doesn't mean I'm in love with her!

KINNICOTT   My daughter feels the same thing.

NOLAN   Slade! You've discussed this with Slade!

KINNICOTT   She's discussed it with me. She's no fool that
girl. She's noticed things lately.

NOLAN What things?

KINNICOTT She says she talks to you and that you're off somewhere else—dreaming. I tried to put her on another scent—but she was positive. She said: "Come on now, dad —don't stall me—come clean!" So I told her!

NOLAN You did!

KINNICOTT Yes.

NOLAN When?

KINNICOTT Yesterday. Told her it happened fifteen years ago, that you were a naïve young feller didn't know anything about women, were just naturally taken in . . .

NOLAN That's not true though. I was not taken in.

KINNICOTT There you go again—defending the woman that's endangering your entire career and using up my energies and yours when you ought to be home right now getting together with folks and thinking how to cinch this here election. Not going to be a walk-over, you know. (*Again trying the window*) How do you open this thing to get some air?

(*Sits window seat*)

NOLAN I don't know. What did Slade say when you told her?

KINNICOTT Nothin'. You know Slade's not the talkin' kind.

NOLAN Funny she didn't mention it to me last night.

KINNICOTT Didn't want to worry yer probably . . . all wool and a yard wide that girl is. I warn you, Leander, don't tamper with the most precious and rare thing. . . .

NOLAN (*Impatient of oratory*) I know—I know. The point is—what are we going to do?

KINNICOTT Course I can get that young fellow—what's his name?

NOLAN Kurt.

KINNICOTT I can get him fired all right. From what you've told me, Leander, he's got something else up his sleeve. . . .

NOLAN I'm afraid so.

KINNICOTT That's what I want to find out from your lady friend. And I've got a pretty sure idea right now what it is.

NOLAN What do you mean?

KINNICOTT   Money!

NOLAN (*Still not understanding*)   Money. . . . ?

KINNICOTT   Blackmail!

NOLAN   You're crazy!

KINNICOTT   You don't know much about women, Leander; when you know the sex as well as I do you'll know that every woman has blackmail up her sleeve.

NOLAN   Look here, Orrin. . . . !

KINNICOTT (*Rises, confronts* NOLAN)   Now, you listen to me for a moment, son . . . This situation's gone about far enough right now. You'd better make up your mind whether you want this blackmailing female or whether you want my daughter . . . and you'd better make it up right quick.

NOLAN (*Flaring up*)   I resent your tone, Orrin and I won't be ordered around as if I were a high-grade servant!

KINNICOTT   Now son, when you get control of your temper, and cool down a little bit, you'll see that my ordering hasn't been so bad for you. I'll acknowledge you were mighty successful as a lawyer, but in politics, you're nothing but a novice.

NOLAN (*Resentful*)   Am I!
   (*Doorbell*)

KINNICOTT   Just look back a bit, that's all—I've had to push and bolster you to get you where you are.

NOLAN (*Desperately*)   I know—I have every reason to be grateful to you—that's the worst of it.
   (MINNIE *enters and crosses to hall door. Both* MEN *turn and watch to see who it is that is calling*)

MINNIE (*Speaking to someone at the door*)   Ja, Fräulein?

SLADE (*Off stage*)   Is Miss Froude in?

MINNIE   Nein, Fräulein.

SLADE (*Entering*)   Well, I'll just wait. (SLADE KINNICOTT *is a good-looking, dark, high-spirited girl, a rather inspiriting and healthy example of the generation growing up on D. H. Lawrence*) (*To her father and* NOLAN *as she crosses downstage between them*)   Hello.

NOLAN   Slade!

KINNICOTT (*Severely*)   Daughter! What are you doing here?

SLADE   Came to have my picture painted. What are you?

KINNICOTT   Your coming here at this time is most inopportune, daughter. We are here on business.

SLADE (*Mischievously*)   I can imagine!

NOLAN   I'm very glad you came, Slade. I want you to meet the woman whom your father has just been accusing of the most reprehensible crimes!

SLADE   I'm pretty anxious to get a load of her myself. (*Looks about the room taking it in and then sits on the left end of the sofa below the piano*) Nice lay-out. Gee, I wish I were artistic. What a lucky gal she is! A paint-brush and an easel and she can set up shop anywhere in the world. That's independence for you! Gosh!
  (*She looks about, admiring and envious*)

KINNICOTT   Why must you come here to get your picture painted? We have tolerable good artists in Knoxville.

SLADE   Well, if you *must* know I'm very keen to have a heart-to-heart talk with my fiancé's old girl. Natural, isn't it?

KINNICOTT   No, it isn't natural!

NOLAN (*Crosses angrily to window and back toward* KINNICOTT *and sits stool down right near sofa in which* SLADE *and her father are sitting*)   This is what you get for telling her, Orrin.

SLADE   If you think I didn't suspect something was up ever since Froude arrived here, you don't know your little bride. Maybe I haven't been watching the clouds gather on that classic brow! Where is my rival? Don't tell me she's holding up two big shots like you two boys.

KINNICOTT   Slade, this is no time . . . please leave us before she comes.

SLADE   Not I! Just my luck when a story is going to come out which has something in it *I* want to read you two killjoys are going to suppress it!

NOLAN   This isn't exactly a joke you know, Slade. . . .

SLADE   I mean it. . . .

KINNICOTT (*Sadly*)   I've spoiled you, Slade—I've been too easy with you. . . .

SLADE At least I hope you'll buy the *manuscript*. My God, Father, I'm curious. Can't you understand that? I want to find out what Leander was like before he became ambitious. I've a right to know! This story might hurt you with the voters in Tennessee, Leander, but it's given me a kick out of you I didn't know was there! How did she make you, Leander —that's what I'd like to know. You've been pretty un-approachable to me but I sort of took it for granted National Figures were like that. Also I'd gotten to the point when I was going to suggest that we break our engagement, but this little incident revives my interest.

NOLAN (*Furious*) Indeed!

SLADE Yes indeed. Where is this woman? What is that secret? How to Make National Figures . . . there's a title for you!

KINNICOTT Slade, you're talking too much! Shut up!

NOLAN (*Rises and moves stool toward them a bit*) No, she isn't at all. . . . (*To* SLADE) If your interest in me requires the artificial stimulus of an episode that happened twenty years ago . . .

SLADE (*Leaning toward him*) It requires something. . . .

NOLAN (*Leaning closer toward her. The three heads are now close together,* KINNICOTT'S *in the center*) Does it!

SLADE It does. We were getting so that conversation, when we were alone, was rather difficult.

(NOLAN *starts to argue*)

KINNICOTT (*Pushes them apart*) Children! Children!

NOLAN We're not children! (*To* SLADE) If our relationship is so——

SLADE Tenuous . . . ?

NOLAN . . . That it requires artificial . . .

SLADE Respiration . . . ?

NOLAN If it's as bad as that then I think perhaps we'd both better . . .

SLADE Call it a day? . . . You'll need me in the Senate, Leander, to fill in the gaps when you get hung up in a speech. Consider carefully what you are discarding. . . .

NOLAN If that is the case I tell you solemnly we'd better separate now.

SLADE (*Mock tragedy*) Father, Leander is giving your daughter the air. Do something!

KINNICOTT I don't blame him for being irritated. You should not be here. Please go home.

SLADE (*Lights cigarette*) Don't worry Dad. I'll get him back.

KINNICOTT This is a bad mess, Leander. And I must tell you frankly that I don't altogether approve of your attitude . . .

NOLAN And I must tell you frankly that I don't approve of *yours.* . . .

KINNICOTT Is that so!

NOLAN I don't like your tone in speaking of a woman with whom at one time I had a relation of the tenderest emotion— for whom I still have a high regard. . . .

KINNICOTT That's evident anyway!

NOLAN When you apply to such a woman the terms you used before Slade came in, when you impute to her motives so base, you cast an equal reflection on my judgment and my character. . . .

SLADE And that, Pop, is lèse-majesté.

NOLAN And it may be perfectly true, Slade, that knowing Miss Froude has spoiled me for the flippant modernisms with which you study. . . .

SLADE I'm dying to ask her one thing: when you made love to her in the old days did it always sound like a prepared speech on tariff schedules?

KINNICOTT This is getting us nowhere. . . .

SLADE Well, Dad, what do you expect? Leander and I have broken our engagement since I came into this room. That's progress, isn't it?

KINNICOTT Your coming here at this time was most unfortunate.

SLADE Leander doesn't think so. (*Ironically*) He's free now to pursue the lady for whom he still has a high regard. (*Rises*) Are we no longer engaged, Leander?

NOLAN That's not for me to say.

SLADE (*Rises and shakes hands with* NOLAN) Gentleman to the last! And at the very moment—

KINNICOTT (*In despair—speaks as* SLADE *starts to speak*) Slade, if you would only go home!

SLADE (*Crosses left*) *Just* at the very moment when I was saying to myself: Well, if a brilliant and beautiful woman who has played footie with royalty in the capitols of the world loved him, maybe there's a secret charm in him that I've overlooked—just when I was saying that and preparing to probe and discover, (*Lightly*) he gives me the air. (*Sits on sofa left*) By God, Orrin, there's life for you. (*Bell rings*) Ah, that must be my rival!

(NOLAN *gets up and fixes his tie expecting* MARION. *But it is* KURT *who comes in. He faces them. He is in a white heat of anger*)

KURT Well, gentlemen, I'm not surprised to find you here! (*Drops hat on model stand and comes down-stage left*)

NOLAN (*About to introduce* KINNICOTT) How do you do Mr. Kurt . . . this is . . . .

KURT I can guess who it is. I can guess why you're here. Having failed to intimidate *me* you are here to intimidate Miss Froude. (SLADE *rises, excited by this tempest*) Well, I can advise you that you will fail with her too.

NOLAN This is his usual style, Orrin. Don't mind him.

KURT I have just come from my office where I have been informed by Mr. Neff— (SLADE *stands below* KURT—*just behind him—watching him*) whom *you* doubtless know, Mr. Kinnicott—that I could decide between publishing Miss Froude's story or giving up my job. I invited him to go to Hell. That invitation I now cordially extend to you two gentlemen.

SLADE Why doesn't somebody introduce me to this interesting young man?

(*She comes toward him.* KURT *is embarrassed, but covers it in a gruff manner. He has actually not been aware of her in the room*)

KURT I'm sorry—I—didn't know. . . .

SLADE   Why are you sorry? I'm Slade Kinnicott.
(*She gives him her hand. He takes it, limply*)

KURT   All right—all right.
(*He is disarmed and feels, suddenly, rather foolish*)

SLADE   Leander, why have you kept me apart from this young man?

KURT   I'm sorry—I . . .

SLADE   Nonsense. What's your name?

KURT   Richard Kurt.

SLADE   Go to it—
(*Turns him toward others*)

KINNICOTT   (*Impressively—interposing   between   them*)
You're being very foolish, young man.

KURT   (*Crosses toward them—to right of model stand*)   Possibly.

NOLAN   You can't argue with him. I've tried it. He's a fanatic.

KURT   But if you ask me I think *you're* being very foolish.

KINNICOTT   (*Who wants to find out what's in* KURT'S *mind*)
Are we? How do you figure that, young man?

SLADE   (*Parroting—crosses and sits on model stand. She is having a wonderful time*)   Yes, how!

KINNICOTT   Oh, hush your mouth.

KURT   Because I'm going to publish Miss Froude's book myself. And I promise you that it'll be the best-advertised first book that's come out in a long time.

SLADE   Thank God! Will you send me the advance sheets? I'll make it worth your while, Mr. Kurt.

KINNICOTT   I can see you are an extremely impulsive young man. Have you ever inquired, may I ask . . . ?

SLADE   (*Edges a bit closer to* KURT)   This is going to be dangerous! Look out, Richard. . . .
(NOLAN *sits on stool, disgusted with* SLADE)

KINNICOTT   (*Smoothly*)   Have you inquired into the penalties for libel, Mr. Kurt?

KURT   Libel! You're going to sue me for libel, are you!

KINNICOTT (*Same voice*)   Yes. You and Miss Froude both . . . yes. . . .

KURT   Well, you just go ahead and try it, that's all I can tell you. Go ahead and sue. (*Crosses to above* NOLAN) It'll put Mr. Nolan in a charming position before those *moral* constituents of his, won't it? (*Includes both* NOLAN *and* KINNICOTT) Go ahead and sue, both of you—sue your heads off. . . . ! I promise the two of you I'll give you the fight of your lives!

SLADE (*Delighted*)   Good for you, Richard!
 (MARION *comes in. She wears a long red velvet coat, and a little red cap stuck on the side of her golden head—she looks a little like* PORTIA. *She is at the top of her form*)

MARION (*Beaming with hospitality*)   Well! How nice! Minnie!

KURT (*Goes up-stage to right of* MARION)   This chivalrous gentleman has just been proposing to sue you for libel—he considers . . .

SLADE (*Who rises and stands just below the model stand*) I'm Slade Kinnicott.

MARION (*Crosses down-stage to her and they shake hands over the model stand*)   How very nice of you to come! (*Turns and faces* KINNICOTT) Is this Mr. Kinnicott? (*He bows*) I'm so glad to see you. (*They shake hands*) I'm so sorry to be late. (*Waves hello to* NOLAN) Hello Bunny.

SLADE (*This is too much for her*)   Oh, my God—BUNNY! (*She sits, overcome*)

MARION (*To* NOLAN)   I'm so sorry . . .

NOLAN (*Glaring at Slade*)   It's all right, Marion!

MARION   Has Minnie given you tea? I'll just . . . Minnie! (MINNIE *enters*) Tea Minnie, please. . . . (*To the men*) Or cocktails—highball . . . ?

KINNICOTT   I never drink alcoholic mixtures.

NOLAN (*Asserting his independence*)   I'll have a highball!

KINNICOTT   I must tell you, Leander, that I do not approve—

NOLAN   I'll have *two* whiskies straight!

MARION   Good! Highball for you, Miss Kinnicott?

SLADE Thanks.

MARION I'll fix them myself, Minnie. Just bring us some tea, Minnie.

KINNICOTT Nor do I wish any tea.

KURT (*Crosses down left*) Nor do I.

MARION Do you mind if I have a cup? Do sit down Miss Kinnicott. A tiring day. . . . (SLADE *sits on model stand.* MARION *goes up to rear of piano*) Minnie, please bring me a cup of tea—

MINNIE Ja, Fräulein. (*Remembering*) A telegram for you, Fräulein.

MARION Oh, thank you, Minnie. Just put it there on the table. (MINNIE *leaves the telegram on the table rear of the sofa left and then exits left.* MARION *removes her coat and hat and crosses to rear of piano and starts to mix the high-balls*) Now then! What is all this nice cheerful talk about a libel suit? That's what they're always having in England, isn't it, on the least provocation. It's when you've circulated a lie about someone—defamed someone—maliciously—isn't it? Bunny! (*She gives* NOLAN *his two drinks. He takes them and returns to his position.* MARION *picks up the other glass and crosses with it to* SLADE) Now then—whom have I defamed?

KURT You've defamed the Honorable Mr. Nolan!

MARION (*Hands drink to* SLADE) Have I? Oh I am tired. . . . (*She sits on sofa*) Sit by me, won't you, Miss Kinnicott?

SLADE (*Sauntering over*) Thanks.
  (*She sits by* MARION *on the sofa*)

MARION You're very pretty. . . .

SLADE (*More warmly*) Thanks!

MARION Bunny, I congratulate you. I've heard so much about you, Miss Kinnicott. And I think it's very gracious of you to come and see me. If Bunny lets me I'd like to paint you— (MINNIE *enters*) and give you the portrait for a wedding-present. (*She rises and crosses to above model stand to get cup of tea from* MINNIE) (MINNIE *exits left*) Thank you, Minnie.

SLADE You're very lovely.

MARION   Thank you, my dear.

SLADE   I can't tell you how curious I've been about you—
I—

KINNICOTT   This is all very well—but I'm a busy man . . .

MARION (*Looks at* KINNICOTT *as she crosses and sits right of* SLADE. *A moment then* MARION *speaks*)   It seems so strange to see you with all your clothes on. It seems a pity—as an artist I must say it seems a pity—to conceal that wonderful chest-development that I've admired so often in The Body Beautiful.

KINNICOTT   That's neither here nor there.

MARION (*This is almost an aside to* SLADE)   It seems to me that it's decidedly *there*.
   (MARION *and* SLADE *laugh quietly together*)

KINNICOTT   Slade, you've upset everything by coming here. . . .
   (KURT *comes forward. He has been eaten up with irritation because the superb indignation he felt should have been so dissipated by this cascade of small talk. He can stand it no longer*)

KURT (*Crosses to right of model stand*)   If you understood better what these gentlemen mean to do . . . !

NOLAN (*Protests*)   It wasn't my idea!

KURT   You wouldn't be quite so friendly, Marion. . . .

MARION   I couldn't possibly be unfriendly to anyone so frank—and—and gladiatorial—as Mr. Kinnicott.

KURT (*Furious at her for not letting him launch into it*)   A libel suit . . . !

MARION   Oh, yes! A libel suit! It sounds so cozy. Sit down, won't you? (KINNICOTT *sits on stool*) A libel suit. Now then —what shall it be about?

KURT   The Honorable Nolan is going to sue you for libel. . . .

NOLAN   I'll punch your head if you say that again. . . .

KURT   On the assumption that when you say in your story that you and he were lovers you are lying and defaming his character!

MARION Dear Bunny, you must want to be a Senator very very badly!

NOLAN (*In despair*) I never said it I tell you!

MARION As a matter of fact how could I prove it? Come to think of it, are there any letters? Did you ever write to me, Bunny?

NOLAN I don't remember.

MARION I don't think you ever did. You see—we were always—during that dim brief period of your youth—we were always so close—letters were hardly necessary, were they? Did I ever send you any letters, Bunny?

NOLAN I don't remember, I tell you.

MARION Neither do I. You might look around in old trunks and places and see if you can find some old letters of an affectionate nature—I'd love to read them—they'd probably make wonderful reading now. Why is it that the things one writes when one's young always sounds so foolish afterwards? Has that ever occurred to you, Mr. Kinnicott?

KINNICOTT I don't admit the fact.

MARION No.

KINNICOTT No. I was looking over some old editorials of mine written in the depression of 1907 and they're just as apropos today. I haven't changed my ideas in twenty-five years.

MARION Haven't you really? How very steadfast. Now if the world were equally changeless, how consistent that would make you. (*To* KURT) Well, there isn't any documentary evidence.

KURT It doesn't matter. . . .

KINNICOTT As I said before, this is getting us nowhere. Don't you think, Miss Froude, that the only way we can settle this is by ourselves? (*She smiles at him*) I can see you're a sensible woman.

MARION I am very sensible.

KINNICOTT And you and I can settle this matter in short order.

KURT You don't have to talk to him at all if you don't want to.

MARION (*Smiling at* KINNICOTT)   But I'd love to. I've always wanted to meet Mr. Kinnicott. There are some questions I want very much to ask him. (*To the others*) You can all wait in my bedroom. It's fairly tidy, I think.

SLADE (*To* KURT— *Rises, crosses to him*)   Why don't you take me for a walk, Richard?

MARION (*As* KURT *hesitates*)   Do that Dickie. A walk'll do you good.

NOLAN   What'll I do?

MARION (*As if it were another dilemma*)   You wait in my bedroom. (*Aware suddenly of the proprieties*) No—in Min- nie's bedroom. It's just next to the kitchen.

NOLAN (*Defiantly*)   I will!
   (*He exits into bedroom*)

KURT (*Sulky—he doesn't quite like the turn affairs have taken*)   We'll be back in ten minutes.

SLADE (*As they go out*)   You can't tell, Richard.
   (SLADE *and* KURT *exit*)
   (MARION *draws a deep breath. She assumes at once with* KINNICOTT *the air of two equals, mature people talking freely to each other after they've gotten rid of the chil- dren*)

MARION (*They cross to sofa left*)   Now we can talk! It's funny—I feel we've put the children to bed and can have a quiet talk after a lot of chatter.

KINNICOTT   Same here!

MARION   Please sit down.
   (*They do*)

KINNICOTT   I feel sure you and I can come to an understand- ing.

MARION   I'm sure we can.

KINNICOTT   Now then about this little matter of the story— You won't mind if I speak very frankly to you. . . . ?

MARION   Not at all.

KINNICOTT   You see, Miss Froude. . . .

MARION   Oh, call me Marion. Everybody does.

KINNICOTT   Thanks. Call me Orrin.

MARION   All right, I'll try. Not a very usual name. Orrin.
Fits you. Strong. Rugged strength.

KINNICOTT   Thank you.

MARION   You're welcome. What were you going to say when
I interrupted you? You were going to say something. . . .

KINNICOTT   I was going to say—you're not at all what I
expected to meet.

MARION   No? What did you think I'd be like? Tell me—I'd
love to know.

KINNICOTT   Well, you're kind of homey—you know—folksey . . .

MARION   Folksey. (*Smiles*) After all there's no reason I
shouldn't be, is there? I'm just a small-town girl from Tennessee. I sometimes wonder at myself—how I ever got so
far away. . . .

KINNICOTT (*Positively*)   Metabolism!

MARION   I beg your pardon. . . .

KINNICOTT   I always say—take most of the bad men and
most of the loose women—and correct their metabolism and
you'll correct them.

MARION   Really?

KINNICOTT (*Seriously*)   Absolutely. Trouble with our penol-
ogy experts—so-called—is that they're psychologists—so-
called—when they should be physiologists.

MARION   That is very interesting indeed. Have you ever
written anything about that?

KINNICOTT   Off and on.

MARION   Any definitive work I mean?

KINNICOTT   I'm considering doing that right now.

MARION   Oh, I do wish you would! It's extraordinary how
little one knows about one's own body, isn't it? I get so
impatient of myself sometimes—of my physical limitations.
My mind is seething with ideas but I haven't the physical
energy to go on working. I tire so quickly—and often for no
apparent reason. Why is that, Mr. Kinnicott?

KINNICOTT   Defective—
    (*She says at same time with him*)

MARION—KINNICOTT Metabolism!

KINNICOTT Tell me—

MARION What?

KINNICOTT Do you eat enough roughage?

MARION I don't know, off-hand.

KINNICOTT (*Firmly*) Well, you should know!

MARION As I say, Orrin—one is so ignorant of these fundamental things.

KINNICOTT (*Definitely aware now of* MARION *as a personal possibility*) I can see this, Marion—if you'd met me—instead of Leander—when you were a young girl—you'd have been a different woman.

MARION I'm sure I would. Imagine—with one's metabolism disciplined early in life—how far one could go.

KINNICOTT (*Confidentially offering her hope*) It's not too late!

MARION Isn't it?

KINNICOTT Er. . . . (*He drops his voice still lower*) What are you doing tomorrow evenin'?

MARION I—I'm free.

KINNICOTT (*Same voice*) Will you have dinner with me?

MARION I'd be delighted.

KINNICOTT Fine! Then we can go over this little matter of the story and Leander quietly. Leander isn't strong on tact. . . .

MARION You know, some men aren't.

KINNICOTT You and I can make a friendly adjustment.

MARION What fun!
    (*They chuckle*)

KINNICOTT What time shall we meet? Say seven-thirty?

MARION Let's say eight . . . do you mind?

KINNICOTT My apartment?

MARION If you like.

KINNICOTT Here's my card with the address. It's a roof apartment. I'm a widower.

MARION   Irresistible combination!

KINNICOTT   By the way—

MARION   What?

KINNICOTT   Don't mention our little date for tomorrow evenin' to Leander.

MARION (*Rising*)   No, I agree with you. I don't think that would be wise.

KINNICOTT (*Nodding trustingly—rises*)   Fine! At seven-thirty?

MARION   No—no. Eight.

KINNICOTT   Oh yes . . . eight.
  (*A moment's pause. He visibly preens before her, buttoning his beautifully-fitting frock-coat across his heroic chest*)

MARION (*Approving*)   Wonderful! Wonderful!

KINNICOTT (*Going toward bedroom. To her*)   Do you mind if I . . . Leander . . .

MARION   Not at all.

KINNICOTT   I'll take the load off his mind.
  (*He goes out. She can't believe it. The whole situation is so fantastic. She flings off her little red cap and shaking with laughter collapses on the couch.* MINNIE *comes in to clear up the tea things*)

MARION (*As* MINNIE *enters*)   It's too good to be true, Minnie. . . .

MINNIE   Vat is too good to be true?

MARION   I must write some of it down before I forget it . . . (*The bell again.* MARION *gets up to make notes on her script*) —A widower's penthouse— (*With an irritated sigh* MINNIE *goes out to answer bell.* MARION *sits at desk jotting notes very fast.* SLADE *and* KURT *come in.* KURT *is morose.* MARION *gets up to greet them*) Well, children?

SLADE   That walk was a total loss.

MARION (*Laughing*)   What did you expect?

SLADE   Well, a little encouragement—just a soupçon . . .

MARION   Dickie's very serious.

SLADE   How did you come out with Dad?

MARION   Wonderful! I'm crazy about him!

SLADE   Bet he got you to renege on the story . . .

MARION   Well, he thinks so. However, we're going to discuss it tomorrow evenin'.

SLADE   Thought he'd date you up—could tell by the way he eyed you. . . .

MARION   He's going to teach me how to live in a state of virtuous metabolism.

SLADE   Oh! Don't you believe it! Dad's an awful old chaser!

MARION (*Rather shocked*)   Slade!

SLADE (*Amused*)   Are you shocked?

MARION   You make me feel a little old-fashioned.
   (KURT *is intensely irritated by this conversation*)

KURT   Where are they?

MARION   They're in there sitting on Minnie's bed. Orrin is probably telling Bunny that everything'll be all right.

SLADE (*Sits left of* MARION)   Marion. . . .

MARION   Yes. . . .

SLADE   What is there about Bunny you can't help liking?
   (*Utterly disgusted,* KURT *goes to sofa down left and sits staring moodily into a gloomily-tinted future*)

MARION   He's a dear—there's something very touching about Bunny—sweet . . .

SLADE   Were you in love with him once?

MARION   Yes.

SLADE   Are you in love with him now?

MARION   No.

SLADE (*In a whisper*)   Are you in love with—someone else?

MARION (*A moment's pause*)   Yes.

SLADE   I thought you were. He's mad about you.—I envy you, Marion.

MARION   Do you? Why?

SLADE   You're independent. You're—yourself. You can do anything you like.

MARION Yes, I know. But it's possible one can pay too much for independence. I'm adrift. Sometimes—you know what seems to me the most heavenly thing—the only thing—for a woman? Marriage, children—the dear boundaries of routine . . .

SLADE If you had married Bunny he would've given 'em to you. He's still in love with you, but he doesn't quite know it. Shall I tell him?

MARION (*Parrying*) What are you talking about?

SLADE I wish we could change places, Marion. You can with me but I can't with you.
(KINNICOTT *and* NOLAN *come in from the bedroom.* KINNICOTT *is at his most oleaginous*)

KINNICOTT (*To* KURT) Well, young man! Over your little temper?

KURT No, I'm not over it! What makes you think I'm over it?

KINNICOTT Well, well, well! As far as I'm concerned there are no hard feelings. I'm going to call up your employer myself when I get home and tell him, that as far as you are concerned, to let bygones be bygones. Can't do more than that, can I?

KURT To what do I owe this generosity?

KINNICOTT To the fact that in Miss Froude you have a most gracious friend and intercepter. (*He gives* MARION *a gallant, old-South bow*) Miss Froude—this has been a very great pleasure.

MARION (*Rises—with an answering bow*) Thank you!
(SLADE *also rises*)

KINNICOTT (*Giving her his hand*) Auf Wiedersehen.

MARION Auf Wiedersehen. Ich kann es kaum erwarten!

KINNICOTT (*Pretending to understand*) Yes, oh, yes, yes, of course! (*To* SLADE) Come, Slade.
(*He goes to hall-door*)

SLADE All right, Dad. (*To* NOLAN) Coming—Bunny?

NOLAN Well, yes—I'm coming.

SLADE (*To* NOLAN) You want to stay. Why don't you?

KINNICOTT (*Quickly marshaling his little following with a military precision*)   I think Leander had better come with us—

SLADE (*To* MARION)   Good-bye, Marion.

MARION (*To* SLADE)   Good-bye, Slade. (*They shake hands*) Come to see me.

SLADE   Thanks, I will.

KINNICOTT (*Smiles at* MARION)   Miss Froude! (*Bows to* MARION *who returns his bow*) Come, Daughter. Come, Leander. (*To* KURT) Good-bye, young man. No hard feelings. (KURT *glares at him*) (KINNICOTT *again bows to* MARION) Miss Froude! (MARION *is startled into still a third bow*) (*He calls without looking back*) Come, Slade! Leander! !

SLADE   Bunny!
   (*As she exits*)

NOLAN (*Lingers an instant then crosses to* MARION)   I'll be back.

MARION   When?

NOLAN   In a few minutes. All right?

MARION   I'll be in. (*He goes out quickly.* MARION *is in wonderful spirits. She runs to* KURT *and throws her arms around him*) Oh, Dickie. That Orrin! That Orrin!

KURT   What did you say to him that put him in such good spirits?

MARION   Everything I said put him in good spirits. I can't wait for tomorrow evenin'. I can't wait for that dinner. It'll probably consist entirely of roughage—just imagine! He's the quaintest man I ever met in my life. He's too good to be true.
   (*Sits right of* KURT)

KURT   Well, he may be quaint to you but to me he's a putrescent old hypocrite and I don't see how you can bear to have him come near you, say less go to dinner with him!

MARION (*Sobered by his intensity*)   You're so merciless in your judgments, Dickie. You quite frighten me sometimes—you do really.

KURT   And so do you me.

MARION   I do! That's absurd!

KURT   You do. It's like thinking a person fastidious and exacting and finding her suddenly . . .

MARION   Gross—indiscriminating?

KURT   (*Bluntly*)   Yes!

MARION   You know, Dickie, I adore you and I'm touched by you and I love you but I'd hate to live in a country where you were Dictator. It would be all right while you loved me but when you stopped. . . .

KURT   It wouldn't make any difference if I stopped—I shouldn't be that kind of a Dictator . . .

MARION   (*Glances at him. Almost sadly*)   I see you've thought of it. . . .

KURT   (*Inexorably*)   What did you say to Kinnicott?

MARION   Your manner is so—inquisitorial. I haven't been able to get used to it.

KURT   (*Angry and jealous*)   I heard you tell Nolan to come back too . . . How do you think I feel?

MARION   Dickie!

KURT   When Nolan sat there and told me he had been your lover, I felt like socking him. Even when we're alone together, I can't forget that . . . yet you encourage him, and Kinnicott— My God, Marion, you seem to like these people!

MARION   I certainly like Slade.

KURT   Well, I don't. She's conceited and over-bearing. Thinks she can have anything she likes because she's Orrin Kinnicott's daughter.

MARION   That's where you're wrong. She's a nice girl—and she's unhappy.

KURT   (*Bitterly*)   Maladjusted, I suppose!

MARION   Dickie, Dickie, Dickie! Studying you, I can see why so many movements against injustice become such absolute—tyrannies.

KURT   That beautiful detachment again. . . .
  (*He is white with fury. He hates her at this moment*)

MARION   (*With a little laugh*)   You hate me, don't you . . . ?

KURT   Yes! Temporizing with these . . . ! Yes. . . . ! I hate you. (*She says nothing, sits there looking at him*) These people flout you, they insult you in the most flagrant way. God knows I'm not a gentleman, but it horrifies me to think of the insufferable arrogance of their attitude toward you . . . as if the final insult to their pride and their honor could only come from the discovery that this stuffed shirt Nolan had once been your lover! The blot on the immaculate Tennessee scutcheon! Why, it's the God-damndest insolence I ever heard of. And yet you flirt and curry favor and bandy with them. And you're amused—always amused!

MARION   Yes. I am amused.

KURT   I can't understand such . . . !

MARION   Of course you can't. That's the difference—one of the differences—between 25 and 35!

KURT   If the time ever comes when I'm amused by what I should hate, I hope somebody shoots me. What did you tell Kinnicott?

MARION   Nothing. Simply nothing. I saw no point in having a scene with him so I inquired into his favorite subject. He gave me health hints. He thinks tomorrow night he will cajole me—through the exercise of his great personal charm—into giving up my plan to publish.

KURT   Well, why didn't you tell him right out that you wouldn't.

MARION   Because I wanted to avoid a scene.

KURT   You can't always avoid scenes. That's the trouble with you—you expect to go through life as if it were a beautifully lit drawing-room with modulated voices making polite chatter. Life isn't a drawing-room . . . !

MARION   I have—once or twice—suspected it.

KURT   (*Rises*)   What the devil are you afraid of, anyway? I had a scene today in the office and I was prepared for one here—until you let me down—

MARION   (*Lightly*)   Prepared? I think you were eager. . . .

KURT   What if I was! It's in your behalf, isn't it?

MARION   Is it? But you forget, Dickie. You're a born martyr. I'm not. I think the most uncomfortable thing about martyrs is that they look down on people who aren't. (*Thinks—looks at him*) As a matter of fact, Dickie, I don't really understand.

Why do you insist so on this story? Why is it so important—now wouldn't it be better to give it up?

KURT Give it up!

MARION Yes.

KURT You'd give it up!

MARION Why not?

KURT (*Obeying a sudden manic impulse*) After all this—after all I've—! Oh, yes, of course! Then you could marry Nolan and live happily forever after. And be amused. Good-bye!
(*He rushes up center, grabs his hat from the stand as he passes it, and continues on out the door*)

MARION (*Rises and runs after him*) Dickie!

KURT (*Going out the door*) Good-bye!

MARION Dickie! Dickie! (*The door slams.* MARION *walks back into the room. A pause. She stands still for a moment; she shakes her head. . . . She is very distressed and saddened and a deep unhappiness is gnawing in her heart, an awareness of the vast, uncrossable deserts between the souls of human beings. She makes a little helpless gesture with her hands, murmuring to herself*) Poor Dickie! Poor boy!
(*In its Italian folder the manuscript of her book is lying on the piano before her. She picks it up—she gives the effect of weighing the script in her hand. Slowly, as if in a trance, she walks with the script to the Franklin stove down-stage left and sits before it on a little stool. She opens the manuscript and then the isinglass door of the stove. The light from behind it glows on her face. She looks again down on her manuscript, at this morsel of her recorded past. She tears out a page or two and puts them into the fire. A moment and she has put the entire script into the stove and she sits there watching its cremation. The doorbell rings. As* MINNIE *comes in to answer it, she shuts the door of the stove quickly*)

MARION It's probably Mr. Nolan.
(MINNIE *goes out.* MARION *makes a visible effort to shake herself out of her mood.* NOLAN *comes in followed by* MINNIE *who crosses stage and goes in the bedroom left.* NOLAN *is excited and distrait*)

NOLAN   Hello, Marion. . . .

MARION   Hello, Bunny dear.

NOLAN   (*Sparring for time*)   Excuse me for rushing in on
you like this . . . I . . .

MARION   I've been expecting you.

NOLAN   That's right! I told you I was coming back, didn't
I? . . .

MARION   You did—yes.

NOLAN   I must have known—I must have felt it—what
would happen. . . . Marion . . .

MARION   Bunny dear, you're all worked up. Won't you have
a highball?

NOLAN   No, thanks. Marion. . . .

MARION   Yes, Bunny . . .

NOLAN   I've done it!

MARION   You've done what?

NOLAN   I've broken with Slade. I've broken with Kinnicott.
I've broken with all of them.

MARION   You haven't!

NOLAN   Yes! I have!

MARION   Oh—oh Bunny!

NOLAN   (*Sits*)   When Orrin told me what you'd done—that
you were going to give up the story. . . .

MARION   But I—

NOLAN   He said he was sure he could get you to do it. It all
came over me—your generosity—your wonderful generosity.

MARION   (*Beyond words*)   Oh Bunny!
   (*Sits*)
   (*She is in a sort of laughing despair. He hardly notices
   her attitude. He rushes on*)

NOLAN   I realized in that moment that in all this time—since
I'd been seeing you—I'd been hoping you wouldn't give up
the story, that you would go through with it, that my career
would go to smash. . . .

MARION   (*Faintly*)   Bunny. . . .

NOLAN I saw then that all this—which I'd been telling my-self I wanted—Slade, a career, Washington, public life—all of it—that I didn't want it, that I was sick at the prospect of it—that I wasn't up to it, that I was scared to death of it. I saw all that—and I told her—I told Slade. . . .

MARION You did!

NOLAN Yes.

MARION What did she say?

NOLAN She said she knew it. She's clever that girl. She's cleverer than I am. She's cleverer than you are. I'm afraid of her cleverness. I'm uncomfortable with it. Marion, I know I seem stupid and ridiculous to you—just a Babbitt—clumsy —but I love you, Marion. I always have—never anyone else. Let me go with you wherever you go— (*Lest she think it a "proposition."*) I mean—I want to marry you.

MARION I'm terribly touched by this, Bunny darling, but I can't marry you.

NOLAN Why not?

MARION If I married you it would be for the wrong reasons. And it wouldn't be in character really—neither for me—nor for you. Besides that, I think you're wrong about Slade. She's very nice, you know. I like her very much.

NOLAN I don't understand her. I never will.

MARION If you did you'd like her. You better have another try. Really, Bunny, I wish you would.

NOLAN Letting me down easy, aren't you?

MARION It's Slade's manner that shocks you—her modern —gestures. If you really understood me—as you think you do—I'd really shock you very much, Bunny.

NOLAN I'll risk it. Marion, my dearest Marion, won't you give me some hope? . . .

MARION (*Sees she must tell him*) Besides—I'm in love.

NOLAN (*Stunned*) Really! With whom?

MARION Dickie . . . You see, Bunny . . . (*He can't get over this. There is a considerable pause*) You see, Bunny . . .

NOLAN (*Slowly*) Do you mean that you and he—you don't mean that . . . ?

MARION   Yes, Bunny.

NOLAN (*Dazed*)   Are you going to marry him?

MARION   No.

NOLAN (*He passes his hand over his forehead*)   This is a shock to me, Marion.

MARION (*Gently*)   I thought it only fair to tell you.

NOLAN (*In a sudden passion*)   You—you. . . . (*He feels like striking her, controls himself with difficulty*) Anybody else but him. . . . !

MARION   You see, Bunny.

NOLAN (*After a moment—rises*)   Sorry! Funny, isn't it? Joke, isn't it?

MARION   I'm terribly fond of you, Bunny. (*Takes his hand*) I always will be. That kind of tenderness outlasts many things.

NOLAN (*Blindly*)   I'll go on, I suppose.

MARION   Of course you will! (NOLAN *crosses to model stand and gets his hat.* KURT *comes in. There is a silence.* NOLAN *forces himself to look at him.* KURT *does not meet his glance.* KURT *is white and shaken—not in the least truculent*) Good-bye, Bunny dear. Bunny!

NOLAN   Yes, Marion.

MARION   Will you do me a favor?

NOLAN   Yes.

MARION   Will you please tell Mr. Kinnicott for me—that as I've been called out of town suddenly—I can't dine with him tomorrow night. You *will* see him, won't you, and you'll tell him?

NOLAN   Yes.
(NOLAN *leaves. A silence again.* . . . *Suddenly* KURT *goes to her, embraces her with a kind of hopeless intensity*)

KURT (*In a whisper, like a child*)   Please forgive me. . . .

MARION   Yes.

KURT   These moods come over me—I can't control myself—afterwards I hate myself—it's because I love you so much—I can't bear to. . . .

MARION I know, dear—I know. . . .

KURT I'm torn up all the time—torn to bits.

MARION I know, dear . . .

KURT When this is all blown over—could we—do you think . . .

MARION What, dear?

KURT If we could only go away together, the two of us— somewhere away from people, by ourselves?

MARION Why not, Dickie? We can go now, if you want to. . . .

KURT Now? But you're crazy. How can we possibly leave now—with the book . . . .

MARION Dickie—I must tell you. . . .

KURT You must tell me what?

MARION You must be patient—you must hear me out for once—you must try to understand my point of view.

(*She leads him to sofa left and sits beside him*)

KURT What do you mean?

MARION You know, Dickie, I've been very troubled about you. I've been sad. I've been sad.

KURT I was angry . . . I didn't mean . . . It was just that . . .

MARION No, you don't understand—it wasn't your anger that troubled me. It was ourselves—the difference between us—not the years alone but the immutable difference in temperament. Your hates frighten me, Dickie. These people— poor Bunny, that ridiculous fellow Kinnicott—to you these rather ineffectual, blundering people symbolize the forces that have hurt you and you hate them. But I don't hate them. I can't hate them. Without feeling it, I can understand your hate but I can't bring myself to foster it. To you, this book has become a crusade. It couldn't be to me. Do you know, Dickie dear—and this has made me laugh so to myself—that there was nothing in the book about Bunny that would ever have been recognized by anybody. It was an idyllic chapter of first-love—that's all—and there was nothing in it that could remotely have been connected with the Bunny that is now. . . .

KURT So much the better—! Think of the spectacle they'll make of themselves—destroyed by laughter. . . .

MARION I don't believe in destructive campaigns, Dickie . . . outside of the shocking vulgarity of it all—I couldn't do it—for the distress it would cause. . . .

KURT You've decided not to publish then. . . .

MARION I've destroyed the book, Dickie.

KURT You've destroyed it!

MARION Yes. I'm sorry.

KURT You traitor!

MARION It seemed the simple thing to do—the inevitable thing.

KURT What about *me?* You might have consulted me—after what I've . . .

MARION I'm terribly sorry—but I couldn't possibly have published that book.

KURT (*In a queer voice*) I see now why everything is this way. . . .

MARION I couldn't . . . !

KURT Why the injustice and the cruelty go on—year after year—century after century—without change—because—as they grow older—people become—*tolerant!* Things amuse them. I hate you and I hate your tolerance. I always did.

MARION I know you do. You hate my essential quality—the thing that is me. That's what I was thinking just now and that's what made me sad.

KURT Nothing to be said, is there? (*Rises*) Good-bye.

MARION (*Rises*) All right! (KURT *starts to go. She calls after him, pitifully*) Won't you kiss me good-bye?

KURT All right.

　　(MARION *goes up after him*) (*They kiss each other passionately*)

MARION (*Whispering to him*) I would try to change you. I know I would. And if I changed you I should destroy what makes me love you. Good-bye, my darling. Good-bye, my dearest. Go quickly. (KURT *goes up-stage and exits without a word. He is blinded by pain*) Dickie. . . . !

(MARION *is left alone. She is trembling a little. She feels cold. She goes to the stove and sits in front of it, her back to it, trying to get warm. She becomes aware that her eyes are full of tears. As* MINNIE *comes in, she brushes them away*)

MINNIE   Are you worried from anything, Marion?

MARION   No, Minnie. I'm all right.

MINNIE   I tink maybe dot telegram bring you bad news.

MARION   Telegram? What telegram?

MINNIE   Dot telegram I bring you.

MARION   Of course—I haven't even—where is it?

MINNIE   (*Gets telegram from table rear of sofa left and hands it to* MARION)   There it is!

MARION   Thank you, Minnie. (*Opens telegram and reads it*) This is from heaven! Minnie, I want you to pack right away. We're leaving!
   (*She springs up*)

MINNIE   Leaving? Ven?

MARION   Right away. Tonight! This is from Feydie! Listen! (*Reads telegram aloud to* MINNIE) "Can get you commission to paint prize-winners Motion Picture Academy—wire answer at once. Feydie." (*Hysterically grateful for the mercy of having something to do at once, of being busy, of not having time to think*) Something always turns up for me! Pack everything, Minnie. I want to get out right away.
   (*She rushes up-stage right, picks up her hat and coat and then runs to the stairs left*)

MINNIE   Don't you tink you better vait till tomorrow?

MARION   No, Minnie. Once the temptation to a journey comes into my head I can't bear it till I'm on my way! This time, Minnie, we'll have a real trip. From Hollywood we'll go to Honolulu and from Honolulu to China. How would you like that, Minnie?
   (*She starts up the stairs*)

MINNIE   (*For her, enthusiastic*)   Fine, Marion! (*Calls after her as she runs up stairs*) Dot crazy Kurt he goes vit us?

MARION   (*As she disappears into her bedroom*)   No, Minnie —no one—we travel alone!

QUICK CURTAIN

☆

Rain from Heaven

★

Rain from Heaven *was produced by the The-atre Guild, Inc., at the Golden Theatre, New York, on Monday night, December 24, 1934, with the follow-ing cast:*

(IN THE ORDER IN WHICH THEY SPEAK)

JOAN ELDRIDGE	Hancey Castle
MRS. DINGLE	Alice Belmore-Cliffe
RAND ELDRIDGE	Ben Smith
HOBART ELDRIDGE	Thurston Hall
LADY LAEL WYNGATE	Jane Cowl
HUGO WILLENS	John Halliday
SASCHA BARASHAEV	Marshall Grant
PHOEBE ELDRIDGE	Lily Cahill
CLENDON WYATT	Statts Cottsworth
NIKOLAI JURIN	Jose Ruben

Scenes

The action throughout takes place in the living room of Lady Wyngate's home, a short distance from London.

ACT ONE	A spring afternoon.

ACT TWO	SCENE I. Afternoon, four days later. SCENE II. About 10:30 the same evening

ACT THREE	The following day.

TIME: *The present.*

ACT ONE

SCENE: *The living room of an English country house not far from Brighton. It is not one of the "great houses" but rambling and informal and spaciously hospitable in a casual way. The garden seems almost to grow into the living room; the French windows at the back merely to beach its efflorescence. Cross the garden and you are in another living room; cross that and you are in another garden. The knack of combining an air of improvisation with solid comfort appears to be a special attribute of the British country house of this type.*

It is a sunny afternoon in spring.

MRS. DINGLE, *the ample housekeeper, and* JOAN ELDRIDGE, *an attractive young American girl, are awaiting the arrival by motor of two visitors. Each time they hear the sound of a car in the road which passes the house,* JOAN *leaps to the piano and strikes up "The Entrance of the Gladiators." At the rising of the curtain* JOAN *is discovered in one of these spasms of optimism.*

JOAN (*As she runs to the piano*) There they are!

MRS. DINGLE (*Lumbering to the window near the hall-door left, whence she may scan the road*) I believe it is, Miss Joan!

(JOAN *plays the music triumphantly. But the motor passes and dies down*)

JOAN (*In despair*) This is impossible. (*She leaves the piano disconsolately*) I wish Lael hadn't left *me* to receive them. I'm getting more nervous every minute.

MRS. DINGLE Nothing to be nervous about that I can see! Your own father . . . and your uncle . . . Tell me, Miss Joan, does your Uncle Rand look like a hero?

JOAN That depends what your notion of a hero is. Besides, you've seen his picture in the papers, haven't you?

MRS. DINGLE   Don't know as I have.

JOAN   He's quite young, you know. And good-looking.

MRS. DINGLE   As good-looking as Lindbergh?

JOAN (*Considering it*)   Different style. Yes. Quite different.

MRS. DINGLE   Do they make a big fuss over him in America?

JOAN   Oh, no end. (*Sound of motor car. Same business.* JOAN *rushes to the piano and plays.* MRS. DINGLE *stands at attention at French window. Same result. Motor car passes and dies down.* JOAN *rises from the piano*) I give up!

MRS. DINGLE   Perhaps they had an accident.

JOAN   I don't think so. It's just Father telling the driver to go slow. He's so damn cautious!

MRS. DINGLE (*Shocked*)   What a way to speak of your own father! In my day . . . !

JOAN   I know. In your day you suppressed your feelings! Such a bother, Lael not having a telephone! I'd like to ring up my young man in London to find out if he's all right.
   (MRS. DINGLE *starts to protest; she decides it's hopeless*)

MRS. DINGLE   You mean Mr.—Mr.—?

JOAN   Barashaev.

MRS. DINGLE   I never will say that name.

JOAN   You will. With practice.

MRS. DINGLE   Is he your young man?

JOAN   I've been trying to persuade him ever since last winter in New York. Like him?

MRS. DINGLE (*Thoughtfully*)   He's a foreigner.

JOAN   Oh, Mrs. Dingle, how British!

MRS. DINGLE   He's worse than a foreigner. He's a Russian. But he can play the piano. I'll say that for him. He makes it talk.

JOAN   Sing, Mrs. Dingle. He makes it sing!
   (*Motor is heard approaching again. This time,* JOAN *doesn't stir*)

MRS. DINGLE (*Excited again*)   Miss Joan, maybe . . .

JOAN   They don't fool me again!

MRS. DINGLE   But maybe . . .

JOAN   I don't care if it is!
(*Motor stops with a squeak of brakes*)

MRS. DINGLE   They've stopped! They've stopped!
(MRS. DINGLE *rushes out*)

JOAN   Really? (*She rushes to the piano and again strikes up the triumphant theme from "Heldenleben." RAND enters, followed by his elder brother HOBART ELDRIDGE. RAND ELDRIDGE is a little over thirty, a Southern American and very attractive. The most attractive thing about him is a kind of shyness, a slightly uncomfortable awareness that he radiates an aura of fame which makes him conspicuous when really he would prefer to be unobserved. HOBART ELDRIDGE, at least fifteen years older than RAND, has none of his younger brother's reticence. He understands completely the sources of his own power and is determined to insure their inexhaustibility. It is impossible for him to visualize a cosmos in which he and his kind are not the central suns*) (JOAN *rushes to her* UNCLE RAND) Hello! Hello!

RAND   (*With his arms around her*)   Joan! How nice! How very nice!

JOAN   (*To her father*)   Hello, Father.

HOBART   (*Annoyed that she is here*)   I didn't know you knew Lady Wyngate, Joan!

JOAN   Oh, yes! We're great friends—met her in New York—She asked me down here to help entertain Uncle Rand!

RAND   Where *is* Lael?

JOAN   She had to run up to London. She left me to do the honors.

HOBART   Run up to London! Didn't she know? . . .

JOAN   It's a long story, Father. She said she'd explain to Uncle Rand.
(*She smiles bewitchingly at her uncle*)

RAND   It's quite all right. I appreciate Lael's not treating me as a guest.

HOBART   (*Grimly*)   If it's informality you're after, you'll get it all right here!

RAND   (*Looking round*)   Sweet place!

JOAN   Wait till you see the garden! (*To her father*) Shall I show him the garden?

MRS. DINGLE   Perhaps Captain Eldridge would like to go to his room?

RAND   No, thank you.

JOAN   This is Mrs. Dingle.
  (MRS. DINGLE *bobs*)

RAND (*To* MRS. DINGLE)   No, thank you, Mrs. Dingle. I'll just stretch here and talk to my brother for a bit. Seems we can't get talked out, doesn't it, Bart?
  (*He takes his older brother affectionately by the shoulder*)

JOAN (*To* MRS. DINGLE)   You might see that Rand's bags are put in his room.

MRS. DINGLE   Certainly, miss, I'll see to it.
  (*She goes out*)

RAND (*To* JOAN, *affectionately*)   Well, Joan, well! Well! It certainly was a great idea of Lael's to have you here.

JOAN (*With real admiration*)   You're looking wonderful. Very, very handsome.

RAND   You, on the other hand, are quite repulsive.

JOAN   Wherever did you get that beautiful tan? I thought it was freezing up there in the Antarctic.

RAND   It's not *up* there—it's *down* there. And coming back I passed through the tropics.

JOAN (*Amazed*)   Tropics!

RAND (*Laughing, to* HOBART)   Geographically, Joan seems a little vague.

HOBART   Vagueness is a charm she inherits from her mother.

RAND   (*To* JOAN)   I'm a little hurt you didn't wait for me in New York. (*Drily*) Seen the reception I had. Might have impressed you.

JOAN   I wish I had! How I should have loved to see you drive up Fifth Avenue. How was it? Were you thrilled?

RAND   Well, as you see, I survived that too.
  (*They laugh*)

HOBART (*Breaking into this*)   What's the inn like here, Joan?

JOAN   Very comfortable. Well, quite comfortable.

HOBART   You might ring up and reserve me some rooms. It's getting so late, I believe I'll stay the night.

RAND   Do, please.

JOAN   There's no telephone in this house. But I'll walk over . . .

HOBART   And while you're about it—would you mind telephoning your mother—she's at Wechsley, you know—ask her to pick me up at the White Hart because I shan't be able to get to Wechsley for her.

JOAN   Right!

HOBART   Thank you very much.

JOAN   (*As she runs out*)   So long, Rand. Be seeing you.

RAND   Oh, Joan.

JOAN   (*Stopping*)   Yes?

RAND   How is she? Lael? Is she all right?

JOAN   Oh, grand! Top of her form. Wait till you see . . .

RAND   (*Smiling*)   I can't!

JOAN   (*To her father*)   I'll get you the Royal Suite. The Royal Suite in the White Hart!
   (*She runs off through the house. There is a long pause. RAND takes a turn about the room. He is sorry LAEL hasn't been there to meet him, not for his own sake alone but because he knows the effect on his brother will be, from his point of view, unfortunate. Nor is he wrong*)

HOBART   Well, this little incident illustrates a bit what I mean about your lady love.

RAND   (*Disingenuous*)   This? What?

HOBART   (*Irritated at his evasion*)   Well, her not being here! It's a bit thick, I must say.

RAND   I don't think so, Bart, really. She'll probably explain it perfectly. After all, she is a busy woman. She wirelessed me to come right down.

HOBART   I know! Come right down. Dying to see you. I won't be there, but come right down!

RAND   (*Remonstrating mildly*)   Bart . . .

HOBART   It all comes under the head of being Bohemian, I suppose.

RAND   Come now! Lael's not Bohemian.

HOBART   Artistic, then. If you're artistic, you can be rude. I must say I'm not comfortable with artists. I get on much better with people who do things.

RAND (*Shyly*)   Bart . . . I . . .

HOBART   Yes, Rand.

RAND   You don't like Lael much, do you?

HOBART   Well, she's not my sort. Not your sort either, Rand —that's what I'd like to make you see.

RAND   Bart . . .

HOBART   She's all right in her place, I suppose, but . . .

RAND   Before you say any more, Bart, I want to tell you— I must tell you . . .

BART   Well?

RAND   I'm going to ask her to marry me. That's why I came to England.

HOBART (*After a moment*)   Rand . . .

RAND   Yes, Bart.

HOBART   You know I love you. You know how proud I am of you. You know how much your career and reputation mean to me.

RAND   And you know how grateful I am to you. I never speak of it, but don't think, Bart, I don't appreciate—deeply —all the money you've spent on my expeditions . . .

HOBART   Nonsense! What's that? What's money compared to what you've done for our name—the Eldridge name. I want that name kept high, Rand—at the highest . . .

RAND (*Pleading for a clean bill*)   There isn't anything against Lael, is there, Bart—nothing—serious?

HOBART   Well, it depends on what you call serious.

RAND   Well, is it anything to do with—anything to do with? . . .

HOBART   Nothing as far as I know—not in that way.

RAND (*Completely relieved*)   Thank God for that! That's all I care about.

HOBART   Her private life's all right, as far as I know, it's what you may call her—public life—that bothers me.

RAND (*Ridicules idea*)   Oh, if that's all!

HOBART   It's more important than you think, Rand. A little affair here and there I would forgive. . . .

RAND (*Pained*)   Please, Bart!

HOBART   Sorry. But the sort of thing Lady Wyngate goes in for . . .

RAND (*Teasing him, completely relieved now and very happy —a sexual aspersion was the one thing he feared*)   Well, now, big brother, what sort of thing *does* she go in for?

HOBART   Hardly know how to explain to you. Her reputation . . .

RAND   What *is* her reputation?

HOBART   Well, she's commonly considered—to put it mildly —eccentric.

RAND   How do you mean eccentric?

HOBART   For one thing her husband was little better than a fire-eater.

RAND   Did you know her husband?

HOBART   No, but I know plenty who did. I know the paper he edited—which her money supported and *still* supports.

RAND   She showed me a copy of it in New York. Seemed harmless—full of book reviews.

HOBART   It's communistic! That's what gets on *my* nerves— a woman of her class—whose fortune has been built up by a lot of hard-working manufacturers, supporting the *Clarion* —a Liberal weekly that's very dangerous—that wants to destroy the system that gives her her income. A woman of fine family whose father was knighted for war work, who might have her house full of the best people, surrounding herself with a lot of riff-raff.

RAND   I don't see any riff-raff.

HOBART   You will if you stay here—but I can't stop for that. What I have to convey to you is this: In the last year or so,

while you've been away in the Antarctic, my mind has gradually crystallized to an important decision. I'm going to settle
down permanently here in England—make my headquarters
here.

RAND   Doesn't Phoebe want to live in America?

HOBART   It's got nothing to do with Phoebe! I've decided to
give myself up, in a manner of speaking, to public service.
I can see my way clear to becoming an influence, a power,
not only here but, from here, in America as well. In fact—
in fact . . .

RAND (*Intrigued by the mystery*)   You're wonderfully clever,
Bart—you always were!

HOBART   I've formed a connection with one of the wealthiest
men in England. You'd be startled, I think, if I told you
who it was.

RAND (*With perfect sincerity*)   The Prime Minister!

HOBART   No, no! Lord—his name would be anathema in this
house—Lord—
   (*He whispers the name to* RAND)

RAND (*Registering the expected astonishment but still not
having the faintest idea*)   Really? Who is he?

HOBART   Well, I'm surprised. Don't you *ever* read the papers?

RAND   We don't get the papers in the Antarctic.

HOBART   Of course. Of course. Anyway, you'll soon learn
about him. He admires you very much.

RAND   Admires me? Really?

HOBART   In fact—curious as it may sound—you are a factor
in our schemes—an unconscious factor—but still a factor—
none the less powerful because unseen—unspoken.

RAND   I? How? But how?

HOBART   Your name. Your magic name.

RAND   Really?

HOBART   Lord—
   (*He can't bring himself to mention the sacred name. He
looks around*)

RAND (*Interested*)   You mean that Lord . . .

HOBART (*Stopping him before he utters the name*)   Yes!
He's one of the most powerful newspaper proprietors in England—in the world. Before a week is out I shall be definitely
associated with him in a newspaper venture of great importance. I'm putting a good deal of money into it, but
what he wants chiefly, I fancy, are my American connections.
And I know you will be glad to hear that in my opinion
your name, your unblemished and heroic reputation, finally
turned the balance in my favor with Lord . . . (*His voice
hushes*) One of those imponderables that sometimes very
subtly outweighs the greatest considerations. Yes, my instinct
tells me you have been invaluable. You have aided me.

RAND (*With complete sincerity*)   Nothing you could say to
me would make me happier.

HOBART   No man ever had a more loyal brother than you are.
I know that. (*A moment's silence*) Now you see, Rand—
you understand what I am telling you is in the strictest confidence. . . .

RAND   Oh, absolutely . . .

HOBART   That includes Lady Wyngate—she's the last person
I'd want to have know.

RAND   Of course, Bart. I never talk to Lael about things like
that.

HOBART   Well, sometimes one thing leads to another.

RAND (*With his half-shy smile*)   I hope so!

HOBART (*Clears his throat*)   You see this venture I am going
into with—the person I mentioned—is more than a newspaper venture. Much more important than that. The affairs of
the world, as you probably know, are in a critical state.

RAND   You mean—the depression?

HOBART   Behind that—beyond that—beneath that.

RAND (*Dimly*)   I see!

HOBART (*Grimly*)   The line is becoming clearly marked.
The issue is joined. At least we know which side we're on!

RAND   I think what you're going to do for the unemployed
young men—get them interested in physical culture, give
them jobs, give them something to live for—it's really wonderful, Bart—just like you—

HOBART   We've got to do something for them—or they'll drift into chaos, crime, anarchy—it's the New Crusade! (*He is struck suddenly by an overwhelming idea*) My God, Rand!

RAND (*Alarmed*)   Bart? What's the matter?

HOBART   Nothing. Nothing. An idea! A terrific idea! The New Crusade—a motto—a picture slogan—for our masthead—don't you see?—The New Crusade—a Crusader in an airplane—don't you see—right on the masthead!

RAND   Masthead?

HOBART (*His hands in front of his eyes to conserve the creative process*)   You at the wheel!

RAND (*Delicately*)   Stick!

HOBART   You at the stick—in a Crusader's costume—driving a plane over a sea of chaos—communism—decadence—into the New Order—it's magnificent—I must telephone at once to Lord . . .

RAND   Won't it look as if you were trying to publicize me?

HOBART   Not a photograph of you—nothing realistic like that—an idealization—if I do say it myself, it's wonderful—how it bridges the centuries—the moral fervor of the . . . (*Feels around for the century—can't remember it, compromises quickly*) Middle Ages—the science and heroism of the twentieth—it's superb!

RAND   Yes, I think it is, Bart. I think Lord . . .

(*He is about to say the sacred name.* HOBART *is terrified*)

HOBART (*Looks about room to see no one overhears them*)   Sh!

RAND   Well, I think he's very lucky to have you for a partner!

HOBART   When I explain to you more clearly what it is we stand for—and when you've had a chance to observe Lady Wyngate in her own bailiwick, so to speak—you'll understand better why a marriage to her would be—well, to put it mildly—inexpedient.

(*Rises and starts to pace back and forth*)

RAND (*Rises*)   But why? I don't see why. She's lovely. Everybody adores her.

HOBART (*Facing* RAND)   The right people don't adore her. After all—what do you know about her? You met her when she was on a flying trip to New York.

RAND   When I went down to Washington to get the—the medal from the Geographic Society.

HOBART (*Turning away*)   Well?

RAND   I met the British Ambassador.

HOBART   Well?

RAND   I asked him about her.

HOBART   Well?

RAND   His face lit up.

HOBART (*Indulgently*)   That, my boy, might mean many things.

RAND   He said he adored her.

HOBART   When he's in Washington, it's safe for him to adore her.

RAND (*In despair*)   But I don't understand—what is it— what is it that—?

HOBART   Shall I be blunt?

RAND (*Dreading it*)   Please—

HOBART   For a man in your position—with your reputation —to marry Lady Wyngate . . .

RAND (*Very tense*)   Well?

HOBART (*Feeling for an analogy that* RAND *will understand*) Well—it would . . . (*Hitting on it at last and pouncing on it happily*) Well—it would be like Lindbergh marrying a young Emma Goldman!
(*At this point, and before* RAND *can protest,* LAEL WYNGATE *comes in. She goes at once to* RAND, *embraces him, kisses him*)

LAEL   Rand!

RAND   Lael, darling!

LAEL   *Can* you forgive me? You must think me most un- believably rude. I left Joan here to receive you. Did she do well by you?
(HOBART *clears his throat*)

RAND   This is my brother, Hobart Eldridge.

LAEL   Joan's father?

RAND   Yes.

LAEL   (*Shaking hands with him*)   I'm so glad to see Mr. Eldridge.

HOBART   (*Formally*)   How do you do?

LAEL   Such a morning! Do sit down! I went up to London to pick up a German refugee. I found him so alone and so charming that I've brought him back with me. You'll adore him.

HOBART   (*Sensing illustrative material*)   German refugee?

LAEL   Yes.

RAND   (*Sensing it equally and to protect* LAEL)   We didn't mind a bit waiting.

HOBART   What sort of refugee?

LAEL   Didn't I say? German!

HOBART   But what sort of German? Communist?

LAEL   I don't know. We didn't talk politics. He's a literary and music critic. A very prominent one. His name is Willens. Hugo Willens.

RAND   No! Willens! Not really!

LAEL   Do you know him?

RAND   I know him well. Where is he?

LAEL   He'll be down in a minute.

RAND   Well, imagine. Hugo Willens! Great chap. We used to go skiing together.

HOBART   Where was this?

RAND   Near Munich. When Phoebe was staying there.

LAEL   Phoebe?

RAND   Yes, Hobart's wife. Met him through Phoebe, as a matter of fact. Great friend of Phoebe's.

HOBART   Oh!

LAEL   Oh, then you know him too, Mr. Eldridge?

HOBART   No. I don't know all my wife's friends. Phoebe travels around quite a bit.

LAEL   Oh, I see. Well, won't it be nice for him to see you again? He hasn't the faintest idea, of course. And Mrs. Eldridge will have to come too. But, Rand, tell me! How splendid you look! How long were you gone this time?

RAND   Eight months!

LAEL   Were you? And did you have a triumphal on your return? Were they glad to see you?

RAND   They seemed to be.

LAEL   Seemed! Don't tell me. When Americans are glad, they're *glad!* How I adore them! And how is my dear, incomparable New York?

RAND   It's still there. Waiting to see you again.

LAEL   (*Makes an impulsive engagement*)   I'll go back with you.

RAND   (*Eagerly*)   Will you?

LAEL   (*To* HOBART)   You must be very proud of him, Mr. Eldridge. You're staying for the week-end, aren't you?

HOBART   It's Tuesday. I'm afraid the week-end's over.

LAEL   I mean next week-end. Do stay. You live in England, don't you, Mr. Eldridge?

HOBART   I intend to.

LAEL   It's a great compliment to us. It's so reassuring for us that we attract Americans like you.

HOBART   (*Bows, and a little angrily*)   Thank you.

LAEL   You know your brother is the most modest national hero I've ever met. That's why I adore him so. I'm so happy to see you again, Rand. What times we had in New York— what *good* times! Really, I believe I never had so much fun anywhere as I did in those two weeks. (*To* HOBART *again*) In any case, Mr. Eldridge, whether you stay the week-end or not, you must stay for dinner.

RAND   I want you to meet Willens, Bart. How'd you corral him, Lael?

LAEL   Through Joan.

HOBART   Joan?

LAEL   When Joan's young man made his début in Berlin,

Herr Willens gave him a great send-off. Yes, decidedly, it's one up for Joan.

RAND (*To* HOBART)   Has Joan a young man? *That's* why she wouldn't wait for me in New York! Well, Bart, are you prepared for that?

HOBART   Oh, Joan's young men come and go. It's not important.

LAEL   Well, anyway, you'll meet him in a minute. He's staying here. A young Russian-American, Sascha Barashaev. Plays the piano.

HOBART   Oh, then it's certainly not important.

LAEL   Between ourselves—all technique—magnificent—but not much feeling. Not what you'd expect, is it? Do you think Latins and Slavs actually have more feeling than we have? Do you, Mr. Eldridge? They're more expressive and that gives the impression of warmth, but actually I don't think they feel more intensely than we do, do you?

HOBART   Latins and Slavs are not my specialty, Lady Wyngate.

LAEL   Oh, well. It's that I get so tired of hearing about Anglo-Saxon coldness. We're such a sloppy, sentimental race. Only yesterday I ran into Lord Abercrombie at lunch . . . (*As she mentions, so casually, the dread name,* RAND *is visibly struck*) What's the matter, Rand? Do you know him?

RAND (*Gasping*)   No! I don't.

LAEL   Very amusing, inflated, wrong-headed little man. Do you know him, Mr. Eldridge?

HOBART (*With some fervor*)   He's the hope of England.

LAEL   Has he told *you* that too? He believes it. He actually believes it. I hate messiahs. Fake ones, charlatan ones I enjoy. It's amusing to watch them do their stuff. I met Aimee McPherson in New York—you know, the woman who was lost in the desert—I found her in a cinema theatre. Now there's the kind of blonde messiah I like. But sincere ones, zealot ones I can't abide. When they tell you they're the hope of anything—and they're not faking—they're hopeless. But I'm not persuaded entirely about Lord Abercrombie. Are you, Mr. Eldridge? Perhaps he practises before a mirror. . . .

HOBART   In my opinion, Lady Wyngate, he is the . . .

LAEL I know! But on the side. Pretty good circulation-booster, isn't he? I haven't quite given him up. He may be —what do they call it in America—delicious word—a phony! Shall we bet on Lord Abercrombie, Mr. Eldridge?

(JOAN *comes in, followed by* MRS. DINGLE *with the tea things*)

JOAN Oh, Lael, I'm crazy about him—I'm just mad about him!

LAEL That's not news. Ah, tea. Thank you, Mrs. Dingle.

JOAN Not Sascha. The new one.

LAEL Oh! Tea! Tea! Aren't you coming, Mr. Eldridge?

HOBART Did you see about the room in the inn, Joan?

JOAN Yes, Dad. I've reserved the Royal Suite for you. He's *so* charming. . . .

HOBART Did you telephone to your mother?

JOAN Yes. She's meeting you. He's so distinguished! So different! And he's been in a concentration camp.

(SASCHA *and* HUGO WILLENS *come in*)

LAEL Oh, here you are! Well, Herr Willens, I hear you're distinguished and different. How different are you, Herr Willens?

RAND (*Stepping forward*) Hello, Hugo!

HUGO (*Astonished*) No. Not really! (*As they shake hands cordially, to* LAEL) Why didn't you tell me?

LAEL I didn't know you and Rand were old friends.

RAND This is my brother, Hobart Eldridge.

HUGO (*Shaking hands with* HOBART) How do you do?

HOBART How do you do?

RAND Phoebe's husband.

HUGO How do you do?

(HOBART *about to sit, looks at* HUGO *after the double greeting*)

LAEL And Mr. Eldridge, Mr. Barashaev.

SASCHA How do you do?

HOBART Oh, so you're Mr. Barashaev.

LAEL And Captain Eldridge, Mr. Barashaev.

SASCHA   How do you do, Captain Eldridge. I've heard a lot about you.

RAND   Thank you.

LAEL   Come on, everybody! Tea! Please sit down!

RAND   Well, well, Hugo! What on earth's happened to you?

HUGO   That's a long story.

LAEL   Herr Willens has just emerged from a concentration camp.

RAND   Whatever for?

HUGO (*Still rather quietly*)   It was rather boring.

RAND   I mean—what did they put you in for?

HUGO   That's part of the long story.

LAEL   What was it like?

HUGO   No luxury. Plain. Simple.

LAEL   Showers or tubs?

HUGO   Barbed wire and truncheons.

LAEL   Both! How generous!
   (*Pours* HUGO'S *tea*)

SASCHA (*Gloomily*)   That couldn't have been any joke.

RAND   Well, I can't conceive—Hugo, why?

LAEL (*Holding* HUGO'S *cup*)   Before I give you tea . . . (*A glance at* HOBART) We must know this—are you a Communist?

HUGO   I assure you, dear lady—I am a music critic.

LAEL   Thank heaven! Cream?

HUGO (*Standing*)   Please.
   (LAEL *pours cream into cup and hands it to* HUGO, *who thanks her and sits down*)

LAEL (*As she pours the second cup*)   Mr. Eldridge?

HOBART   Straight, please. I beg your pardon—plain.

LAEL   Rand? I know how you take yours. (LAEL *hands* HOBART *his cup. She pours* RAND'S *tea.* JOAN *rises and pours for* SASCHA *and herself. Gives* SASCHA *his cup then sits down again*) You know, Herr Willens, Captain Eldridge has just discovered a new world—a bright, new, fresh, untainted world.

HUGO   Yes! I know! (*Quietly—to* RAND) What a let-down it must be to return to this old one!

RAND (*Quite buoyantly*)   Oh, I don't know. I like it down there, but it's nice to be back too, Lael!

LAEL (*Holds out* RAND'S *cup for him. He rises and gets it and sits down again*)   It seems to be easier to discover new worlds than to run them once you've found them.

HOBART   England has done pretty well.

LAEL   Has she? It's generous of you to say so, but some of us don't feel in the least complacent about it.

HOBART   There's plenty of strength in England. In America, too. It's not unified. It's not co-ordinated. Power not in the right hands, that's all.

LAEL   So Lord Abercrombie was telling me just the other day—his very phrase—"Power isn't in the right hands." He means to put it there.

HOBART (*To* HUGO)   Tell me Herr—Herr . . .

LAEL   Willens.

HOBART   Herr Willens. You say you're a music critic.

HUGO   I was.

HOBART   You're not a political writer then?

HUGO   Not at all.

HOBART   You don't mind I hope, if I—?

HUGO   Not at all.

HOBART   Then may I ask why you were put into a concentration camp?

HUGO   I wrote a pamphlet.

HOBART (*In triumph*)   Ah! Communist!

HUGO   Not at all! It was satiric.

HOBART   Making fun of the government!

LAEL   If he did make fun of the government, Mr. Eldridge, does that justify, in your opinion, his being put in a concentration camp?

HOBART   It's a government trying to make headway against tremendous odds. They're justified in putting down opposition. The Communists about whom we're so sentimental nowadays . . .

LAEL   Are we?

HOBART   They did it with bullets. They weren't sentimental. We might learn from them.

HUGO   As a matter of fact, Mr. Eldridge, my pamphlet had nothing to do with politics. It was pure fantasy.

LAEL   Really?

RAND   What was it about?

HUGO   I called it "The Last Jew."

LAEL   Where have I . . . ?

HUGO   They did me the honor to burn it—(*Deprecatingly*) with other important works.

LAEL   Hugo Willens! Of course! I remember reading the title in the—fire list. "The Last Jew"—Hugo Willens. I remember thinking: Now who is Will—? I beg your pardon.

HUGO   Well, now, you know. I thought it amusing, really. As a writer on music I had, as a matter of course, innumerable Jewish friends. I was touched personally by their sudden misfortunes. Also, as a lover of music, I was devastated by what the Aryan standardization was doing to my world. I resented this gratuitous disturbance of my professional routine —so I sat down and wrote this pamphlet.

LAEL   What was it about?

HUGO   Well—

LAEL   Oh, do tell us, we want to know.

RAND   Yes, do.

HUGO   With the extermination of the Jews, the millennium has been promised the people. And with the efficiency of a well-organized machine the purpose is all but accomplished. They are all dead—but one—the last Jew. He is about to commit suicide when an excited deputation from the All-Highest comes to see him. There has been a meeting in the sanctum of the Minister of Propaganda. This expert and clever man has seen that the surviving Jew is the most valuable man in the Kingdom. He points out to the Council their dilemma. Let this man die and their policy is bankrupt. They are left naked, without an issue, without a programme, without a scapegoat. The Jews gone and still no millennium. They are in a panic—till finally a committee is dispatched— and the last Jew is given a handsome subsidy to propagate—

LAEL (*Claps her hands in delight, jumps up*) Where is it? I must get my hands on it. I want to publish it in my magazine.

HOBART (*Maliciously*) The Jew accepts the subsidy, I suppose!

HUGO (*Calmly*) Not only does he accept it—he makes them double it. You see, Mr. Eldridge, he is not an idealist—he is a practical man. Idealism he leaves to his interlocutors.

LAEL Why not? A subsidy to propagate for destruction. As an Imperialist Fascist, Mr. Eldridge, you must understand that perfectly. Where is your pamphlet, Herr Willens?

HUGO It is destroyed. I have no copy.

LAEL You must rewrite it—from memory.

HUGO Why? Why should I be the Jewish apologist? I'm not a Jew. That is to say—

LAEL Oh! Oh!

HUGO I had a Jewish great-grandmother.

LAEL But what an indiscretion! What an indulgence!

RAND (*To* HUGO, *sympathetically*) Well, I never heard such nonsense! Do you mean to say they actually—

HUGO Yes, and my father was a minister in the Protestant Church.

LAEL (*Inexorable*) Still—that speck—that unfortunate— speck.

HUGO Curiously enough, I was rather proud of that speck— when I thought of it—which wasn't often—it was not unpleasant to remember I had it. This odd and mysterious strain —did it give me sympathy and flavor, intellectual audacity, impudence and intensity? You see, Mr. Eldridge, it was rather like being left gold bonds in a vault—bonds which couldn't be touched but which, nevertheless, paid one an unseen and incalculable dividend. That's how I felt about—the speck. I was a Nordic with an interesting racial fillip. I was secretly vain about it—until it began!

LAEL The chromosome-hunt!

HUGO   The chromosome-hunt! A curious experience—to find myself overnight a marked person, a special person. Curious discomfort. I kept saying to myself: What is it? What is it you feel? You are the same—in spite of these looks, these sudden stillnesses in conversation, this restraint—you are the same. But within forty-eight hours, it was not the same. Spiritually, I was in the ghetto.

HOBART   Imagination, of course!

HUGO (*After a look at him—agreeing*)   Of course—imagination—the only reality. The world in which one really lives and feels. And then the strangest thing happened. I cannot—still I cannot understand it. Atavism? The—*speck*—took possession of me. I became its creature. I moved under its ordering. I began to ask myself whether subconsciously I hadn't written the pamphlet to defend my antecedents.

LAEL   But—how absurd! Really, do you have to go to Freud to explain an act of simple humanity? You wrote the pamphlet because you are a generous human being. Don't you think—don't you really think—that the subconscious has been done to death and that it's high time someone re-discovered the conscious?

HUGO (*Amused*)   I admit that leaving the Fatherland has restored my balance a bit. I am quite over this aberration. I've returned to my Aryan inheritance.

LAEL   And very welcome you are.

RAND (*Rises and puts down cup on tray. Warmly*)   You bet you are! It's grand seeing you, old boy!

LAEL   Joan, will you like him even if he is an Aryan?

JOAN   I'll try. Sascha, come and play for me now, will you? I want to hear music.

LAEL   What's the matter with *this* piano?

JOAN   Sascha likes the tone of the upstairs one better.

LAEL (*Realizing that they might want to be alone*)   Oh.

JOAN (*To* SASCHA)   Come on.

SASCHA (*Surly*)   What if I don't feel like playing?

HUGO   Sascha, I'd love some Bach.

SASCHA (*Capitulating at once*)   Of course.

HUGO (*Rising*)   If Lady Wyngate will excuse us?

LAEL   Certainly.

JOAN   He'll play for you, Herr Willens. I'm jealous.
(*She slips her arm through* SASCHA's)

LAEL   How did you get this hold on Sascha, Herr Willens?

HUGO (*Quizzically*)   By appreciating him—publicly.

SASCHA (*Eagerly*)   You know, I still carry that notice around
with me. Whenever I get depressed, I read it.

LAEL   Where is it now?

SASCHA (*Taking a German newspaper clipping from his breast
pocket*)   Right here!

LAEL   Really!

HUGO   Let me see it!
(SASCHA *hands it to* HUGO)

LAEL   May I see it?

JOAN (*Wearily*)   He's read it to me fifty times.
(HUGO *and* LAEL *look at the yellowed clipping. In it he sees
epitomized his vanished career, and another life. After a
moment he gives the clipping back to* SASCHA)

HUGO   Thank you. (*A moment's pause. Then in a bantering
tone*) I wanted to assure myself that I had actually once had
an identity. I must have had. I told people to go to concerts
and they went. I told them to stay away—they stayed away.
Quite incredible, but it seems to be true!

SASCHA   My next appearance after that notice was sold out.

JOAN   Yes, but what about the Bach?

SASCHA   I'm out of practice.

JOAN   Are pianists ever in practice, Herr Willens?

HUGO   Not good ones.

LAEL (*As they go out*)   I'll join you presently. (*To* RAND *and*
HOBART)   Now then! Isn't he nice?

RAND   Oh, he's swell!

LAEL   Imagine your knowing him!

HOBART (*Rises*)   If you'll excuse me, I'll walk down to the
post office. I have to send a telegram.

LAEL   I can give Robert the message and he can . . .

HOBART   Thank you. As a matter of fact, Phoebe—my wife . . .

LAEL   Where is she?

HOBART   She's picking me up at the White Hart. We were driving on to Boxwood.

LAEL   You'll bring her back to dine, of course. I'd love to meet her.

RAND   She'll probably want to see Hugo.

LAEL   Yes, of course.

RAND   Be sure you tell her he's here.

HOBART   I will.

RAND   She and Hugo were great pals.

LAEL   Oh, were they? Do make her come then. It will be so nice bringing them together again.

HOBART   I'll do my best. Thank you very much! I'm sure she'll be delighted. Besides, Mrs. Eldridge hasn't seen Rand yet. In his eagerness to come here he stopped for nothing—for nobody.

(*Piano is heard from upstairs—"Organ Fugue in G Minor"*)

LAEL   I'm very flattered.

HOBART (*Heavily facetious*)   The bridegroom runneth to his chambers.

LAEL   Now you're committing him and you don't want to be committed, do you, Rand? I'll expect you both for dinner. Tell Mrs. Eldridge she needn't fuss.

HOBART (*Grimly*)   She loves to fuss. Thank you very much. Good-bye.

LAEL   Good-bye.

HOBART   See you later, Rand.

(*He goes out. In the moment that follows* LAEL *and* RAND *turn and face each other*)

LAEL   Well, Rand . . .

RAND   Awfully good of you to invite my entire . . . (*They are in each other's arms. After a bit, from this close embrace emerges a whispered conversation*) Why did you run away from me?

LAEL (*Muffled*) Had to.

RAND It was hateful of you . . .

LAEL It was. But I had to . . .

RAND You won't again.

LAEL I will again. I'll have to again.

RAND Why? Why?

LAEL If you give me a chance I'll tell you . . .

RAND My dearest! I'll never let you go again—never let you go again!
(*They stand in silence a moment longer, locked in each other's arms. Then they separate—still standing quite close, looking at each other*)

LAEL Tell me now—what was it like?

RAND What?

LAEL Your triumphal return. I saw pictures in the news-films. How I wish I could have been there! How I wish I could have fluttered telephone books at you! I'd have given anything—I adore parades.

RAND Shall I tell you how it was? It was incomplete. It didn't mean much—because you weren't there. I'll never forgive you—for not being there.

LAEL How very sweet of you! I've never had a nicer compliment.

RAND It's true.

LAEL What was it like? What were you thinking about? I'm enormously interested in fame. What is it like to be famous? To know—to be aware—that when you enter a room, its temperature alters? To be the Prince of Wales or Einstein—or yourself?

RAND (*Embarrassed*) I never think of it.

LAEL Not even when you're shaving? (*They laugh*) Oh, come now, you must think of it when you're shaving. As a matter of fact I've never—and I've known very many famous people—I've never met anyone so genuinely modest, so unconscious of being haloed, as you.

RAND (*Quite unaffectedly*) It bewilders me. I don't understand it. You know—I was thinking in New York—riding up

Fifth Avenue—when they were making all that fuss—I was thinking—I remembered . . .

LAEL   That's just what I'd love to know—what does one think of on climactic occasions like that?

RAND   I remembered—it'll sound foolish. . . .

LAEL   Please tell me!

RAND   When I was a kid—I hated school—I simply couldn't study. . . .

LAEL   Did you like mathematics?

RAND   I loathed it.

LAEL   Do you know, Rand, that to this day I can't add or subtract? And these days with the papers full of that awful rigamarole about inflated currencies and what not I'm very unhappy—when I read about frozen assets I really shiver—and the very idea of earmarking gold makes my nerves tingle, like gears grinding. But go on—tell me.

RAND   There was a hill—Mount Wachusett—it wasn't much more than that—I could see it out of the window of the little country schoolhouse, misty blue and very far away. One spring morning, when I should have been studying, I found myself looking at it—I had such a wish to climb it—to climb it, to discover it, for myself. I've never understood what came over me. But I just put down my book, left the schoolhouse and made for it.

LAEL   How old were you?

RAND   I was eight. It was farther away than I thought. When I got to it, it was nightfall. I spent the night in a barn. At sunrise I got up and climbed to the top. I'll never forget that instant—when I got to the summit and looked around at what seemed to me the whole world.

LAEL   How glorious! Like finding a Pole.

RAND   Much more thrilling because more definite. You wouldn't know you were at the Pole if your instruments didn't tell you so. When I got to the top of Mount Wachusett, I *knew!* But what I didn't know was that my poor mother, frantic with anxiety, was scouring the countryside for me.

LAEL   Did you catch it?

RAND Did I? That's what I remembered—that incident — riding up Fifth Avenue. And it seemed so funny—all this acclaim for doing what I'd been spanked for as a kid—the same thing exactly—for having fun—it was fun for me then —it is still— I don't know what they make all that fuss over —I honestly don't.

LAEL (*Sincerely and tenderly*) I'm really frightfully flattered —that you should have left all that adulation and come to see me.

RAND (*Hating to confess it*) And all the time I was remembering that I felt bitter against you—for not being there.

LAEL I'm sorry.
    (*A moment's pause*)

RAND (*To reassure her*) I kept your photograph in my cabin on the *Odyssey*.

LAEL Did I give you a photograph?

RAND I cut it out of the rotogravure section in a New York newspaper.

LAEL Did I behold those awful vastnesses? Did I share those lonely vigils?

RAND (*Laughing a bit*) We both did.

LAEL Do you know, when I was a young girl, I met Admiral Scott?

RAND (*Excited*) Did you really? What was he like?

LAEL Well, rather like you. Very good-looking.

RAND You'll give me a swelled head.

LAEL I don't think so. Did you ever read Scott's "Diaries"?

RAND Yes.

LAEL Do you remember that passage about the death of Captain Oates? (*Quoting from memory*) "We knew that poor Oates was walking to his death, but though we tried to dissuade him, we knew it was the act of a brave man and an English gentleman. We all hope to meet the end with a similar spirit and assuredly the end is not far."

RAND Think of your knowing that—by heart. You're wonderful!

LAEL (*Quietly*)   Anyone can memorize a heroic bit of prose, Rand. To live that sort of thing—as you do—is much more difficult. (*He is embarrassed. She laughs*) Sorry! You can't bear praise, can you? I won't do it again. Promise! (*A pause. He is hung up. He wants to make love to her; he doesn't know how to bridge the gap. She shifts into a less delicate field. She hesitates, herself, to approach the explanation she must give him*) Your brother doesn't like me much, does he? I shock him, don't I? And, I must tell you, Rand, I don't mind a bit shocking him. I enjoy shocking him. What did he say to you about me? I wager he's frightened to death.

RAND (*Very uncomfortable*)   Well, you know Bart; he's a little strict.

LAEL   Oh, that's what it is. Strict!

RAND   He's the kindest brother a fellow ever had, only . . .

LAEL   Rand?

RAND   What?

LAEL   'Fess up. Are you afraid of your older brother? You are! It's too delicious! Never mind, Rand, I'll do my best to protect you. Tell me, what did he say about me?

RAND   He didn't say anything.

LAEL (*Very severe with him*)   Rand! What did he say?

RAND (*Miserably*)   Well, he thinks your friends are a little peculiar.

LAEL   Peculiar. He thinks my friends are peculiar. Well, did you defend me? What did you say?

RAND   Oh, that you were just kind-hearted—that you didn't mean anything, no matter whom you associated with. . . .

LAEL (*Understanding perfectly*)   Amiable but misguided.

RAND   I want you to know, Lael—anything you do is all right with me.

LAEL   Please don't idolize me, Rand. I'm not worth it.

RAND (*Simply*)   I love you.

LAEL   Rand—

RAND   I want to marry you, and I'm going to.

LAEL   Rand—

RAND   That's why I came over here.

LAEL (*Overwhelmed, doesn't know how to explain to him, worried about herself*) Oh, dear!

RAND Are you in love with anybody else?

LAEL I wish I were!

RAND What does that mean?

LAEL That would make it simple.

RAND Why did you run away from me in New York?

LAEL That is precisely what I did. I ran away from you in New York. I ran away from you this morning. I'm going to stop running away from you. I'm going to face you, Rand. (*She looks at him squarely*)

RAND What is it? What is it, Lael?

LAEL How can I tell you? I must make it plain to you.

RAND What?

LAEL I've thought of marrying you, Rand. I've thought of it often.

RAND (*Overjoyed*) Lael!

LAEL No—wait. It's not as simple as that—I've been greatly tempted to marry you—but it's a temptation I've finally managed to put aside—and it's not been easy to put aside.

RAND But, Lael, you're crazy—if you love me—and I love you—

LAEL We should marry and be happy forever after, eh?

RAND Yes!

LAEL That's what we shouldn't be!

RAND But why—why? We have everything to go on with!

LAEL No, we haven't. That's just the point. We have very little. What we have would soon exhaust itself and— "Two opinions do not accord well on the same bolster."

RAND What are you talking about?

LAEL That's a saying by an old English worthy named John Aubrey. It's profoundly true. Hasn't it occurred to you, Rand, that there's hardly anything in the world—hardly one single important thing—that you and I agree about?

RAND No—it hasn't. We've never discussed anything— How can you tell?

LAEL (*Laughs*)   We haven't discussed anything because I've steered clear— I knew if we discussed things—important things—we should quarrel and I couldn't bear to quarrel. It's so uncharacteristic of me, Rand, all this. I don't understand it myself—it's an aberration.

RAND   But why? What's the matter with me?

LAEL   I'm not—in a sense—I'm not up to you, Rand.

RAND (*Hurt*)   Don't make fun of me.

LAEL   I mean it literally. You're direct and sincere. You have an adorable simplicity—I'm involved and—compared to you—I'm—Machiavellian.

RAND   I don't believe it.

LAEL   It's true. For instance, just now, with your brother— I was having him on!

RAND   Really? How?

LAEL   I see a few people. I know about his scheme to start a paper with Lord Abercrombie—to enlist the Anglo-American youth for Fascism.

RAND   Well, what's wrong with that?

LAEL   From my point of view, a good deal. Do you know, Rand, I think, with practice, I could work up a first-rate feud with your brother.

RAND   Please don't. I can't tell you how much I want you two to like each other.

LAEL (*Unable to resist*)   Do you want us, as you say at home, to get together?

RAND (*Literally*)   Yes. I do.

LAEL   Oh, Rand, you make me ashamed of myself. You'd probably always make me a little bit ashamed of myself.

RAND (*Miserably*)   I don't know what you mean—really I don't—we like each other and . . .

LAEL (*Determined to be ruthless*)   But don't you see— We're worlds apart.

RAND   Simply because you imagine we disagree theoretically—

LAEL   Your defence of me to your brother was touching but it only proves how little you know me. What did you say? I'm

good-hearted and mean nothing by what I do. But I do, Rand
—I try to mean a great deal. I'm a determined woman. Are
you terrified?

RAND   No.

LAEL   How can I put you off? How can I finally put you
off?

RAND   Do you want to?

LAEL   No!

RAND   There you are!

LAEL   (*Self-reproachful*)   You bring out the worst in me,
Rand—the most feminine. I haven't had this kind of conversation since before I married, when I lived in Heartbreak House.

RAND   Where?

LAEL   It's a fancy by Mr. Shaw. I'd like you to meet him.
He'll probably put you in a play. Being a sedentary vege-
tarian he adores men who fly to unknown worlds and ad-
minister torrid continents. You and Lawrence . . .

RAND   Lawrence . . .

LAEL   Colonel, not D. H. . . . I refer to the exploit with
Arabia—not with Lady Chatterley.

RAND   (*Laughs*)   I don't mind. Usually I'm uncomfortable
with brilliant people, but I'm not with you.

LAEL   You make *me* though!

RAND   (*Very sceptical*)   Oh, yes! I'm sure I do!

LAEL   You do. Also you make me feel a little—horrid.
(RAND, *stung by this, suddenly takes her in his arms and
kisses her passionately*)

RAND   Do I! Do I! Do I!

LAEL   (*After recovery*)   It is pleasanter off the pedestal, I
admit. (*Sighs*) Oh dear!

RAND   What is it now?

LAEL   I have an awful foreboding that eventually I'll suc-
cumb to you but I feel I owe it to my conscience to put up
an awful fight.

RAND   I want you—forever.

LAEL   No, you don't.

RAND I'll never want anyone else but you.

LAEL If you thoroughly knew me, you'd be bewildered by me—you might even be horrified by me.

RAND (*His arms still around her*) You mean—darling, tell me—do you . . .

LAEL What?

RAND Do you have affairs with men?

LAEL (*Between annoyance and laughter*) My dear!

RAND Do you? I must know.

LAEL (*Disengaging herself from him finally*) Well, if it's any comfort to you, I may tell you that though I'm intellectually sympathetic to any indulgence, emotionally I'm fastidious and even puritanic.

RAND (*Fervently*) Thank God!

LAEL (*Bursts out laughing*) Oh, Rand!

RAND (*Offended*) What's so funny?

LAEL You make me feel that any progress is hopeless. How are we going to break down the indurated conservatism of men?

RAND What's progress got to do with it?

LAEL Imagine finding you—a great explorer, a hero—so—sex-ridden. It's disillusioning. I'm ashamed of you, Rand.

RAND Sex-ridden? I love you!

LAEL I mean your assumption that as long as I'm sexually monogamous, no other foible I might have could matter to you. I might be nourishing an idea to destroy the universe. I might be the incarnation of malice, a well, deep and poisonous; I might be anti-Christ, but so long as I didn't—well—you wouldn't mind, you wouldn't enquire. Your psyche, my dear Rand, is sex-ridden. It's obsessed. It's maggoty with possessive desire.

RAND How can you say that when I want to marry you?

LAEL How dare you marry me without knowing me! Much better if we—er—well—till you find me out!

RAND I couldn't. You mean more to me than that.

LAEL If I didn't know this rejection sprang from the purest chivalry, I should be humiliated.

RAND   Please don't be clever.

(HOBART *enters*)

LAEL (*Addressing them both*)   Most men simply can't imagine any woman except in relation to themselves. Are you like that too, Mr. Eldridge? I imagine you are!

HOBART (*Wary*)   I wouldn't think of answering a question like that without preparation.

LAEL   I'm sure you are. An amusing instance of it happened during the one serious quarrel I ever had with my husband. It was during the Sacco-Vanzetti trial in America. I'd read everything there was to be found about it and felt passionately. I was coming up here one day in the train—I was living here alone then—for the moment Nick and I had separated. I had just read Vanzetti's farewell letter; I sat there thinking of this man being shunted in and out of the death-house, facing ignominious death and sitting down to write this patient, forgiving, beautiful letter and I began to cry. I just sat there —crying. A stranger was in the same carriage; I had forgotten his existence—a nice old Anglo-Indian colonel. He put his hand on my arm—"My dear young lady," he said, "Come! Come! A pretty young woman like you!" Life didn't seem long enough to explain to him that I was not crying about a lost lover but about Sacco and Vanzetti. "Think of all life has in store for you," he said. I was thinking about death but I couldn't help laughing. "Do you think so?" I asked. "That is right," he answered. "Keep a stiff upper lip!"

HOBART   Maybe your soldier friend wasn't far from right. Maybe your personal unhappiness was mixed up with those tears, Lady Wyngate.

LAEL   There you are!

HOBART   Maybe it was yourself you were crying for, after all.

LAEL   I see your resemblance to your brother, Rand. I'm sure you despise women, don't you, Mr. Eldridge?

HOBART   Well, I wouldn't exactly say that.

LAEL   Have you men been so successful in running the world that you can take the position of despising us?

HOBART   Surely you can't complain of Rand on that score? He's idolatrous.

LAEL (*With a dazzling smile at* RAND) I certainly do. I complain of his idolatry more than of your contempt. He tells me, for example, that I don't mean anything at all. . . .

RAND I didn't say that.

LAEL You know better than that, don't you, Mr. Eldridge? You know that I mean a great deal.

HOBART (*Showing* RAND *how fair he is*) I think that you do mean a great deal—but—you'll forgive me—I think that you're not nearly so certain of what it is that you mean. If you could visualize the ultimate implications of your conduct, I'm sure that you'd probably . . .

LAEL What nonsense! But that would mean foreseeing to the end of time. It's difficult enough to visualize the immediate implications—and you talk about ultimate implications. What —you will forgive me—what conceit! Where is Mrs. Eldridge? Didn't you go to fetch Mrs. Eldridge?

HOBART She hadn't arrived at White Hart. I left word for her to join me here. I hope you won't mind.

LAEL Of course not! That's utterly delightful! You know, I can hardly wait to know you better because I am certain that the better we know each other the less we shall agree. I foresee enchanting vistas of antagonism. I love opposition. It solidifies my own position.

HOBART What—you will forgive me—what conceit!

LAEL (*Delighted—vamping* HOBART) I am beginning to see why you and Lord Abercrombie hit it off. He's a Puck.

HOBART I beg your pardon!

LAEL He's a Puck—and so are you—a malevolent Puck . . . (JOAN *comes in*) Hello, Joan. What's Herr Willens doing?

JOAN Arguing music with Sascha.

LAEL That's one thing musicians can do. It appears music's more controversial than politics. Poor Herr Willens! What is he going to do? I have it! (*To* HOBART) Why don't you let him review music for your new newspaper?

HOBART We're not going in for that sort of thing.

LAEL What are you going to fill it with?

HOBART I'll send you advance sheets of the first issue.

LAEL   Please don't trouble. I can imagine. Racial solidarity and a higher tariff on wool. Rand, would you like to see the river view?

RAND (*With alacrity*)   I would indeed!

LAEL   We must find something though for that poor fellow Willens. To find yourself suddenly without a job and without a country . . . I'll take you on the most enchanting walk you ever . . . (*To* HOBART) Won't you come too, Mr. Eldridge? Do you mind if I call you Hobart? Even if we do disagree to the death, there is no reason we can't be friends, is there? You will come, won't you, Hobart?

HOBART   No, thank you.

LAEL   I'm so sorry. Joan, will you be a dear and go tell Herr Willens that if he's bored with Sascha he might join us? We'll be walking the river path—slowly. Come on, Rand.

CURTAIN

ACT TWO | Scene One

SCENE: *The same as* ACT ONE.

    Afternoon, four days later.

    CLENDON WYATT'S *voice,* SASCHA *accompanying on the piano, is heard singing a spiritual.* NIKOLAI JURIN *sits by, listening. The curtain rises during the first lines of* WYATT'S *'song.* WYATT *is an attractive young Southern American who won a Rhodes Scholarship for making a spectacular dash on the football field.* JURIN *is an aristocratic Russian, middle-aged, tired, very gentle.*

WYATT'S VOICE

        Away up thar
        My massa's settin'
        Settin' on
        His judgment chair
        He looks down on
        All creation
        He sees sorrow
        He knows care . . .
        He sees sorrow
        He knows care.

(*There is a moment's pause when he finishes singing*)

JURIN   Thank you, Mr. Wyatt. I have always wanted to hear one of these songs. Sascha, please . . .

SASCHA   Yes?

JURIN   This spiritual which Mr. Wyatt has just sung for us— did it make you think of anything, did it remind you of anything?

SASCHA   Musically, you mean?

220

JURIN (*Eagerly*)   Yes. Musically.

SASCHA   Not especially. Why?

JURIN   Ah, that's because you were never in Streilna before the Revolution, where Maria Nikolaevna used to sing the gypsy songs. (*He closes his eyes and sings*)

> Utro Tumannoye
> Utro Sedoye
> Nivi Pechalnia
> Snegom Pokritiya

Do you see what I mean about the resemblance?

WYATT   I see what you mean. . . .

SASCHA (*Argumentative*)   Not a bit alike! The Russian is sensuous, earthy . . .

(LAEL *comes in. Grouped around the piano, the others don't see her at once*)

JURIN (*Trying to persuade* SASCHA)   But in the melancholy of both, there's . . .

WYATT   I know what it is they have in common—resignation!

JURIN   Yes! Resignation. Yes!

LAEL (*Coming up to them*)   What's this about resignation? (*They all rise*) I don't approve of it. I think people ought to fight,

JURIN (*Standing above his chair*)   There comes a day, dear lady, when you cannot fight—then you need resignation.

LAEL (*Briskly*)   I don't admit that day!

JURIN   Had you been in Russia when the Bolsheviks came, you would have recognized such a day.

LAEL   Well, I'm prepared to admit that resignation may have its uses, a recuperative interval, a kind of hibernation of the soul—but you can't be resigned forever. That's Buddhism.

JURIN   No, pardon me, dear lady, but I do not agree with you. There comes a day when you wake up and you find yourself, though you are living and breathing, a part of the past. (HUGO *enters*) You are historic. You realize that you have survived yourself. That's sad. That's strange. And for that day you need resignation.

LAEL   Oh, I understand it, but temperamentally I'm against it.

JURIN   But really to understand it, you have to undergo persecution and contempt.

SASCHA   It's no joke the way things are going nowadays.

LAEL   It was never a joke at any time the way things were going. Was there ever a moment in history when you weren't surrounded by blood and tears? (HOBART *enters. He is fingering a telegram and is very businesslike*) It depended always on where you looked. (*The last of this she has said looking at* HOBART) Oh, hello, Hobart.

HOBART (*Aggressively*)   I've got to go up to London. Where's Rand?

WYATT   On the tennis-court I believe. Shall I get him for you?

HOBART   If you please.
   (*With a look at* LAEL, WYATT *goes out*)

LAEL   I'll join you in a minute, Clen.

JURIN   What a nice boy that is. How does he, an American, happen to be at Oxford?

LAEL   He's a Rhodes Scholar. He says he's so grateful to Mr. Rhodes for letting him stay at Oxford that he's always wanting to write him a bread-and-butter letter.

JURIN (*Puzzled*)   But I thought Rhodes was dead?

LAEL (*Laughs—in explanation to* JURIN)   American humor, Jurin!
   (JURIN *rises and kisses her hand*)

SASCHA   I'll find Joan and we'll play doubles. Mrs. Eldridge doesn't want to play. What do you say, Jurin?

JURIN   I'll do my best. (*To* HUGO) Perhaps you would like to play, Herr Willens?

HUGO   Thank you, no.

LAEL (*To* SASCHA *and* JURIN)   We'll be out in a second to watch you. (SASCHA *and* JURIN *exit*) Now, then, Hobart, why must you go up to London? Why can't you relax? You're always so busy.

HOBART   I've just been down to the post-office . . .

LAEL   I could have a ticker-tape in your room?

HOBART (*Smiling grimly*)   A telephone would be some help. But this isn't the Stock Market. I've got to go up to London.
   (RAND *comes in flushed from tennis*)

LAEL (*To* RAND)   Your brother's going up to London. I'm hurt!

HOBART   Just for a few hours. And I've got to take Rand with me.

RAND (*Appalled*)   Oh, now, Bart . . .

HOBART   We'll be back in time for dinner. Right after, anyway. . . .

RAND   But I'm right in the middle of a set.

HOBART   An hour to London—half hour in Fleet Street—an hour back.

LAEL (*Unable to resist it*)   Shall I ask Lord Abercrombie here?

HOBART (*Horrified*)   Rand!

LAEL   Nonsense. Rand didn't tell me. I told him. *Shall* I ask him here?

HOBART (*Recovered*)   Don't think you could get him.

LAEL (*Wickedly*)   Shall I try?

HOBART (*Fearful of her magic*)   No, thank you. I'm afraid you might succeed and I'd rather see him in London—away from you. Probably, like everyone else, Lord Abercrombie can't resist you.

LAEL   Well, up to a point he can't resist me.

HOBART (*Looking at his watch*)   Please get ready, Rand. The longer you take . . .

RAND (*Turning to obey*)   Right! (*Stops*) Why don't you drive up with us, Lael?

LAEL   Shall I, Hobart? Look how frightened he is. No, I can't leave my guests.

RAND (*To* HOBART)   Sure we will be back for dinner?

HOBART   If you hurry.

RAND   Be right down.
   (RAND *exits*)

LAEL (*To* HUGO)   Mr. Eldridge is organizing an Anglo-American Youth League.

HOBART (*Surprised that she should speak of it to* HUGO) Hum?

LAEL (*To* HOBART)   Oh, it's everybody's secret. What are you going to ask the Anglo-American Youth to do for you?

HOBART (*As if he had memorized it*)   We are appealing to the generous spirit of the youth of both countries to mobilize against the subversive forces current in the world today.

LAEL   Are you appealing to it because it's generous or because it's uncritical?

HUGO   It's a myth about the generosity of youth. Youth is bloodthirsty and savage—it's only the exceptional youth that's generous—just as it's only the exceptional man.

LAEL   I don't agree with you, Hugo. I think the impulse of youth is to be generous.

HUGO   When it's well-fed and romping it may be occasionally, out of excess of energy—but normally it isn't. But then, normally, who is? No point in being quixotic, is there? Excuse me, Lady Wyngate, I think I'll watch the tennis.

(HUGO *saunters out*)

LAEL   I hate Youth Movements. They all come to the same thing. Boy Scouts with bayonets. Do you want a private army, Hobart? Have you a little dictator hatching in your brain?

HOBART (*Urbanely*)   As a matter of fact, Lady Wyngate, it's commonly acknowledged that democracy is passé. At home, the historic system of "checks and balances"—(*He utters the phrase derisively*)—has brought us where we are. And your Parliament is—what does Lord Abercrombie call it?

LAEL   Vestigial! He calls it vestigial!

HOBART   Exactly. Vestigial!

LAEL   I hate dictatorship because it implies omniscience, and I don't believe in omniscience. That's theology applied to politics, and I believe it's dangerous. I can believe in God only if He's invisible.

HOBART (*Patronizingly*)   Very good!

LAEL   Thank you!

HOBART   There's one thing about you—and people like you —that I *don't* understand . . .

LAEL   Oh, is there?

HOBART   . . . that I'd like to have explained to me.

LAEL   I have no secrets from you, Hobart.

HOBART   I can understand people who haven't anything being Communists. Naturally they want to take things away from the people who have. But why people like you, who have everything to lose by the destruction of our system, should be Communists, I never will understand. It baffles me. Frankly, it does.

LAEL   Well, in the first place, I'm not in the least bit a Communist. That's just an epithet that people like you apply to anyone like me who doesn't happen to share your prejudices. In the second place . . . Oh, dear . . .

HOBART   (*Patiently*)   In the second place? . . .

LAEL   Dear, oh, dear, I find the prospect of arguing with you appals me.

HOBART   Why?

LAEL   Because the possibility of enlightening you—if you'll forgive me, Hobart, seems so—shall we say—remote? (*He smiles benignly, patiently*) That benign smile!

HOBART   At least, I know where my interests lie.

LAEL   I'm sure you do.

HOBART   You don't. I am fighting your battles.

LAEL   Thank you!

HOBART   You ought to pray for my success.

LAEL   I will, if you insist.

HOBART   It means the continuance of a world in which you can entertain Communists like Mr. Jurin and . . .

LAEL   Because he is a Russian—and my guest—you assume —you put two and two together—get a colossal sum—typical financier. As a matter of fact, Mr. Jurin is a victim of the Communists—as anti as possible.

HOBART   Humph!

LAEL   That irritates you, doesn't it?

HOBART (*Still very bland*)   Dear Lady Wyngate, inconsistency of any sort irritates me.

LAEL   Yes, I suppose it would.

HOBART   If I favor dictatorship as against democracy, it is because I've applied dictatorship in my business and in my private life, and have made it successful.

LAEL (*Who is pondering, while he is talking, another problem*)   Have you?

HOBART   I flatter myself I have. I am a very rich man, Lady Wyngate. I should never have become so through a system of divided powers. In the political realm also such a system is impractical. The state of the world today proves how impractical it is.

LAEL (*On whom a light breaks*)   Of course!

HOBART (*Misunderstanding*)   Don't tell me you agree with me. That would make me dubious of the soundness of my own premises.

LAEL   Lighter, Bart, lighter . . . I'm afraid these heavy broadsides are wasted on me. Do you know what's been worrying me while you've been making these pronunciamentos? Rand! What has Rand to do with all this? Why are you rushing him into town to meet Lord Abercrombie? Of course it's perfectly obvious—the whole scheme. Really, it is a trifle shabby.

HOBART (*Olympian*)   What is shabby, Lady Wyngate?

LAEL (*Deliberately and firmly*)   Exploiting your brother's name and reputation for a movement the real motive of which he doesn't understand and which he'd loathe if he did understand.

HOBART   And may I ask what makes you think he'd loathe it?

LAEL (*Warmly*)   Because he's generous-hearted and your movement isn't!

HOBART   In your opinion it isn't. As a matter of fact my brother does understand it and approves thoroughly.

LAEL   Will you risk my explaining it to him—from my point of view?

HOBART   That would hardly be fair.

LAEL   Why not?

HOBART   Because you are a lovely woman with whom he happens to be in love.

(*This gives her pause*)

LAEL (*Slowly, realizing* HOBART *is cleverer than he seems*) That's the most effective appeal you could have made. But perhaps I'll stop Rand joining you anyway. I must remember that people like you regard chivalry in others exactly as strategists in war regard weakness in defence. Shall I stop him? I can, you know.

HOBART (*Steely now*)   If I were you, Lady Wyngate, I really shouldn't try.

LAEL   Probably not. After all, why should I?

HOBART   That's wise.

LAEL   It's because I don't believe in your survival, no matter how many Youth Leagues you organize. But don't threaten me—even by implication. Because if you do—I *will* stop him. I'm perverse, you know, Hobart . . .

(RAND *comes back. He has changed into a traveling suit.* HOBART *rises—looks at watch*)

RAND (*Transparently reluctant*)   Well, here I am!

LAEL (*Her customary chatter*)   Of course, any hostess with a nature less adorably angelic than mine would simply poison you for taking away her most celebrated guest in the middle of the day like this. The trouble is you're so used to Rand you have no idea the glamor he sheds.

HOBART (*Significantly*)   I have some idea.

LAEL   I take it back. Of course you have!

RAND   I hate to go. (*He smiles at his brother*) I wish, Hobart, you weren't so important!

HOBART   You two make me feel like the villain in the play separating the lovers. But it has to be done. Please, Rand . . .

RAND (*Obedient but not apologetic*)   I want to talk to Lael— for just a second.

HOBART (*Looking at his watch*)   I'll give you ten. (*Faces* LAEL) Not so bad, am I? Any message to Lord Abercrombie?

LAEL   Give him my love—that's ambiguous enough.

HOBART (*With a laugh*)   I will! (*Holds up both his hands to* RAND) Ten!
  (*He goes out.* RAND *goes to her. Takes her in his arms. She is not very responsive*)

RAND   What a bore! I have to go!
  (*He sits on arm of* LAEL'S *chair*)

LAEL   I think so!

RAND   I can't very well refuse Bart, can I?

LAEL   I suppose not.

RAND   He's done so much for me. It seems little enough to do in return.

LAEL   Does it?

RAND   After all—a few hours in London— I'll be back at the latest by . . .

LAEL   I wasn't referring to the time involved.

RAND   To what then?

LAEL   This illustrates what I mean when I . . . Oh, well, never mind.
  (*She was about to tell him how it illustrates the essential incompatibility between them—his leaving her to go on a mission she detests—but she is inhibited by recalling* HO-BART'S *accusation of unfairness*)

RAND   But you must tell me. This illustrates—what?

LAEL   I can't tell you now—your brother's waiting for you—there isn't time.

RAND   There is. Tell me. Please, Lael, tell me.

LAEL   I promised your brother I wouldn't.

RAND   But . . .

LAEL   Oh, dear, life is very complicated!

RAND   You make it so.

LAEL   Do I?

RAND   I love you.

LAEL   You shouldn't.

RAND   I do though.

LAEL   Well, then—I shouldn't.

RAND   As long as you do! . . .

LAEL   You'd better go now, Rand, but when you come back . . .

RAND   Will you tell me then what all this mystery is?

LAEL   I will. I'll tell you then.

RAND (*Smiling at her*)   A showdown!

LAEL   That's it! A showdown!

RAND   That's what I've been waiting for. We've got to get clear. (*Takes her in his arms*) Good-bye, darling.

LAEL   Good-bye.

RAND (*Starts to leave, stops and faces her*)   Come with me to the car, Lael, please.
   (*He has returned to her*)

LAEL (*Crosses the room, stops at door and faces him*)   All right. Rand—

RAND   Yes, Lael?

LAEL   Will you do me a favor?

RAND   Anything.

LAEL   After you've talked to Lord Abercrombie, tell him that before you make a final decision about anything you have promised to consult me.

RAND   Certainly I will.

LAEL   That'll cheer him up.
   (*They exit through arch in alcove, laughing*)
   (HUGO *comes in through the French windows from the garden, crosses to the end-table by sofa, picks up a cigarette and lights it. From the garden also* PHOEBE ELDRIDGE *comes in, blonde, exquisitely dressed, an adorable Kewpie*)

PHOEBE   Are you afraid of me?

HUGO   Why, Phoebe?

PHOEBE   You seem to avoid me.

HUGO   Not at all.

PHOEBE   You've changed. You know that. You've got a lot of new lines in your face.

HUGO   Well, don't rub it in.

PHOEBE   At lunch I watched you. I thought: What is it about him that's changed?

HUGO   Age, my dear.

PHOEBE   No, not age. You don't somehow look older. Trouble, suffering. And I stopped hating you.

HUGO (*Suddenly Mephistophelean, making passes with his fingers over his forehead*)   Look, I erase the little lines.

PHOEBE (*Piteously*)   Do you want me to hate you?

HUGO   I don't want to be loved for a blemish. I am too vain!

PHOEBE   I didn't say that I loved you. I only said that I didn't hate you.

HUGO   In that dubious region between love and hate . . .

PHOEBE   What?

HUGO   Nothing. I succumbed to the cadence of that opening phrase. It seemed to be an opening phrase. Seemed to lead somewhere into some superb aphorism. But it doesn't. It doesn't lead anywhere. It gets ready to be magnificent and then dries up.

PHOEBE   There's one thing that I'd like to know—that I have a right to know.

HUGO (*After a moment*)   Well?

PHOEBE   About her?

HUGO   Her?

PHOEBE   The woman.

HUGO   What woman?

PHOEBE   The woman for whom you left me in Munich.

HUGO   Oh! That woman! What do you want to know?

PHOEBE   Are you still in love with her?

HUGO   You overestimate my fidelity.

PHOEBE   Are you trying to comfort me? It's nothing to me. I'm just curious.

HUGO   Well?

PHOEBE   Where is this mysterious woman now?

HUGO   I haven't the least idea.

PHOEBE Haven't you? Are you sure you haven't?

HUGO Quite.

PHOEBE You must wonder why I'm so curious. . . . Really it's for the most trivial reason. You know how feminine I am.

HUGO Yes, Phoebe, I do—I do. I assure you, Phoebe, that like the whole of my life—this woman—is part of the past.

PHOEBE When you left me in Munich—that last time— where did you go to meet her?

HUGO Where?

PHOEBE Yes.

HUGO Oh, er—Bayreuth, wasn't it?

PHOEBE You know perfectly well it was Bayreuth. As a matter of fact, you heard "Tristan" with her—and you were going to take me. (*She bursts out suddenly at him*) You don't see her any more, do you? You don't know where she is, do you?

HUGO What are you? . . .

PHOEBE This Wyngate woman . . .

HUGO What!

PHOEBE The moment I saw you together I knew it. I felt it. And then I found out. I was talking to her before luncheon. It wasn't difficult, clever as she's supposed to be.

HUGO Phoebe, Phoebe! Of all your intuitions, this is the most brilliant.

PHOEBE I found out where she was that summer—in Bayreuth—where you went to hear "Tristan" . . . "Tristan." You and your wonderful titled Englishwoman!

HUGO Phoebe, does it occur to you that there must have been several hundred titled Englishwomen in Bayreuth that summer, that month, that day? You must believe me, Phoebe. This is a fantastic caprice of your imagination.

PHOEBE Is it?

HUGO I never saw Lady Wyngate until the other day—when Sascha brought her up to London to meet me.

PHOEBE It's no use, Hugo.

HUGO   Very well, have it your own way. There's nothing to be done about it, is there?

PHOEBE   I can't help it, Hugo. I love you still. I've never stopped thinking of you. I can't do anything about it. I used to wonder who the other woman was. For three years I've wondered. I felt if I knew, it would be easier. Well, now I know—and it isn't.

HUGO   Phoebe! Phoebe, whatever you think about Lady Wyngate and me, it isn't true.

PHOEBE   Why did you come here then?

HUGO   I had to go somewhere. Phoebe, I assure you . . .

PHOEBE   Do you still love her?

HUGO   Oh, Phoebe!

PHOEBE   Is there anything between you now?

HUGO   Not a thing. You've got to believe me.

PHOEBE   Promise?

HUGO   Promise.

PHOEBE   Word of honor?

HUGO (*Stands at attention and clicks his heels*)   Word of honor.

PHOEBE (*Leans back in chair, then speaks*)   Still—I suppose I'd better leave here today.

HUGO (*In panic—dreading a scene*)   No, no! Don't do that! You mustn't do that! (*Going closer to her*) Phoebe, I want you to stay.

PHOEBE (*Coquettishly*)   You don't—you don't in the least.

HUGO   I do. When I saw you here today, I felt . . .

PHOEBE   No, you didn't—you didn't feel anything.

HUGO   That's not true. Stay, Phoebe, and I'll show you how wrong you are.

PHOEBE (*Rises—about to put her arm about his neck*)   All right, Hugo. I'll give you a chance to explain.
    (JURIN *enters from the French windows. He sees that he is interrupting and starts to leave*)

HUGO   Phoebe . . . (HUGO *sees* JURIN *and is delighted, grasping this as a means of escape from* PHOEBE. *He calls out to* JURIN, *but remains standing at right of* PHOEBE) Oh, come in, Mr. Jurin, come in! I've been wanting to speak to you. It's most important that I speak to you!

JURIN   (*Crossing to left of* PHOEBE's *chair*)   Please?

HUGO   Are you fond of music, Mr Jurin?

JURIN   Naturally.

HUGO   Ah! Then you can help me. You can help me no end!

JURIN   Can I?

HUGO   Yes. I want to do an article on Russian music.

JURIN   (*Interested*)   Oh?

HUGO   Russian music since the Revolution. From Glazounov to Sostakhevitch. Did you by any chance know Glazounov, Mr. Jurin?

JURIN   No. (*Sensing something is amiss, glances amusedly at* PHOEBE, *then continues*) I admire him greatly—but as a matter of fact . . .

HUGO (*Interrupting him*)   You see the point I want to make, Mr. Jurin, is that music is the only Russian art which has eluded political dictatorship—now Sostakhevitch . . .

JURIN   As a matter of fact, Herr Willens, Sostakhevitch . . .

PHOEBE (*Unable to bear any more, rises and speaks to* JURIN *—rather coldly*)   When you've both finished this fascinating subject . . . (*To* HUGO—*warmly and sincerely*) I'll be waiting for you down by the river, Hugo.
   (HUGO *and* JURIN *bow to her. She goes to the French windows and exits.* JURIN *and* HUGO *watch her go and then* HUGO *looks at* JURIN *and sinks into the chair*)

JURIN (*Quite aware of the situation—slightly teasing*)   You see, Herr Willens—I left Russia in 1917. Sostakhevitch is a post-Revolutionary phenomenon. The first time I heard anything by Sostakhevitch was not in Russia but in the Bowl.

HUGO (*Absent-mindedly*)   The Bowl?

JURIN   Yes, the Bowl, in Hollywood.

HUGO   Oh.

JURIN   But it is a very interesting topic, although I am very much afraid, Herr Willens, that you will have some difficulty in proving your point. These days it would seem nothing eludes political dictatorship. Not even music. To hear people talk you might think that music is a form of political pamphleteering. Hindemith is Bolshevik. Strauss is reactionary. Sostakhevitch is the orchestrator of the Five-Year Plan. Even dead composers are pulled out of their graves to hang in effigy. (HUGO *is slumped in his chair.* JURIN *goes to him and glances off after* PHOEBE) However, my dear chap, if I can help you still further in any way, I shall be delighted.

HUGO   Thanks.

JURIN   You're welcome.
   (LAEL *enters*)

HUGO   (*Suddenly conscious of* JURIN)   Mr. Jurin, have you been wandering over the face of the earth since 1917?

JURIN   Since 1917.

LAEL   (*Amused*)   You ought to publish a refugee's handbook, Jurin.

JURIN   A time-table?

LAEL   There ought to be a marvelous place set aside somewhere for all the refugees.

JURIN   But I thought it was *here,* Lady Wyngate!

LAEL   A little bigger, Jurin. My accommodations are so limited. A semi-tropical paradise set aside by the League of Nations. A government of refugees—by refugees—for refugees. What sort of a government would it be, I wonder.

JURIN   (*Humorously*)   Probably a—dictatorship!
   (JURIN *exits through French windows into the garden*)

LAEL   Great charm, that man! One of those rare souls whom suffering doesn't embitter but makes mellow somehow. Oh, dear—I'm very depressed, Hugo. I'm in a funk. I want building up.

HUGO   Then I'm afraid I'm the last person you want.

LAEL   If you let me talk I'll gradually build myself up. I'm irrepressible. Do you ever despise yourself, Hugo?

HUGO   Just now—before you came in here—I had occasion to despise myself.

LAEL   Did you? So did I! What a beautiful coincidence! Just now with Rand . . .

HUGO (*Quickly*)   Yes?

LAEL   I was strongly tempted to coquette him into doing something for me—like a film vampire shedding sex-appeal. Not nice!

HUGO   Well, we're even.

LAEL   How do you mean?

HUGO   Just now I overheard myself almost beginning to make insincere love to a woman for whom I feel nothing whatever —God knows why—but it was probably the only thing to do at the moment.

LAEL (*After a moment—understanding*)   Oh. Mrs. Eldridge?

HUGO   You know then?

LAEL   I found out today.

HUGO   Did you?

LAEL   Yes, just before luncheon.

HUGO (*Realizing that* PHOEBE *hadn't put anything over on* LAEL)   Oh.

LAEL   Nothing so thankless as to warm over an old love affair, is there?

HUGO (*Rises*)   Two weeks ago I was in a land suddenly hostile to me. I thought: If ever I get out of it—I'll live austerely. Now I am out and I find myself dawdling about and being agreeable where agreeableness is indicated. Really, human nature is too resilient!

LAEL   Isn't it lucky it is— How often—if it didn't bend, it would break!

HUGO   Better to break!

LAEL   That's too austere. That's Calvinist.

HUGO (*Smiles*)   Just now, while I was being agreeable to Phoebe, I kept saying to myself: "Why don't you tell her the plain truth—that you can't endure her?" I couldn't though. I kept on being agreeable.

LAEL   But of course you had to. The other would be too cruel.

HUGO   Would it? I wish I'd told her long ago in Munich—instead of what I did tell her then.

LAEL   What did you tell her then?

HUGO   I was so desperate to get rid of her and so determined to be ruthless that I told her there was another woman.

LAEL   Wasn't there?

HUGO   Not a soul. Pure improvisation. "Titled English-woman." I told her I was leaving her for a "Titled English-woman," a phrase from a tenpenny novel of "High Life." I heard it again today, the same phrase—she's treasured it: "Titled Englishwoman!"

LAEL   Did she demand to know who the "Titled English-woman" was?

HUGO   She did. Morbid curiosity.

LAEL   Not morbid at all. I'd have wanted to know too.

HUGO   (*Suddenly overcome by the grotesqueness of the situation, he bursts into laughter*)   Really, it's too funny!

LAEL   I suppose you couldn't tell her there was nobody. No, that would be too pointed.

HUGO   Having improvised a rival, she tried to force me to produce one for her and since, for obvious reasons, I couldn't do that, she's done the job for me—conjured one out of the clear air! You!

LAEL   What?

HUGO   You! You are the "Titled Englishwoman." She is certain of it. Nothing I can say will dissuade her of it.

LAEL   But I . . .

HUGO   One of those sudden, irrational convictions jealous people get. The evidence is incontrovertible. A: You *are* a titled Englishwoman, aren't you? B: You *were* in Bayreuth during the Wagnerian cycle of the summer of '32, weren't you? C: So was I. A—B—C

LAEL   (*Laughing*)   Q. E. D.

HUGO   (*Ironically. Rises and bows to her*)   I congratulate you!

LAEL   (*Enjoying it all*)   But I think it's marvelous! (*All graciousness*)   And I may say—I congratulate *you!*

HUGO (*Sits again on sofa beside* LAEL)   I'm terribly sorry.

LAEL   But why? I don't mind, if you don't.

HUGO   It's too silly. It's so unfair to you.

LAEL   Nonsense! If I were to be upset by rumors about me —this is mild compared to some. I've given up years ago worrying about what people say. Do you know why? Because everybody else in the world is anonymous really except those few—it can never be more than a very few—who really matter to me. One, at most two absolute friends.

HUGO (*Not too seriously*)   There's no such thing as absolute friendship. Like everything else, friendship is relative—a thermometer of expediency.

LAEL   That's too cynical. Not bad as an epigram though. But you can't compress the truth about anything into a sentence. It's like pressing a drop of blood on a slide and saying: "This is the stuff that flows in your veins!" It isn't though. When it's in your veins it's something different.

HUGO   I'm glad you can believe in friendship. It must be a great comfort to you!

LAEL   Don't you? Don't you really?

HUGO   I did once.

LAEL   During the trouble at home—did no one stand by you?

HUGO   I was aware of one friend. He was an unknown playwright. I felt this man to be, though he was even then middle-aged, the freshest and the most living voice, since Ibsen, in Europe. In my first published book a large part was devoted to him. But the book brought me more success than it brought him—as a result of it I was invited to lecture in America. I took his plays with me, I translated them and lectured on them from New York to San Francisco. Now, you must understand that in all this, I was exalting myself; it was the most any critic can be, a disciple of greatness.

LAEL (*Knowing he has begun to be afraid she will think him conceited*)   I understand, Hugo.

HUGO   And I had the greatest reward such discipleship can have. As a result of my enthusiasm a curious phenomenon took place; the fame I created for him in America reverberated to Germany—and we began to accept him at home!

LAEL   You mean Lehrmann, I suppose?

HUGO   Yes, Lehrmann.

LAEL   He's your Grand Old Man, isn't he?

HUGO   Something like that. He's over sixty. I've hero-worshipped him for thirty years. I came to see him, sure that in his mellow greeting I would be in some sense—restored. Because I actually felt a wavering of sanity. I had sent him the manuscript of my pamphlet. I began to tell him how disturbed I was by the New Dispensation when I detected a new look in his eyes, a new manner. He had not smiled in greeting; he had not given me his hand. He refused point-blank to read my pamphlet; in a hard voice he advised me to tear it up. "This is a new day," he said to me. "There is no place in it for Oriental decadence!" Oriental! My family had lived in Germany for hundreds of years. I sat there staring at him. In his eyes, already glazed with mortality, I saw something impenetrable, incurably hostile, something that no appeal to the past could soften. That look did for me. I'd never had such a sense of helplessness. For in his youth this man had been the voice of the submerged—he had written the saga of the oppressed and the poor; he had been a living instrument of justice. There he sat, impersonal, hard, fanatical. He let me go without asking me to come to see him again, as you let go a servant who has cheated you and to whom you refuse to give a reference. . . . Friendship! (*A pause. He tries to gather himself together and speaks lightly*) After all—it's none of your affair, is it?

LAEL   (*Very quietly*)   That's the unkindest thing, I think, that anyone's ever said to me.

HUGO   I'm sorry. But, really—I came here a complete stranger to you—you invite me to stay out of a fantastic goodness of heart. The least I can do in return is to be—jolly. As a matter of fact, I'm going away and that is partly why. It's too unfair to you.

LAEL   You mustn't go until you've had a chance to get a perspective on yourself. Besides, where would you go?

HUGO   I was going to borrow from Sascha passage-money to America. They've started something there they call the University in Exile. Maybe I could get into that. I've cabled the director.

LAEL We'll see what can be done for you *here*.

HUGO It won't be easy. To be at once an émigré and a critic —that is a double parasitism. Before I can be eloquent I need a masterpiece and before I can be witty I need something which fails to be a masterpiece.

LAEL (*Amused*) Have you heard yet from America?

HUGO Not yet.

LAEL Well, I do wish you could feel welcome here, Hugo. Don't you like me?

HUGO You've been very—gracious. It's that—! I feel—!
(*He doesn't finish. She gives him a quick look. She realizes that she has a problem on her hands that will not yield to simple tact merely*)

LAEL Hugo—

HUGO Yes?

LAEL Do you mind if I speak to you—frankly? That is to say, critically?

HUGO (*Smiles quizzically*) Do you think I'm thin-skinned?

LAEL I've avoided rather speaking to you about your—special experience. I've avoided it in a mistaken effort to keep your mind off it—but aren't you mistaking a mass antagonism for a personal one? Hugo, you don't want to develop a persecution mania.

HUGO Is it a mania for the persecuted to believe in the reality of persecution?

LAEL No. The truth is there's a pest over all the world just now, an epidemic of hatred and intolerance that may engulf us all. That is perfectly possible. People have suffered too much during the last twenty years—they can't stand any more, that's all. In one way or another they're letting off steam—the form it's taken against you is peculiarly detestable. Everyone here abhors it. The whole world revolts against it. That is what you must remember. This is a different climate, Hugo; you are like a man who continues to shiver when he's left the Arctic—and moved into the tropics. There are other worlds, you must remember, than the one you've left. . . .

HUGO Are there?

LAEL   Oh, I know what you're saying to yourself: "It's easy enough for her to talk. She's at home, she's comfortable, she's secure." Am I though? There is no longer, in this curious moment of history, any security for anybody. What security should I have, as a liberal person, if the world goes Communist? Or Fascist? I think Hobart Eldridge and Lord Abercrombie might be—to say the least—unsympathetic to me. In any dictatorship, subtleties of opinion and temperament are swept away; you're either black or white.

HUGO (*Quizzically*)   But you're not a luxury commodity!

LAEL   I beg your pardon!

HUGO   Like the race of which I find myself suddenly an involuntary member!

LAEL   But, Hugo, these days *every* hereditary aristocracy is a luxury commodity!

HUGO (*He takes her hand and kisses it*)   You're very sweet —but I'm afraid the analogy is not quite complete. They, I suppose I ought to say we, are like passengers on a vessel that lets them stay on board—and even enter the first-class salons occasionally—as long as the weather is fair—but ho! for the sharks the minute there's a storm. Our science and our art are tolerated and even praised while the economic level is high. Once the golden stream is dammed and constriction sets in we are the first to be squeezed. Of course the world has suffered, we among the rest, but, in its misery it singles us out to levy a secret and an ageless revenge.

LAEL (*After a moment*)   Where is your legendary patience, your legendary capacity for endurance, your legendary—resignation?

HUGO (*Almost gleefully*)   I haven't it! That's my special dilemma. I am neither patient, nor resigned, nor enduring. You forget I am only a Jew by fraction! I suffer the disabilities without the hereditary armors. The Aryan seven-eighths of me wars against the Semitic eighth—wars and retreats—and I'm afraid nothing can be done for me.

LAEL   That, Hugo, is a challenge to my resourcefulness! Promise me that you won't run away—if only because I like you and find you very sympathetic. (*Humorously*) If you don't enjoy adapting yourself to Phoebe—adapt yourself to me.

HUGO (*A slight pause, sincerely*)   Shall I?

LAEL (*After a second—candidly*)   No. Don't.

HUGO   The idea tempts me.

LAEL (*Resolutely*)   It was automatically flirtatious. You deserve better than that of me—and so do I!

HUGO (*Rather darting out at her*)   You're in love with Rand!

LAEL (*After a moment*)   One's an awful mixture, Hugo.

HUGO (*Accepting it instantly as a fact*)   Don't you feel a sense of—incongruity?

LAEL   All the time. Yes. Keenly. It doesn't help though. (*A moment's pause. She walks about the room impatiently. He watches her*) One gets so tired of one's own complexities. There's Rand, a symbol of simplicity, courage and directness. There, in a world of cruelty and chicanery, are honest purpose and generosity.

HUGO   So eloquent—and so unconvinced!

LAEL (*Looks at him quickly, then away*)   You're shrewd, Hugo. You're diabolically shrewd.

HUGO (*Watching her*)   Am I?

LAEL   Of course I'm unconvinced, but whether I'm convinced or not—there it is!

HUGO (*Shrugging his shoulders*)   Why attempt to rationalize the—elemental?

LAEL (*As if to herself*)   Isn't it extraordinary how one can go on being agreeable and alert—so-called normal—and all the time nourish an obsession that has a life of its own, independent and arrogant—a fugue that seeks stubbornly its own resolution—at no matter what cost—to oneself? (*Rises and faces him*) Hugo . . .

HUGO (*Rises*)   Yes?

LAEL (*Throwing away her pretences and appealing to him pitifully*)   In you I feel—a special friend. Don't go. Please stay.

HUGO (*Crosses to her*)   All right. I'll stay. (*With great intensity*) But not as a friend.

LAEL (*Almost whispers*)   Hugo . . .

HUGO   Not even as a special friend.

LAEL   On any terms.

HUGO   But because an obsession—may be destroyed.

LAEL (*Realizes the implication of what he has said and looks at him in surprise*)   Hugo!

HUGO (*Terrific determination*)   Yes! It may be destroyed!
(*His hand closes on her arm. They stand near together, close and warm spiritually also.* PHOEBE *comes in. She is eaten with jealousy, blind with rage, behaves almost like a person paralyzed with drugs. Speaks and walks as if in automatism*)

PHOEBE   Do forgive me!

LAEL   Hello, Phoebe. Won't you . . .

PHOEBE (*Without waiting to discover the invitation*)   No, thank you very much. (*She stands at door leading to staircase and addresses* HUGO) Liar! Liar! Liar!
(*She disappears*)

LAEL   Hugo! What does she mean? What did you tell her?

HUGO (*Drily*)   Well, she demanded to know whether there was anything between us, and I said there was not.

LAEL (*Mischievously*)   Well, you really shouldn't have lied to her, Hugo.

HUGO   That was twenty minutes ago—and I didn't know . . .
(*She is amused and provoked and still a little disturbed by* PHOEBE'S *plight. He stands looking at her, enchanted by her*)

QUICK CURTAIN

ACT TWO | Scene Two

SCENE: *The same.*
   Later that evening. Around 10:30.
   JURIN *and* WYATT *are playing double patience and talking.*

WYATT   I wonder why the two Eldridges went so abruptly to London?

JURIN   I cannot suspect why.

WYATT   Didn't you feel a strain at dinner?

JURIN   Not especially. Mrs. Eldridge seemed a bit . . .

WYATT   Didn't she?
   (*A moment's pause. They play in silence*)

JURIN   The way Lady Wyngate rushed them all off to see the cinema in the village . . . They had no chance at all, did they? Whether they wanted to or not, to the cinema they went. You could tell she didn't mean to stand an evening of that by herself.

WYATT   The German didn't help much, did he?

JURIN   Not much.

WYATT   A burst of brilliance and then . . .

JURIN   A burst of brilliant silence! What do you think of him?

WYATT   I don't know. I can't tell. I think Lady Wyngate likes him. Do you like him?

JURIN   As a fellow refugee, I feel a sympathy for him. Poor fellow, he doesn't realize yet what being a refugee means.

WYATT   Maybe he does!

JURIN   He's new! I've had seventeen years of it.

WYATT   I can imagine—it's no fun.

JURIN   Half mendicant—half vagabond.

WYATT   Surely not for you—with your gift for languages.

JURIN   The English are really very kind. You'd be surprised how many of them are willing to begin to study Russian! (WYATT *laughs*) They start with such enthusiasm, a mingling of philanthropy and really a romantic yearning to learn the language. But very soon, unhappily, they find that between the yearning to learn and learning is a gap which can only be bridged by a certain amount of hard work. This work is irksome and soon they begin to look on me, unconsciously perhaps, as a disagreeable taskmaster. They begin to miss lessons. They insist on paying for these missed lessons—at first I refuse to accept—now I accept for a little while till it becomes only too apparent that the fees are only gifts. My pride intervenes. And I think: you have two children who must be fed—what right have you to pride? Pride is the last luxury one can train oneself to give up—like the traditional dress suit of the impoverished swell. So it goes. Ah! The king I wanted.

   (*He puts the king in place*)

WYATT   Does Lady Wyngate miss many lessons?

JURIN   Oh, she misses them but with her it is different. When she misses a lesson it is because she really has something else to do. She works at it; she has made progress. But there is only one Lady Wyngate.

WYATT   Yes, isn't it lucky there is one!

JURIN   Oh, then why didn't you go along to the film?

WYATT   I have to cram for an exam.
   (*He gets up*. HUGO *and* PHOEBE *come in,* PHOEBE *in evening dress*)

JURIN   So soon back from the film?

HUGO   I left at the point where the first Lord Rothschild makes a loan to the Allied Powers out of sheer altruism!

PHOEBE   The stuffy place gave me a headache.

WYATT   Where is Lady Wyngate?

HUGO   Still there, I suppose. We couldn't find seats together —we got separated.

WYATT   Captain Eldridge came back just after you all left. Did he catch up to you?

HUGO   Yes, he did.
   (*A moment's pause*)

JURIN (*Looking triumphantly at his cards*)   There—I've defeated myself—a brilliant victory—but a financial loss.

WYATT   How is that?

JURIN   I bet against myself—quietly.
   (PHOEBE *goes to fireplace and sits by herself staring into it.* WYATT *gets up*)

WYATT   Of course, Mr. Jurin, what you've been saying makes me timid about asking you to give me Russian lessons.

JURIN   My dear friend!

WYATT (*To* HUGO)   Mr. Jurin's been telling me what a hard time an émigré has even in a country as friendly as this is.

JURIN   Oh, please, I beg of you, do not repeat what I've been saying to Herr Willens!

HUGO   Why not?

JURIN   We don't want to discourage a novice!

HUGO   There is no novitiate in being a refugee. You are a veteran after you've left your country one day.

JURIN (*Deprecatingly*)   Well . . .

HUGO   To be a refugee is to belong to a lost cause. And people are bored by defeat.

JURIN   There have been refugees who have returned.

HUGO   Like Napoleon! When you still hope to return, you are not a refugee.

JURIN (*Wistfully*)   May not a lost cause be glamorous?

HUGO (*Brutally*)   In the amber of literature or history—yes. But not when it is contemporaneous. For a moment sympathetic people and generous people may be kind to the victim, but the average man has nothing but contempt for anyone who has been so footless as to put himself permanently in the wrong in the country of his origin. I saw it in people's faces the moment I crossed the frontier. A flicker of chivalry —merging almost instantly into a guarded boredom. No, it's a shabby martyrdom at best and if you will tell the truth, Mr. Jurin, you will have to admit that this is true.

JURIN (*Sadly*)   There are exceptions—that is to say, there is an exception—but in the main—yes—it is true.

(*A moment's pause*)

WYATT   Mr. Jurin, if you don't mind I shall insist on studying Russian with you—not because you are a refugee—but because I want to learn the language.

JURIN   You will be unique among my pupils.

WYATT   Good night.

(*He goes out*)

(JURIN *and* PHOEBE *and* HUGO *sit in silence.* JURIN *looks from one to the other, has some understanding of the situation and tries to stir up a little fire of conversation in these ashes*)

JURIN   Evidently, Lady Wyngate likes the picture better than you did.

HUGO   I don't know. We weren't sitting together.

JURIN   It wouldn't matter if she didn't like it. She never can bear to leave anything in the middle. She always feels, she says, there may be something wonderful at the end.

PHOEBE   Oh, does she?

JURIN   Incorrigible optimist, isn't she? (*A moment's pause.* JURIN *continues to* PHOEBE) Are they coming back after the film?

PHOEBE   I don't know. They said something about going to a Pier dance at Brighton. (*With perceptible irony*) Lady Wyngate thought that would be fun!

JURIN   I won't wait up then. Will you say good night to her for me if she does come back?

PHOEBE   Yes, I will.

JURIN   Thank you, Mrs. Eldridge. (*To both of them*) Good night. (*He walks to French windows, stops*) I think I'll stroll through the garden. Really, the roses are overpowering at night. In the daytime I think they relax.

(*He goes out through the garden windows.* HUGO *and* PHOEBE *are left alone. He is so angry at her, he cannot bring himself to face her. He paces the room*)

PHOEBE (*At her most martyrish*)   You're terrible! You act as if *I* had committed the grievance, as if *I* had hurt *you!* (*A silence. He says nothing. He continues to pace*) You didn't say a word to me all the way here. Didn't you want me to leave the cinema with you? I couldn't sit there alone. How would it have looked afterwards—with Lady Wyngate and Rand? If you didn't want me to go, why didn't you say so?

HUGO   You've got it into your head that Lady Wyngate is the woman for whom I left you in Munich and nothing I can say will dissuade you of it. If you want to know the truth, there was nobody—nobody at all. I left you—not to meet Lady Wyngate nor anybody else—but for the blissful release of being away from you.

PHOEBE   You're very chivalrous, where she's concerned, aren't you? Anything to protect her!

HUGO   Well, whatever you may think, I want to be left alone now!

PHOEBE   I said I wanted to leave here this afternoon. Oh, no, you wouldn't have it! I mustn't go. Why? You'll be much more comfortable here without me, I should think. As for me, I'm quite reconciled, I assure you!

HUGO (*Tensely*)   Are you?

PHOEBE   You flatter yourself!

HUGO   You're behaving like a jealous schoolgirl. You're not a schoolgirl after all, Phoebe. You're the mother of a grown daughter.

PHOEBE   I know.

HUGO   You might behave with some dignity.

PHOEBE   Well, you needn't worry about it any longer.

HUGO   You say I needn't, but I do just the same. You act the martyr. You suffer. You whine.

PHOEBE   Hugo . . .

HUGO   *Um Gottes Willen,* I want to be left alone!

PHOEBE   Why didn't you tell me the truth then?

HUGO   Truth! Truth! What truth?

PHOEBE   This afternoon when I asked you if you still loved

Lady Wyngate? You said you didn't. Why didn't you tell me the truth?

HUGO   Because I wanted to spare your feelings. Like all my other lies to you to spare your feelings!

PHOEBE (*Gets very comfortable, then speaks*)   Thank you, you needn't.

HUGO   Besides, you've always bullied me in your quiet way and I won't let you bully me any more. For that cowardly consideration I've always displayed to you—I apologize to you. I'll tell you the truth now—for all time. . . .

PHOEBE   Hugo . . .

HUGO   The truth is I can't endure you. Whether I love Lady Wyngate or anybody else can't possibly matter to you because I don't love you and never have. I detest your best qualities: your amiability, your patience, your clinging sweetness! You make me feel a cad and a sadist. You've done it for years and I'm sick to death of it. I repudiate it. I can't endure it. You drive me mad with boredom. You have almost from the beginning.

PHOEBE   That's a lie. I didn't before she came. You loved me before she came.

HUGO   You bored me before anybody came. The only reason our affair lasted as long as it did was because we were separated months at a time, because I hardly saw you for more than a few weeks each year. I beg of you, Phoebe, get interested in somebody else. Take up folk-dancing, or needlework, but for pity's sake, don't cling to me. Leave me alone.

PHOEBE (*Not militantly*)   All right, Hugo. You needn't worry. I will.

HUGO   You have a way of cringing before a blow when I speak harshly to you that's made a liar and a hypocrite of me for years. This conquest of me through meekness and patience and understanding has eroded me for years, and I'm not going to let it any longer. Do you understand that finally —not any longer!

PHOEBE   It's a pity your charming hostess won't make up her mind.

HUGO   I tell you she has nothing to do with it!

PHOEBE (*Sweetly*) Whether she wants Rand or you. She sets her cap for him in New York and she got him over here. Why doesn't she make up her mind? Or maybe she's just using him. That's not very generous, I should say!

HUGO (*In despair of her understanding—rises and faces her, then, as though explaining to a child*) Nothing would make any difference between you and me. How can I make it clear to you that if Lady Wyngate were blind or deaf or in a nunnery, it would make no difference to you and me? Nothing would make any difference between you and me!

PHOEBE All right, Hugo. (*He sits back in chair. She faces front. A pause*) No! No matter what you say to defend her —it was all right between us till she came. (*With quiet hatred*) I owe this—to her!

(JURIN *enters from the French windows*)

JURIN (*Seeing them*) Oh! Really, it is criminal to stay indoors on such a night. It is pure magic out there. Forgive me —one drink and I go.

(JURIN *comes to the secretaire and begins to mix himself a highball.* PHOEBE *and* HUGO *sit occupied with their own thoughts.* HOBART *enters. His face is set and grim. He has not had a happy or successful evening.* LORD ABERCROMBIE *has proved, at the critical moment, to be elusive*)

HOBART (*Taking in the frozen group*) Um! How very cozy!

JURIN Oh, good evening, Mr. Eldridge.

HOBART Good evening. I'll take a whiskey and soda, too, if you don't mind. I need it. Where's everybody?

PHOEBE Rand is at the cinema with Lady Wyngate. So are Joan and Sascha.

HOBART Should be back soon, shouldn't they?

PHOEBE They said something about going to Brighton to a Pier dance hall.

HOBART (*Incredulous*) What?

PHOEBE (*Sarcastically*) Mingling with the people!

HOBART Damn nonsense! I want to see Rand!

PHOEBE You may have to wait up pretty late.

JURIN Whiskey and soda, Hugo?

HUGO (*Rises eagerly*)   Yes, thanks.

JURIN (*After a moment*)   Why don't you all come out into the garden?

HOBART   Why? What's in the garden?

JURIN (*Poetically*)   The night. (HUGO *understandingly pats* JURIN'S *arm and then goes to left of the sofa.* HOBART *looks at* JURIN *disgustedly and crosses to get another drink.* JURIN *then turns to* MRS. ELDRIDGE *and speaks to her from rear of the sofa*) Will you come, Mrs. Eldridge?

PHOEBE   No, thank you, Mr. Jurin.

HUGO   I'll go with you.

JURIN (*Gallant*)   I'd rather have Mrs. Eldridge, if *you* don't mind.

PHOEBE   I'm sorry.

JURIN   Then, thank you, Hugo. (*Crosses to above the left end of the sofa, glances at* PHOEBE *and* HOBART *and indulging suddenly a personal sense of humor begins to declaim*)

> The moon shines bright: In such a night as this,
>   When the sweet wind did gently kiss the trees . . .
> (HOBART *crosses to the right end of the sofa with his drink. He and* PHOEBE *exchange an incredulous glance and then he continues to the stool where he sits*)
>   And they did make no noise, in such a night
>   Troilus methinks mounted the Trojan walls . . .
> (JURIN *stops, glances at* HUGO, *then leans over and speaks to* PHOEBE)

What comes next? (*Phoebe looks at him and then at* HOBART. JURIN *then turns to* HUGO) What comes after that?

HUGO (*Smiling*)   I only know the original . . .

> *In solcher Nacht*
> *Erstieg wohl Troilus die Mauern Trojas*
> *Und seufzte seine Seele zu den Zelten*
> *Der Griechen hin, so seine Cressida*
> *Die Nacht in Schlummer lag.*
> (JURIN *taking his arm affectionately*)

JURIN   Still you must admit—"And Sigh'd his soul toward the Grecian tents, where Cressid lay that night" is not bad.

HUGO Not bad—for a translation!

(*They both go out, carrying their highball glasses with them.* HOBART *has drained his highball and he goes to the tabouret to pour himself another.* PHOEBE *watches him*)

PHOEBE (*Dovelike to him suddenly*) What's the matter, Bart?

HOBART (*Gruffly*) Why?

PHOEBE Whenever you start drinking in that determined way, I know you're disappointed about something.

HOBART Tired. Long day.

PHOEBE (*After a moment*) Why didn't you and Rand come back together?

HOBART I had to stay on to finish up with Lord Abercrombie.

PHOEBE Did you finish up?

HOBART Extraordinary interest you take in my affairs suddenly.

PHOEBE If I know anything about them at all, it isn't because *you* confide in me.

HOBART (*Mechanically*) What's the matter?

(*He knows there is something, but he's not interested much. He cannot possibly attribute gravity to* PHOEBE'S *preoccupations*)

PHOEBE Nothing. Why?

HOBART (*After a moment, drinking*) Rand get back in time for dinner?

PHOEBE No. Just after we all left for the cinema.

HOBART Everything go off all right?

PHOEBE Of course. Not that it would matter—Rand is so in love he's in complete oblivion as far as anything outside Lady Wyngate is concerned. He wouldn't notice anything anyway.

HOBART What would there be to notice?

PHOEBE Nothing. Nothing much.

HOBART Well, what do you mean nothing much? What's on your mind? Speak up!

PHOEBE Bart . . .

HOBART   Well?

PHOEBE   I think Rand ought to be warned . . .

HOBART   Warned?

PHOEBE   . . . about Lady Wyngate.

HOBART   How do you mean warned?

PHOEBE (*With an air of dropping the whole thing*)   Well, perhaps I'm crazy. (*A pause.* HOBART *pours himself a third drink.* PHOEBE *walks about. He stands still, thinking, drinking his drink more slowly*) I think I'll take a turn in the garden.
(*She starts for garden doors, throwing a glance at him. He doesn't turn his head. She has to go through with it now and starts out, through the garden doors. At the last second, he calls her back*)

HOBART   How do you mean warned? About what?

PHOEBE   It doesn't matter.

HOBART (*Steely*)   Come here.

PHOEBE   You're obviously in no mood to talk.
(*A pause. He goes to her*)

HOBART   What did you mean?

PHOEBE   I meant . . .

HOBART   Well?

PHOEBE (*Her feelings get the better of her and she pours them out*)   I meant simply this: that Rand's precious idol is having an affair with that—immigrant—this Hugo Willens!
(*This makes considerable of an impression. So much so that, the moment she has uttered it,* PHOEBE *feels a bit frightened*)

HOBART (*After a pause*)   What!

PHOEBE   Yes.

HOBART   Since coming to this house, you mean?

PHOEBE   Oh, no. It's been going on for years.

HOBART   How do you know?

PHOEBE   I know.

HOBART   How? This is important to me, Phoebe. More important than you realize. How do you know?

PHOEBE (*More scared still and fighting for time—she realizes she hasn't worked her scheme out sufficently in her mind*) I can't tell you that.

HOBART You've got to.

PHOEBE I can't.

HOBART You've got to. You will.

PHOEBE Later perhaps—now I can't.

HOBART Why not?

PHOEBE It involves a friend.

HOBART Who?

PHOEBE That I can't tell you. You'd guess if I told you. I mean . . .
(*She has said it before she realizes it might be a clue. She is in a funk now about the whole thing. There is a pause. HOBART gathers himself together*)

HOBART (*At his cunningest*) Nonsense.

PHOEBE What?

HOBART You're crazy.

PHOEBE What do you mean?

HOBART It's absurd. Your notion is absurd. It's not possible. Willens? It's not possible. Somebody's been pulling your leg, my dear.

PHOEBE (*Now she feels her quarry slipping from her and she is furious—determined not to let it go at all costs*) Have they?

HOBART Of course they have! (*He pours himself another drink*) Better go to bed, Phoebe. You're overwrought.
(*He turns away from her, his back to her as he drinks his highball. She feels the ground slipping from beneath her, her enemy escaping. A mania seizes her, a mania of cruelty and revenge—at any cost she must destroy LAEL. That is the first condition of her further being. Mixed in it is a desire to wound HOBART also, to destroy his complacency, to hurl a dart into that strong arrogant back*)

PHOEBE (*A new voice*) Am I?

HOBART (*Without moving*) Of course you are.

PHOEBE (*After a second*)   Do you really want me to tell you —how I know?

HOBART (*Knows he's got her, but his face revealing nothing —the poker face*)   In the morning will do. I'm not interested much in female gossip.

PHOEBE (*Her voice rising*)   Aren't you?

HOBART   I advise you to go to bed, my dear.

PHOEBE (*With an outburst of hysterical laughter*)   You fool . . . You complacent fool! Can't you see that . . .
   (*The sound of laughter and voices off stage—*RAND *and* LAEL)

HOBART (*Very annoyed at this interruption, still making the best of it*)   You'd better . . .

PHOEBE (*Hate in her voice*)   She's back! I can't bear to . . .

HOBART (*Close to her, quickly*)   Go to your room. I'll join you there in a minute.
   (*She crosses the room swiftly to opposite door and goes out. Left alone,* HOBART *decides rather quickly. He is pretty grim. He concludes there is no point in meeting* LAEL *now. Besides, it will delay the revelation he knows now he can get from his wife if he follows it up. He follows* PHOEBE *out. For a moment the stage is deserted—the voices and laughter of* RAND *and* LAEL *growing louder. They come in. They are in full evening dress. One gets a sense from* LAEL *that she has missed* HUGO *and is rather on the look-out for him*)

LAEL   Where is everybody?

RAND   Do you miss them? I don't.
   (*Following her*)

LAEL   After all, I am a hostess.

RAND   Let's go to the Pier dance.

LAEL (*Looking around toward the garden*)   Shall we? Oh, Rand, remember that wonderful dance place in New York you took me to—all crystal and chromium and stratosphere!

RAND   I went there once afterwards without you; it was no good.

LAEL   Sometimes I get such a sudden homesickness for New York. I feel I want to be there on the instant—must walk those glittering streets, breathe that electric air.

RAND   Come back with me. I'll let you walk and breathe all you like.

LAEL   Don't spoil me.

RAND   (*Putting his arm around her shoulder*)   Wouldn't I love to!

LAEL   (*In a dream of her own—rather drifts away from him*) Oh, Rand!

RAND   (*A slight pause—feels her mood*)   Now, Lael, don't do that.

LAEL   What?

RAND   Drift away from me. Every once in a while you drift away from me.

LAEL   (*Coming back to the moment*)   Little excursions. You take such big ones. Don't deny me the tiny ones.

RAND   Well, I don't like it.

LAEL   Tyrant!

RAND   I want to be with you on all the little excursions, do you hear? On all of them.

LAEL   Oh, you don't know what you're letting yourself in for. If you knew—in a day—in an hour—the thousand absurd and silly impulses I get. I wake up in the morning a sober woman with a sense of responsibility. An hour later I feel that I ought to be somewhere in Bali or Tahiti going native.

RAND   Well, why don't we?

LAEL   A graph of my impulses, Rand dear, would make you rather dizzy. (*They both laugh.* LAEL *sits on arm of* RAND'S *chair*) I wonder—I wonder where Hugo is?

RAND   (*Immediately and sharply*)   Why? Do you like him?

LAEL   (*His tone attracts her attention*)   Yes, very much. Don't you?

RAND   (*Coldly*)   I was brought up not to like his kind.

LAEL   (*Looking at him*)   Oh! (*Looking away from him*) One is brought up with so many prejudices.

RAND   (*After a pause—attempts to recapture the lost gaiety of a few moments before*)   Let's go to the Pier dance, Lael.

LAEL   No, thank you, Rand.

RAND   Why not?

LAEL   I don't feel like it, really, Rand.

RAND   You said we'd drop in here to see where the others were and that if they weren't about you'd go on with me to Brighton.

LAEL   (*Rises*)   I felt gay before. I don't any more.

RAND   (*Watches her*)   Do I depress you?

LAEL   (*Sadly—facing him*)   Rand.

RAND   I'm sorry.

LAEL   It's my fault. I'm sorry, Rand.

RAND   (*Irritated into demanding results*)   Now, look here, Lael—you promised me a showdown and I mean to have it.

LAEL   (*Backing away a step*)   Please, Rand, not now.

RAND   (*Following up*)   Now! You're not going to put me off any longer. You're going to give me an answer. And it's going to be yes!

LAEL   Thank you for the choice.

RAND   Well, if it's no—I'm going to damn well know why. Lael, you're mixed up with a lot of funny notions about politics and theories and God knows what!

LAEL   Am I? Perhaps I am.

RAND   Do you think I'm going to let a lot of complicated *isms* stand between us? Well, I'm not. You've told me enough to let me see that once you let yourself go I can make you happy. All this "highbrow" atmosphere and these seedy people you have surrounded yourself with—it's all not you, Lael. I want to get you out of it—into some different environment where you can stop all this thinking. And where you can breathe deeply, and I'm going to do it.

LAEL   Oh, Rand, I'm so fond of you.

RAND   That's not enough,

LAEL   (*Finally*)   It's all I can offer you. (*A moment's pause*) I'm sorry.

RAND   But you told me only the other day that some day you'd give in to me—and I believed you, Lael—I believed you.

LAEL   What I told you then was true. But since then . . .

RAND   What's happened since then?

LAEL   I can't bear to hurt you, Rand.

RAND   What's happened since then? I must know, I tell you. I've *got* to know.

(HUGO *and* JURIN *appear in the French windows; they are talking German to each other.* LAEL *rather rushes to them, grateful to have escaped the immediate necessity for inflicting on* RAND *the dreaded "showdown"*)

LAEL   My two lost children! Hugo, I'll never forgive you —never as long as I live!

HUGO   Won't you?

LAEL   For leaving that film—for missing the glory at the end of that film. Do you know what happened?

HUGO   Did Lord Rothschild go to heaven?

LAEL   He did and in color, my dear, in color! Suddenly and with divine unreasonableness, Lord Rothschild and everybody else became iridescent. (*Everyone laughs*) He went to a big ball in the palace to be slapped on the back by the King. Good old Rothschild lends money to the Allies for patriotism and four per cent. You could see his pearl shirt-studs glisten with pride—you simply must come with me to see the end of that picture!

JURIN   I want to see it too.

LAEL   We'll all go. (HOBART *enters. He has received* PHOEBE'S *information and stands there looking like Thor*) Now let's have some supper, shall we? Oh, there you are Hobart—just in time for supper. Mrs. Dingle's outdone herself. (*She sees* HOBART *standing there like an angry and sullen god*) What's the matter, Hobart? You stand there looking like the Lord High Executioner. Did you give Lord Abercrombie my love? Did he send me his?

HOBART   He did!

LAEL   Well, that evens things up, doesn't it? (*Crosses the others and goes to* HOBART) Let's go to supper—come on, everybody!

HOBART   I'm in no mood for supper, thank you!

LAEL   Oh, Hobart, do something for me, will you? Try to enjoy life. What can we do to cheer you up?

HOBART   Nothing, I'm afraid.

LAEL   (*Turns to others, appealing*)   Jurin, Hugo, Rand—think of something. (*To* HOBART) Lord Abercrombie is much more cheerful than you are, Hobart. I can always make him laugh.

HOBART   I'm sorry. My sense of humor is defective, I guess.

LAEL   Too bad. I wonder what we can do about it. Now let me see—I've known some very difficult cases but you—you—maybe you weren't a happy baby. Is that what it is? But anyway, do you mind if we have supper?

HOBART   No, thank you! I must speak to Rand alone.

RAND   What about?

LAEL   You're always taking him away from me.

HOBART   (*His tone is such that a chill falls over them*)   Does that distress you, Lady Wyngate?

RAND   Bart!

LAEL   (*Quietly*)   Of course it distresses me. (*To* HUGO *and* JURIN) Shall we go?

RAND   I don't like your tone, Bart. I must tell you I don't like your tone to . . .

LAEL   Nonsense, Rand, Hobart and I understand each other. . . .

HOBART   No, we don't, Lady Wyngate—we don't in the least understand each other.

LAEL   Hobart, if you have a grievance against me I wish you'd tell me what it is.

HOBART   Shall I?

LAEL   Please do.

HOBART   Even you, Rand, will find out sooner or later; so you may as well know now. . . . (*To* LADY WYNGATE) I hope at least, Lady Wyngate, that you're giving Rand value received.

RAND   What!

HOBART   You fool—you blind fool! The least she can do for you is to give up her present lover and take you on!

RAND Hobart!

(HUGO *and* LAEL *exchange a sudden look of comprehension. It dawns on them both at once what has happened*)

HOBART (*Thundering at* RAND *and pointing accusingly at* LAEL *and* HUGO) Look at them! You have only to look at them!

RAND Lael!

HOBART Phoebe's just told me. And she ought to know because Lady Wyngate is her successor!

RAND (*To* LAEL) So that's what you were going to tell me. That's why you kept putting me off! You were wondering where he was. Well, here he is!

HUGO Captain Eldridge—

RAND (*Turns on him*) You dirty Jew!

LAEL (*Horrified*) Rand!

HUGO It's all right, Lael. This makes me feel quite at home.

HOBART You swine! Maybe those people over there are right.

LAEL Hobart, please remember—Herr Willens is not only my lover; he is also my guest. (*Smiles at* HUGO) Hugo darling!

CURTAIN

ACT THREE

SCENE: *The same.*

SCENE: *The same.*
Afternoon of the next day.
JOAN *and* SASCHA.
JOAN *is rather drawing* SASCHA *out; he is sulky and uncommunicative. He is at the piano with sheets of manuscript paper open before him making notes for an arrangement.*

JOAN Something certainly happened last night, but I can't discover what it is. It's very tantalizing! (SASCHA *doesn't answer. She looks at him. He has been especially taciturn lately. Also, there are other things which make her less than contented with him*) Have you seen Hugo?

SASCHA Yes.

JOAN Did *he* say anything?

SASCHA What about?

JOAN About—anything.

SASCHA There was some sort of row!

JOAN Was there?

SASCHA Between him and Rand. I must say I blame Hugo for it.

JOAN What was it about?

SASCHA I can't tell you exactly. I wish Hugo would forget this race business.

JOAN (*Studying him*) Why do you want him to forget it?

SASCHA He'll bring a lot of trouble on himself. He has already.

JOAN You manage to avoid trouble.

SASCHA If everybody were as sensible about it as I am there'd be no problem.

JOAN By sensible you mean—ashamed.

SASCHA There's too much said about it. It's not important.

JOAN I notice any time the question comes up you shy off.

SASCHA Well, Hugo's too conscious about it. He's out of Germany now. Why doesn't he forget about it? It's the individual that's important.

JOAN (*Slowly*) I understand better now, Sascha, your enthusiasm last night at the Pier dance for Lady Worrell.

SASCHA Oh, that's it. Now it comes out. (*As one above that sort of thing*) Jealous!

JOAN Isn't she a bit elderly for you, Sascha?

SASCHA I think she's marvelous. She's a marvelous woman.

JOAN How could you tell?

SASCHA Well, she's so—for one thing, she's so musical.

JOAN Is she?

SASCHA She invited me to play at Brierly.

JOAN Did you tell her your fee?

SASCHA Don't be vulgar!

JOAN When is it going to be?

SASCHA Thursday.

JOAN Funny she didn't invite me.

SASCHA I'll ask her if you like.

JOAN No, thanks. I'm proud. As long as you're back on Friday for our jaunt to Cornwall.

SASCHA Oh, Joan . . .

JOAN Yes?

SASCHA I'm staying the week-end at Brierly.

JOAN (*Who knew it was coming, flaring up*) Are you? What about our date for Friday?

SASCHA (*Rather miserably. He has dreaded it*) I thought I'd better pass it up. On account of . . . Frankly, Lady Worrell can do a lot for me.

JOAN   I dare say she can. You'll meet a lot of duchesses at Brierly. You'll like that!

SASCHA   What's wrong about liking duchesses? They're as good as other people, aren't they?

JOAN   Better. Their blood is so much bluer!
   (*A moment's pause*)

SASCHA   (*Deciding it's expedient to conciliate her, faces her*) I thought you were interested in my career. After all, I'm only doing it for you, you know—in a way. Once I get really established here in England I can turn my back on anybody I want to.

JOAN   Can you?

SASCHA   Except you. I can be independent. And then we— you and I—

JOAN   (*Turns away from him*)   No, Sascha, this is the end.

SASCHA   (*Aggrieved*)   Simply because I'm going to Lady Worrell's for the week-end! (*Realizes his mistake and controls himself—quietly*) Now, Joan, please, I'll get her to ask you and we'll go together.

JOAN   I don't want to go. I'm through.

SASCHA   I'm not quite sure I understand.

JOAN   (*Turns on him—emotionally*)   I think you do! Not that I'm not in love with you. I am and I'll have to take it, but I've always felt it. You're cold and calculating, and this about muffling your race is characteristic!

SASCHA   What do you want me to do? Shout it from the house-tops?

JOAN   It's characteristic! Instead of being proud and thrilled about it you are ashamed. That's contemptible, Sascha.

SASCHA   Oh, come now, Joan, don't take it so big. We'll talk it over when I get back on Monday.

JOAN   (*Very quietly*)   Will we?

SASCHA   I'm going up to practise.
   (SASCHA *walks up the stairs leaving her alone. She crosses to the piano seat and sits down. After a moment* HUGO *enters from the garden through the French windows*)

HUGO   What's the matter, Joan?

JOAN (*After a slight pause*)   Well, the jig's up, Hugo. . . .
Between Sascha and me. He prefers duchesses.

HUGO   Does it surprise you that he should?

JOAN   Yes. It surprises me.

HUGO   But why should it? Like so many insecure people,
Sascha is a snob.

(LAEL *comes in. She takes them in. A moment's pause*)

LAEL   Hello, Joan. You must have come back very late
last night. How was the dance? Did you have a good time?

JOAN   Not very.

LAEL   I'm sorry. How was the Pier dance? Was it fun?

JOAN   It was very fashionable. It was overrun with duchesses.
I wonder, really, where the lower classes go to dance.

(*She goes out.* LAEL *watches her. A moment's pause*)

LAEL   What is it? Sascha?

HUGO   Yes.

LAEL   Sascha's stupid.

HUGO   Yes. He is stupid. He is also cunning and unscrupulous
and greedy—and an exquisite artist, a superb artist!

LAEL   It's unfair that these attributes should go together.
Poor Joan! What a pity she can't love the artist—and let the
rest go!

HUGO   Pity the psyche isn't operable!

LAEL (*Lightly*)   According to you—it is! An obsession, you
say, may be destroyed! (*He looks at her. A pause. He lights
a cigarette. His hand trembles slightly as he does so. She
notices it*) Hugo! Your hand is trembling. Hugo . . .

HUGO   No sleep.

LAEL   I'm glad at least that you didn't sleep. I know I
didn't. (RAND *enters*) Oh, hello, Rand.

RAND (*Stiffly—it's a great effort for him to do it*)   Herr
Willens . . .

HUGO   Yes, Captain Eldridge.

RAND   I want to apologize to you—for last night. For making
a scene.

HUGO   Please don't. I understand it perfectly.

RAND   Whether you understand it or not—I beg you to accept my apology.

HUGO   Of course. (*To* LAEL) You will excuse me.

LAEL   You needn't go, Hugo.

HUGO   I want to speak to Sascha.
(HUGO *exits through French windows*)
(LAEL *looks at* RAND. RAND *is abject and broken. He has aged overnight. The fresh look in his face is gone.* RAND *looks at her, unable to speak.* LAEL *is stirred with pity for him*)

LAEL   (*Involuntarily, moving toward him*)   Rand . . .

RAND   (*In a dim voice*)   I beg you—Lael—don't be nice to me!

LAEL   (*Devastated by him*)   Rand!

RAND   (*In an ecstasy of self-reproach*)   The Death of a Hero!

LAEL   What do you . . .

RAND   There was a picture of me once in the Sunday section of the newspaper in my home town. In color—very beautiful. Crossed flags over my head. Rosy cheeks. Perfect uniform. Clear-eyed look. Heroic expression. I joked about it when I saw it but now I realize—now that it is gone forever—that I took that picture seriously. I did. It was this picture of me which I've carried about in my mind all these years. It was my notion of myself. Decent fellow. Clean-cut. Well, he went to pieces last night—this wonderful effigy —smashed to bits like a lot of cheap crockery.

LAEL   After all, you thought you had some provocation. You mustn't . . .

RAND   (*Pacing about*)   Don't tell me. I wanted to kill him. I wanted to tear him to bits. I wanted to lynch him. (*Faces her suddenly*) All last night I was up—walking those roads —wishing I had him home. So I might lynch him. That's what I am!

LAEL   Poor Rand!

RAND   That's what I am!

LAEL   (*Rises and going to him*)   In one way or another— that's what everybody is. Why do you suppose we're all staggering pitifully toward some incalculable abyss? Because, in one way or another, that's what everybody is. I'm sorry, Rand dear, that I had to take you out of the Happy Hunting Grounds into the Cave of Despair.

RAND (*Sits in chair before her*)   Well, you've done it all right.

LAEL (*Gently*)   Well, it's better than whistling away in the Never-Never Land.

RAND   What is there left?

LAEL   Instead of an effigy—a human being.

RAND   Pretty poor specimen.

LAEL   Not so bad, really. I like you!

RAND (*Bitterly, without looking at her*)   Do you?

LAEL   Now you can begin to live more—

RAND   After all these years!

LAEL   Why not? You're so young! And you'll find it's much more wholesome!

RAND (*Jumps to his feet facing her*)   Wholesome! Do you call this wholesome? Do you think that because I've apologized to him that I've forgiven him? Or you? Do you think my telling you cures me? I forced myself to apologize to him and while I was doing it I—and for me you're . . . in spite of anything I can say to myself—you're—you're—tainted! Now you know!

LAEL (*Greatly troubled*)   Poor Rand—what have I done to you?

(*He looks at her a moment, turns and walks out swiftly. LAEL starts to follow him, stops, realizing that her explanation will only increase his despair. She is overwhelmed herself with a kind of despair. The difficulty and the complexity of bringing human motives into some conformity with sanity and decency overwhelm her. Into the disturbed silence comes the sound of* SASCHA *upstairs playing the "Intermezzo in A Major" by Brahms. She lights a cigarette. HUGO comes in. He looks at her a moment standing there and comes to her impetuously. He is very tense. He has reached a decision and he must unburden himself to her*)

HUGO   Lael—I must speak to you.

LAEL   Yes, Hugo . . .

(*Before he can go on* HOBART *enters. He sees them together; to him this is another "Love Scene." He is carrying a high-ball glass and crosses to the secretaire to mix himself another drink. He has been drinking steadily since last night. His eyes are bloodshot and he is quite drunk really but he holds his liquor wonderfully well, and, though he is quite shaky, you wouldn't know he was drunk first off unless you watched him closely*)   •

HOBART   (*Seeing them*)   Well, still at it, I see! And so am I . . . (*Holds up his glass*) . . . at this! Just different ways of killing time, that's all. I'm not what you call a drinking man ordinarily . . . (*Takes a drink*) . . . but lot to be said for it—makes you see things in—proportion! (*To* HUGO) What is there about you fellows anyway that makes women go crazy about you? (*To* LAEL) What is it, Lady Wyngate? Mystery? Romance? Passion? What is it?

LAEL   (*Starts to go*)   Perhaps I'd better . . . Is Mrs. Eldridge? . . .

HOBART   Don't go. I'm not drunk—not very, anyway. I won't be objectionable—promise. Been all day without a soul to speak to. Phoebe has one of her headaches—she's had 'em for years. You can't go near her when she has a headache. (*With a glare at* HUGO) I can't anyway. (*He and* HUGO *look at each other.* HUGO *says nothing.* HOBART *goes on, laughing boisterously*) Maybe you think it's on account of Phoebe I'm drinking? Do you think *that* is the sorrow I'm trying to drown? That's good! That's very good! I've got more to worry about than that, my good fellow. You'll be glad to hear, Lady Wyngate, that my negotiations with Lord Abercrombie have broken down.

LAEL   Have they? I'm sorry.

HOBART   Why should you be sorry? Besides, you're not sorry! You're glad! He's a very clever man, isn't he, Lady Wyngate?

LAEL   Yes. He's clever!

HOBART   Knows a hell of a lot, doesn't he? That little smile of his—those little wrinkled eyes. Well, I thought I had him. Thought he realized how serious things were for us—the haves against the have-nots—the last fight. Thought he knew

it, thought I'd convinced him of it. Thought it was all settled
—feather in my cap—when all of sudden—last night—felt
him slipping away from me—he began to joke—little jokes
—flippant—then he told me . . .

LAEL (*Curious*) What?

HOBART That, "on mature consideration," he'd decided the
idea of Anglo-American Youth League wouldn't go down.
He'd be glad to advise me on any project I'd care to under-
take, but he made it clear he couldn't be in on it. Press of
business in London—demands of his papers—all that rot. He'd
just decided—God knows what decided him—to let me down.
(*Fanatically*) I tell you he doesn't understand—none of them
understand!

LAEL Understand what?

HOBART (*Same voice*) The danger—the danger they're heading for—we're all heading for—all last night I sat up facing
it. . . .

LAEL Facing it! Facing what?

HOBART Losing everything I have, my fortune, my position,
everything I've worked for. For money—for money—I've
given up everything. My wife hates me, and my daughter—
all of that—but my fortune and the power it gave me—were
mine. Now they're threatened. They're in danger—terrible
danger—and nobody'll do anything about it—nobody. (*Turns
on* HUGO *suddenly*) They're in danger from you! You think
it's my wife I'm worried about? I've got a deeper grievance
against you than that. You think it's because you killed
Christ that we fear and hate you— No! It's because you gave
birth to Lenin!

HUGO (*Murmuring*) You over-estimate us!

LAEL Really, Hobart, you mustn't drink any more. . . .

HOBART (*In despair*) What is there left but to drink?

LAEL Nonsense. Your fortune'll last you your lifetime. You
needn't worry.

HOBART What do you know about it—or the danger? Where
it's a question of money in danger I'm as sensitive as a cat.
I can tell you because I know. Better than Abercrombie with
his cynical manner and his flippancy, better than anybody.

We're doomed—all of us rich men. It's a question—as such things are reckoned—it's a question of minutes—and it'll overwhelm us all.

LAEL   Well, you'll be no worse off than the rest of us, will you?

HOBART   No worse off! No worse off! Where's the comparison? You don't care about money. You're sloppy about money. You don't love it as I do. You don't count on it as I do. It doesn't sustain you, it doesn't compensate you for everything else you've missed. And yet you say I'll be no worse off. You're as near-sighted as Abercrombie.

LAEL   He has as much to lose as you. His lightness should give you hope.

HOBART   (*Contemptuously*)   Abercrombie! He's just a newspaperman—not a financier! When the Last Trumpet calls, it'll be just another headline to him!

LAEL   Well, you've had your innings—and a very good time too. If you have to give way—well, put a good face on it. Buck up. Be sporting.

HOBART   Can't—can't . . . Who's going to pay for everything—that's what I'd like to know? (*He again confronts* HUGO) Who's going to pay? Will you Communists pay?

HUGO   If you capitalists lend us the money . . .

HOBART   (*A bit taken back*)   Well, you shan't have it! And there's Rand . . . (*Very confidentially to* HUGO) Do you know what his expeditions have cost? Do you know what I've spent in my lifetime for hospitals, scientific research, even art? Who's going to pay after we're gone? Who's going to pay?

LAEL   Bart, please . . .

HOBART   Poor Rand! Poor Rand! No more South Poles!

LAEL   Bart, please . . .

(*Into the room from upstairs comes the sound of* SASCHA *playing the "Intermezzo in E Flat Minor" of Brahms*)

HOBART   (*Turning to* LAEL *for sympathy this time*)   Do you know, since the surtax, my income's shrunk to nothing? Do you know what I pay each year to the Government—State and Federal? (*He begins to weep. He becomes aware of the music and rushes to the foot of the stairs in the alcove, crying as he goes*) There's another one! Listen to him up there! (*At the foot of the stairs*) Who's going to pay for your Goddamn concerts! (*Rushes to the secretaire and grabs a bottle of whiskey*) You'll see! (*He starts out, crying like a baby, and through his blubbering says*) You'll want us back!

(*He goes out. There is an embarrassed pause. During the following scene between* LAEL *and* HUGO, *the Brahms goes on*)

HUGO To have in the world only one thing—and to face losing that—well, as Sascha might say, it's no joke!

LAEL In the sixteenth century—when people went to the Tower to be executed—it's always struck me how casually they died. Something beyond gallantry. Just before they put their heads on the block—it's extraordinary how they prayed for king and country. We've lost that.

HUGO They merely faced death. Mr. Eldridge faces extinction.

LAEL That's true. Suspicion and fear . . .

HUGO To be accused simultaneously of killing Christ and giving birth to Lenin—quite a feat, I must say! Just the same, Mr. Eldridge would do pretty well if he had the upper hand.

LAEL (*Smiling*) Hobart's an American and doesn't really understand democracy.

HUGO He's drowning in a reality he doesn't understand. He hates me because . . .

LAEL He doesn't hate you. He's afraid of you. Suspicion and fear. They're suffocating the world.

HUGO How're you going to get rid of them? Through some cosmic psychoanalysis?

LAEL Through understanding.

HUGO While you're understanding the enemy, he will destroy you.

LAEL The eternal impasse.

HUGO Unless—you destroy him first.

LAEL (*A moment's pause*) You're inexorable, Hugo, ruthlessly analytical. You're always looking for the motive behind the motive.

HUGO (*He looks at her a moment, then crosses to her, sitting beside her on the sofa*)   Yesterday I fell in love.

LAEL   Hugo.

HUGO   All through dinner, sitting near you in the car going to the cinema, in the theatre—I was in love.

LAEL   I know. I too.

HUGO   I thanked God for the miracle that filled me with longing for you. From my being alone, from my isolation, from the less than nothing I had to offer, from all these I gathered strength. When Mr. Eldridge turned on me, and Rand, too, I felt strong, omnipotent—but when you turned to me so magnanimously before them all, that did for me. I felt like a thief in the pillory to whom a sentimental bystander throws a rose.

LAEL   Your pride is devastating.

HUGO   Yes. And then I went up to my room. I sat at the window and looked over the garden, asleep in the moonlight. Enchantment. And suddenly the unreality of everything, of my presence here in this house overcame me. I thought: What can I hope for—what can I foresee—vistas of bliss in this pleasant country-house—with you. But what would it end in —a self-indulgent day-dream. I thought: What am I doing here? What *am* I?

LAEL   What am *I*?

HUGO   It's your home. You belong here. But for me . . .

LAEL   But, Hugo, don't you see? I wanted my love to shield you from the odium of a graceless world.

HUGO   I hoped for love—without philanthropy.

LAEL   How untrue half truths are. I sat up last night too —thinking—about Rand and you—everything— For the first time in months it seemed to me I felt clear—I felt free. I had thought that never again would I be lost in an emotion that I could accept entirely without reservation. To love and not to be ashamed to love. This miracle I felt would never happen to me again—and now it has.

HUGO (*Kisses her hand*)   You are all there is left in the world for me to love. I'll never forget you. Your radiance, your goodness, your compassion.

LAEL (*After a moment*)   That has a valedictory sound, Hugo.

HUGO   Yes. I must leave you. I must go.

LAEL   Where?

HUGO   Back to Germany.

LAEL (*Almost in terror*)   Oh! But you can't go back, Hugo. They'll—stop you.

HUGO   I must risk it.

LAEL   Don't go, Hugo!

HUGO   I must. I must. Look at my career—a public taster of the arts—a dilettante in everything, except that I was paid. Behind this decorative curtain I was forced to discover that there is a harsh reality. Well, I must investigate this reality further. To stay here, to go to America would only be a continuation of my life before. Intellectual squirearchy! I was able to feed my vanity with the comfort of knowing that I made and unmade reputations. Lehrmann—I made Lehrmann—I created a world in which Lehrmann was king; and what sort of a world is it? Out of egotism and vanity I created worlds without testing the foundations on which they rested. A criminal architect who builds houses that topple on their hapless tenants. I see now that there is only one thing left: To destroy the inhuman—to discover humanity.

LAEL   You talk about humanity—discovering humanity— as if it were an abstraction—an essence like the elixir of life which you might find somewhere in a bottle and dispense. Hugo, listen, humanity is here, all around us. I tell you what I wish you'd do. Humor me. Let me take you for a holiday through our shires and let me show you our common folk. You'll find them kindly and gentle. In their faces you'll see how impossible, how far beyond them, are ferocity or brutality or mass-hate. Let me take you, Hugo, and you'll see— you'll be comforted.

HUGO   But I don't want to be comforted. I don't want to be soothed. What you say about England is true. I feel it in you who are the best of England. But what right have I to this immunity? A sybarite in a famine.

LAEL   You're an artist, Hugo. What have you to do with feuds and hatreds and rebellions? Can't you try to see it as I see it? You see, I believe in England. I believe in gradualness. I believe in muddling through. I believe—a poor foolish illusion, I suppose—I believe that in the main people are reasonable and corrigible and sweet—fragments of God.

HUGO   That isn't a belief. It's a mirage. A self-hypnosis. A wish-fulfillment.

LAEL   I allow for that. And is it your dream that the world, overnight, can be scrubbed clean of injustice and left glowing with humanity?

HUGO   It's that I must find certitude at last, and, having found it, if necessary, die for it.

LAEL   Or kill for it?

HUGO   Or kill for it.

LAEL   You are leaving to fight a mania as ravaging as a forest fire that burns down everything before it, leaving stumps and ashes where there had been strength and growth. I don't want it to consume you, Hugo, dearest Hugo. Don't go. You may be lost in it—and to me.

HUGO   Dearest Lael—I can't stay because of one thing—that I remember the past year. And what I remember . . .

LAEL (*Understanding completely*)   Wouldn't let you rest.

HUGO   No. I'm determined at last to view the world—including myself—completely without illusion. It's a matter of life and death. I see now that goodness is not enough, that kindness is not enough, that liberalism is not enough. I'm sick of evasions. They've done us in. Civilization, charity, progress, tolerance—all the catchwords. I'm sick of them. We'll have to re-define our terms.

LAEL (*Seeing the inevitability of their separation*)   The iron has entered into your soul, Hugo. You have crossed some frontier—into some region—where I cannot follow you.

HUGO   If I can ever return—it will be to you.

LAEL (*Faces him*)   You will find me here. There is a genius for wandering and a genius for remaining behind. There is the shooting star and the fixed. Perhaps when you come back —you will find that in our own way we have realized your dream.

HUGO   I know this—that while you live—one needn't despair.

LAEL Then you need never despair. For nothing will destroy me. (*With deep feeling, her valedictory*) I shall live forever and so will you. Our enemies will beat against us and find that we have a strength beyond their clamor, beyond their forces.

(HUGO *and* LAEL *look deeply into each other's eyes without moving. Then* HUGO *turns and goes out.* LAEL *watches him until he has left the room, starts instinctively to follow him, stops.* RAND *enters from the garden*)

RAND Lael!

(LAEL *stops but doesn't face him. She is looking away into some vision of her own*)

RAND Joan's just told me, Lael—that you never saw Willens until you met him in London. I can't tell you how I feel— how humiliated— If there was any way I could make you see how deeply ashamed I am—you'd—you'd . . .

(*There is the sound of a motor leaving the driveway*)

LAEL Hugo's gone.

RAND I know now, Lael—whether he goes or stays—there's some awful fence in my mind and in my spirit, and you're on the other side, and no matter what I do I'll never be able to break through to you—never.

LAEL We're all shut in behind our little fences, Rand—

THE CURTAIN FALLS

☆

End of Summer

★

for May and
Harold Freedman

End of Summer *was produced by the Theatre Guild, Inc., at the Guild Theatre, New York, on Monday night, February 17, 1936, with the following cast:*

(IN THE ORDER OF THEIR APPEARANCE)

WILL DEXTER	Shepperd Strudwick
MRS. WYLER	Mildred Natwick
PAULA FROTHINGHAM	Doris Dudley
ROBERT	Kendall Clark
LEONIE FROTHINGHAM	Ina Claire
SAM FROTHINGHAM	Minor Watson
DR. KENNETH RICE	Osgood Perkins
DENNIS MCCARTHY	Van Heflin
DR. DEXTER	Herbert Yost
BORIS, COUNT MIRSKY	Tom Powers

Scene

The action of the play takes place in the living room of Bay Cottage, the Frothinghams' summer place in Northern Maine.

TIME: *The present.*

ACT ONE

SCENE: *The verandah-living room of the Frothingham estate.*
Bay Cottage in Northern Maine. It is a charmingly fur-
nished room with beautiful old distinguished pieces. A
chintz couch and chairs give the room an air of informality.
Beyond the door back you see a spacious, more formal
room. Through the series of glass windows over the curv-
ing window seat on the right wall you see the early budding
lilac and sumach. Woodbine and Virginia creeper are
sprawling over the fence of native stone. Silver birch and
maple are beginning to put out their leaves. The tops of
red pine and cedar are visible over the rocks which fall
away to the sea.

    Time: The present. A lovely afternoon in May.

    At Rise: MRS. WYLER, *a very old lady and* WILL DEXTER,
an attractive, serious boy, are engaged in conversation.
MRS. WYLER *is knitting.*

WILL   When you were a young girl in Cleveland, did you
see much of Mr. Rockefeller?

MRS. WYLER   Not much. Of course my husband saw him
every day at the office. But he never came to our house. We
were young and worldly. He was strict and religious.

WILL   Did you suspect, in those days, how rich you were
going to be?

MRS. WYLER   Mercy no! We debated a long time before we
moved up to Cleveland from Oil City. My mother thought
Oil City was no place to bring up a young girl. She finally
persuaded my father to let us move up to Cleveland. But there
was a lot of talk about the expense.

WILL   Was Oil City lively?

MRS. WYLER (*Demurely*)   It was pretty rough! I remember
the celebration when they ran the first pipe-line through to
Pittsburgh. That was a celebration!

WILL   The oil just poured, didn't it? Gushed out of the ground in great jets, and the people swarmed from everywhere to scoop it up.

MRS. WYLER   I remember we had a gusher in our backyard. We put a fence around it to keep the cows from lapping up the oil.

WILL   Were you excited?

MRS. WYLER   Not by the oil.

WILL   I should think you would have been!

MRS. WYLER   (*Dryly*) We weren't. Oil was smelly. We wanted to get away from it. We discovered bath-salts.

WILL   You didn't know it was the true fountain of your— dynasty?

MRS. WYLER   We left it to the men—as I look back over my life the principal excitement came from houses—buying and building houses. The shack in Oil City to the mansion on Fifth Avenue. We had houses everywhere—houses in London, houses in Paris, Newport and this—and yet, it seemed to me, we were always checking in and out of hotels.

WILL   It seems strange to think—

MRS. WYLER   What?

WILL   This golden stream—that you stumbled on so accidentally—it's flowing still—quenchless—and you on it—all you dynastic families—floating along in it—in luxurious barges!

MRS. WYLER   When I read these books about the early days of oil—these debunking books, you call them—they make me smile.

WILL   Do they? Why? I'd like to know that.

MRS. WYLER   They're so far from the truth.

WILL   Are they?

MRS. WYLER   Of course they are!

WILL   Why?

MRS. WYLER   Because they're written from a foreign point of view—not *our* point of view. We did as well as anybody could have done according to our lights.

WILL   Yes, but what sort of lights were they?

MRS. WYLER (*Tolerantly*)   There you are!

WILL   How lucky you were!

MRS. WYLER (*Teasing him*)   Our young men didn't moon about. They made opportunities for themselves!

WILL   Or did the opportunities make them? All you had to do was pack your week-end bag and pioneer.

MRS. WYLER   Is the world quite exhausted then?

WILL   Possibly not, but our pioneering might take a form you would find—unpalatable.

MRS. WYLER   Yes, yes. (*Benevolently*)   I suppose you're one of those young radicals our colleges are said to be full of nowadays. Tell me, what do you young radicals stand for?

WILL   I haven't decided exactly what I'm for, but I'm pretty certain what I'm against.

MRS. WYLER (*Pumping him*)   Most young people are bored by the past. You're full of curiosity. Why is that?

WILL (*Not committing himself*)   I'm interested.

MRS. WYLER   At my age to be permitted to talk of one's youth is an indulgence. Ask me anything you like. At my age also one has no reason for restraint. I have had the bad judgment to survive most of my contemporaries.

WILL   I love talking to you, Mrs. Wyler. I think you're very wise.

MRS. WYLER (*With a sigh*)   Go on thinking so—I'll try not to disillusion you! (*A moment's pause*)   Are you staying on here at Bay Cottage?

WILL   Oh, no, I have to go back to Amherst to get my degree.

MRS. WYLER   And after that?

WILL (*Humorously*)   The dole!
    (*The old lady laughs*)

MRS. WYLER   My daughter tells me she's invited your father here.

WILL   Yes.

MRS. WYLER   I shall be so glad to meet him. He's an inventor, isn't he?

WILL   He's a physicist. Specializes in——

MRS. WYLER Don't tell me—in spite of my great wisdom I can't keep up with science. Whenever anybody makes a scientific explanation to me I find there are two things I don't know instead of just one.

WILL (*Cheerfully*) Anyway, Dad's been fired.

MRS. WYLER I am very sorry to hear that.

WILL He's been working on a method for improving high-speed steel.

MRS. WYLER Did he fail?

WILL He succeeded. (MRS. WYLER *is surprised*) They decided that his discovery, if perfected and marketed, might increase the technological unemployment. They have decided therefore to call a halt on scientific discovery—especially in those branches where it might have practical results. That is one of the differences, Mrs. Wyler, between my day—and yours—in your day, you put a premium on invention—we declare a moratorium on it.

(*The old lady gives him a shrewd look*)

MRS. WYLER Yes, yes. I am perfectly sure that you're in for a hard time, Will.

WILL (*Lightly, shrugging his shoulders*) As I have been elected by my class as the one most likely to succeed, I am not worrying, Mrs. Wyler. All I have to do is bide my time.

MRS. WYLER (*Amused*) I am perfectly certain you'll come out! Paula tells me you and your friend, Dennis McCarthy, want to start some kind of magazine.

WILL Yes. A national magazine for undergraduate America. You see, Mrs. Wyler, before the rift in our so-called system, college men were supposed to live exclusively in a world of ukuleles, football slogans, and petting-parties—*College Humor* sort of thing. But it was never entirely true. Now it is less true than ever. This magazine—if we can get it going—would be a forum for intercollegiate thought. It would be the organ of critical youth as opposed—to the other.

MRS. WYLER What other?

WILL The R.O.T.C., the Vigilantes and the Fascists—the Youth Movement of guns and sabres—

MRS. WYLER I see. Well, I wish you luck, Will.

WILL Thank you.

(PAULA FROTHINGHAM *comes in, a lovely young girl in gay summer slacks*)

PAULA (*To* WILL) Aren't you swimming? Hello, Granny.

WILL Your grandmother and I have been discussing life.

PAULA With a capital L, I suppose?

WILL Enormous! I've been getting data on the pioneer age. Your grandmother thinks the reason we're in the condition we're in is that we're lazy.

MRS. WYLER (*Mildly*) Lazy? Did I say that?

WILL In a way.

MRS. WYLER If I said it, it must be so. Everybody over seventy is infallible!

PAULA (*Nestling to her*) Darling!

MRS. WYLER Survival is quite a knack. You children don't realize it.

WILL Oh, don't we though! It's getting harder every day.

MRS. WYLER Nonsense! At your age you can't help it.

WILL In your stately opulence that's what you think, Mrs. Wyler. You just don't know!

MRS. WYLER Nonsense! Do you think your generation has a monopoly on hard times?

WILL Now please don't tell me we've had depressions before?

MRS. WYLER (*Rising to go*) Paula, your young man is impertinent. Don't have anything to do with him.

(*She goes out*)

PAULA What a conquest you've made of Granny! Way and ahead of all my beaus!

WILL That undistinguished mob! Who couldn't?

PAULA As long as you admit there is a mob . . .

WILL Why wouldn't there be? Everybody loves you for your money!

PAULA (*Confidently*) I know it! And of all the fortune-hunters I've had dangling after me you're easily the most . . .

WILL Blatant!

PAULA   That's it! Blatant! Like my new slacks?

WILL   Love 'em.

PAULA   Love me?

WILL   Loathe you.

PAULA   Good! Kiss?
(*They kiss quickly*)

WILL   Funny thing about your grandmother . . .

PAULA   Now I won't have you criticizing Granny . . .

WILL   I'm crazy about her. You feel she's been through everything and that she understands everything. Not this though. Not the essential difference between her times and ours.

PAULA   Oh, dear! Is it the end of the world then?

WILL   The end of this world.

PAULA (*Goes to window seat right, with a sigh*)   Such a pretty world. (*She points through windows at the garden and sea beyond*) Look at it! Too bad it has to go! Meantime before it quite dissolves let's go for a swim.
(*She starts for door*)

WILL (*Abstracted*)   All right. . . .
(*Following her to window seat*)

PAULA (*She turns back*)   What's on your mind?

WILL   Wanted to speak to you about something. . . .

PAULA   What?

WILL (*Embarrassed slightly*)   Er—your mother. . . .

PAULA   What's Mother gone and done now? Out with it. Or is it you? My boy-friends are always in love with Mother. I've had to contend with that all my life. So if it's that you needn't even mention it . . . come on.

WILL   No, but really, Paula. . . .

PAULA   Well then, out with it! What is it!

WILL   This. (*He gives her note*) Found it on my breakfast tray this morning in a sealed envelope marked "Confidential."

PAULA (*Reading note aloud, rather bewildered*)   "To give my little girl a good time with. Leonie Frothingham."

WILL   And this!

(He hands her check. PAULA *takes it and looks at it)*

PAULA   A hundred dollars. Does Mother think her little girl can have a good time with *that?* She doesn't know her little girl!

WILL   But what'll I do with it? How'll I get it back to her?

PAULA   Over my dead body you'll get it back to her! You'll spend it on Mother's little girl. Now come on swimming!

WILL   Does your mother put one of these on every breakfast tray?

PAULA   Argue it out with her.

WILL   I can't. It would seem ungracious. You must give it back to her for me.

PAULA   Catch me! Don't take it too seriously. She slips all the kids something every once in a while. She knows my friends are all stony. You overestimate the importance of money, Will—it's a convenience, that's all. You've got a complex on it.

WILL   I have! I've got to have. It's all right to be dainty about money when you've lots of it as you have. . . .

PAULA   Rotten with it is the expression, I believe. . . .

WILL   I repudiate that expression. It is genteel and moralistic. You can't be rotten with money—you can only be *alive* with it.

PAULA   You and the rest of our crowd make me feel it's bad taste to be rich. But what can I do? I didn't ask for it!

WILL   I know. But look here . . . I've got a brother out of college two years who's worked six weeks in that time and is broke and here I am in an atmosphere with hundred-dollar bills floating around!

PAULA *(With check)*   Send him that!

WILL   Misapplication of funds!

PAULA *(Warmly)*   Mother would be only too . . .

WILL   I know she would—but that isn't the point. . . . You know, Paula—

PAULA   What?

WILL   Sometimes I think if we weren't in love with each other we should be irreconcilable enemies—

PAULA   Nothing but sex, eh?

WILL   That's all.

PAULA   In that case—
(*They kiss*)

WILL   That's forgiving. But seriously, Paula—

PAULA   Seriously what?

WILL   I can't help feeling I'm here on false pretences. What am I doing with a millionaire family—with you? If your mother knew what I think, and what I've let you in for in college—she wouldn't touch me with a ten-foot pole. And you too—I'm troubled about the superficiality of your new opinions. Isn't your radicalism—acquired coloring?

PAULA   I hope not. But—so is all education.

WILL   I know but—!

PAULA   What are you bleating about? Didn't I join you on that expedition to Kentucky to be treated by that sovereign state as an offensive foreigner? My back aches yet when I remember that terrible bus ride. Didn't I get my name in the papers picketing? Didn't I give up my holiday to go with you to the Chicago Peace Congress? Didn't I?

WILL   (*Doubtfully*)   Yes, you did.

PAULA   But you're not convinced. Will darling, don't you realize that since knowing you and your friends, since I've, as you say, acquired your point of view about things, my life has had an excitement and a sense of reality it's never had before. I've simply come alive—that's all! Before then I was bored—terribly bored without knowing why. I wanted something more—fundamental—without knowing what. You've made me see. I'm terribly grateful to you, Will darling. I always shall be.

WILL   You are a dear, Paula, and I adore you—but—

PAULA   Still unconvinced?

WILL   This money of yours. What'll it do to us?

PAULA   I'll turn it over to you. Then you can give me an allowance—and save your pride.

WILL   I warn you, Paula—

PAULA   What?

WILL   If you turn it over to me, I'll use it in every way I can to make it impossible for anyone to have so much again.

PAULA   That's all right with me, Will.

WILL   Sometimes you make me feel I'm taking candy from babies.

PAULA   The candy is no good for the baby, anyway. Besides, let's cross that bridge when we come to it.

(ROBERT, *the butler, enters*)

ROBERT   I beg your pardon, Miss Frothingham.

PAULA   Yes, Robert?

ROBERT   Telephone for you.

PAULA   Thank you, Robert. (*She crosses to table back of sofa for telephone*) (*At phone*) Yes—this is Paula—Dad! —Darling!—Where are you? . . . but how wonderful . . . I thought you were in New York . . . well, come right over this minute. . . . Will you stay the night? . . . Oh, too bad! . . . I'll wait right here for you. Hurry, darling! Bye! (*She hangs up*) Imagine, Dad! He's motoring up to Selena Bryant's at Murray Bay—I'm dying to have you meet him. He's the lamb of the world.

WILL   Not staying long, is he?

PAULA   No. He wants to see Mother he says. I wonder . . . oh, dear!

WILL   What?

PAULA   I was so excited I forgot to tell him. . . .

WILL   What?

PAULA   That a new friend of Mother's is coming.

WILL   The Russian?

PAULA   The Russian's here. He dates from last winter. You're behind the times, Will.

WILL   Who's the new friend?

PAULA   I'm not sure about it all yet. Maybe Mother isn't either. But I've had some experience in watching them come and go and my instinct tells me Dr. Rice is elected.

WILL   Who is Dr. Rice?

PAULA   Psychoanalyst from New York. (*Burlesquing slightly*)
The last word, my dear—

> (*At this point the object of* PAULA'S *maternal impulse
> comes in, running a little and breathless, like a young girl.*
> LEONIE FROTHINGHAM, *as she has a daughter of nearly
> twenty, must be herself forty, but, at this moment, she
> might be sixteen. She is slim, girlish, in a young and quiv-
> ering ecstasy of living and anticipation. For* LEONIE, *her
> daughter is an agreeable phenomenon whom she does not
> specially relate to herself biologically—a lovely apparition
> who hovers intermittently, in the wild garden of her life.
> There is something, for all her gaiety, heartbreaking about
> LEONIE, something childish and child-like—an acceptance
> of people instantly and uncritically at the best of their own
> valuation. She is impulsive and warm-hearted and generous
> to a fault. Her own fragile and exquisite loveliness she
> offers to the world half shyly, tentatively, bearing it like a
> cup containing a precious liquid of which not a drop must
> be spilled. A spirituelle amoureuse she is repelled by the
> gross or the voluptuary; this is not hypocrisy—it is, in
> LEONIE, a more serious defect than that. In the world in
> which she moves hypocrisy is merely a social lubricant but
> this myopia—alas for* LEONIE!—*springs from a congenital
> and temperamental inability to face anything but the pleas-
> antest and the most immediately appealing and the most
> flattering aspects of things—in life and in her own nature.
> At this moment, though, she is the loveliest fabrication of
> Nature, happy in the summer sun and loving all the world*)

LEONIE   My darlings, did you ever know such a day?

WILL (*He is a shy boy with her*)   It's nice!

LEONIE   Nice! It's . . . (*Her gesture conveys her utter inadequacy to express the beauties of the day*)   It's—radiant!
It knows it's radiant! The world is pleased with herself today.
Is the world a woman? Today she is—a lovely young girl in
blue and white.

WILL   In green and white.

LEONIE (*Agreeing—warmly*)   In green and white!—It depends where you look, doesn't it? I'm just off to the station
to meet Dr. Rice. Will, you'll be fascinated by him.

PAULA (*Cutting in—crisply*)   Sam telephoned.

LEONIE Sam!

PAULA Your husband. My father. Think back, Leonie.

LEONIE Darling! Where is he?

PAULA He's on his way here. He telephoned from Miller's Point.

LEONIE Is he staying?

PAULA No.

LEONIE Why not?

PAULA He's going on to Selena Bryant's.

LEONIE What is this deep friendship between Sam and Selena Bryant?

PAULA Now Leonie, don't be prudish!

LEONIE (*Appealing for protection to* WILL) She's always teasing me. She's always teasing everybody about everything. Developed quite a vein. I must warn you, Paula—sarcasm isn't feminine. In their heart of hearts men don't like it. Do you like it, Will? Do you really like it?

WILL I hate it!

LEONIE (*In triumph to* PAULA) There you see! He hates it!

PAULA (*Tersely*) He doesn't always hate it!

LEONIE (*Her most winning smile on* WILL) Does she bully you, Will? Don't let her bully you. The sad thing is, Paula, you're so charming. Why aren't you content to be charming? Are you as serious as Paula, Will? I hope not.

WILL Much more.

LEONIE I'm sorry to hear that. Still, for a man, it's all right, I suppose. But why are the girls nowadays so determined not to be feminine? Why? It's coming back you know—I'm sure of it—femininity is due for a revival.

PAULA So are Herbert Hoover and painting on china.

LEONIE Well I read that even in Russia . . . the women . . . (*She turns again to* WILL *whom she feels sympathetic*) It isn't as if women had done such marvels with their—masculinity! Have they? Are things better because women vote? Not that I can see. They're worse. As far as I can see the women simply reinforce the men in their—mistakes.

WILL (*To* PAULA) She has you there!

LEONIE (*With this encouragement warming to her theme*) When I was a girl the calamities of the world were on a much smaller scale. It's because the women, who, after all, are half of the human race, stayed at home and didn't bother. Now they do bother—and look at us!

PAULA Well, that's as Victorian as anything I ever—

LEONIE I'd love to have been a Victorian. They were much happier than we are, weren't they? Of course they were.

PAULA (*Defending herself to* WILL) It's only Mother that brings out the crusader in me— (*To* LEONIE) When you're not around I'm not like that at all. Am I, Will?
   (*But* WILL *is given no chance to answer because* LEONIE *is holding a sprig of lilac to his nostrils*)

LEONIE Smell. (WILL *smells*) Isn't it delicious?

WILL It's lovely.

LEONIE Here . . . (*She breaks off a sprig and pins it into his lapel. While she is doing it she broaches a delicate subject quite casually to* PAULA) Oh, by the way, Paula . . .

PAULA Yes, Mother?

LEONIE Did you mention to Sam that—that Boris—

PAULA I didn't, no. It slipped my mind.

LEONIE It doesn't matter in the least.

PAULA Father isn't staying anyway . . .

LEONIE Well, why shouldn't he? You must make him. I want him to meet Dr. Rice. He's really a most extraordinary man.

PAULA Where'd you *find him?*

LEONIE I met him at a party at Sissy Drake's. He *saved* Sissy.

PAULA From what?

LEONIE From that awful eye-condition.

PAULA Is he an oculist too?

LEONIE (*To* WILL) She went to every oculist in the world —she went to Baltimore and she went to Vienna. Nobody could do a thing for her—her eyes kept blinking—twitching really in the most unaccountable way. It was an ordeal to talk to her—and of course she must have undergone agonies of embarrassment. But Dr. Rice psychoanalyzed her and completely cured her. How do you suppose? Well, he found that the seat of the trouble lay in her unconscious. It was too simple. She blinked in that awful way because actually she couldn't bear to look at her husband. So she divorced Drake and since she's married to Bill Wilmerding she's as normal as you or me. Now I'll take you into a little secret. I'm having Dr. Rice up to see Boris. Of course Boris mustn't know it's for him.

PAULA What's the matter with Boris?

LEONIE I'm not sure. I think he's working too hard.

WILL What's he working at?

LEONIE Don't you know? Didn't you tell him, Paula? His father's memoirs. He's the son, you know, of the great Count Mirsky!

WILL I know.

LEONIE I must show you the photographs of his father—wonderful old man with a great white beard like a snow-storm—looks like Moses—a Russian Moses—and Boris is sitting on his knees—couldn't be over ten years old and wearing a fur cap and boots—boots!—and they drank tea out of tall glasses with raspberry jelly in—people came from all over the world, you know, to see his father . . . !

WILL Isn't it strange that Count Mirsky's son should find himself in this strange house on this odd headland of Maine —Maine of all places!—writing his father's life? It's fantastic!

PAULA (*With some malice*) Is Dr. Rice going to help you acclimate him?

LEONIE I hope so. You and Paula will have to entertain him—you young intellectuals. Isn't it a pity I have no mind? (*She rises and crosses to table right to arrange lily-of-the-valley sprigs in a vase*)

PAULA (*To* WILL) She knows it's her greatest asset. Besides she's a fake.

WILL (*Gallantly*) I'm sure she is.

LEONIE Thank you, my dears. It's gallant of you. (*She crosses to* PAULA—*embraces her from behind*) But I'm not deceived. I know what Paula thinks of me—she looks down on me because I won't get interested in sociology. There never were any such things about when I was a girl. The trouble is one generation never has any perspective about another generation.

WILL   That's what your mother was saying to me just a little while ago.

LEONIE   Was she? (*She sits left of* WILL) I'm sure though Mother and I are much closer—that is, we understand each other better than Paula and I. Don't you think so, Paula?

PAULA (*Considering it*)   Yes. I do think so.

LEONIE   I knew you'd agree. Something's happened between my generation and Paula's. New concepts. I don't know what they are exactly but I'm very proud that Paula's got them.

PAULA (*Laughing helplessly*)   Oh, Mother! You reduce everything to absurdity!

LEONIE (*Innocently*)   Do I? I don't mean to. At any rate it's a heavenly day and I adore you and I don't care about anything so long as you're happy. I want you to be happy.

PAULA (*Helplessly*)   Oh dear!

LEONIE   What's the matter?

PAULA   You're saying that!

LEONIE   Is that wrong? Will—did I say something wrong?

PAULA   You want me to be happy. It's like saying you want me to be eight feet tall and to sing like Lily Pons.

LEONIE   Is it like that? Why? Will . . .

WILL (*Gravely feeling he must stand up for* PAULA, *but hating to*)   Paula means . . .
   (*Pause*)

LEONIE   Yes . . . ?

WILL (*Miserable*)   She means—suppose there isn't any happiness to be had? Suppose the supply's run out?

LEONIE   But, Will, really . . . ! On a day like this! Why don't you go swimming? (*Rises*) Nothing like sea-water for—morbidity! Run out indeed! And today of all days! Really! (*Gets gloves*) I'm disappointed in you, Will. I counted on you especially . . .

WILL (*Abjectly*) I was only fooling!

LEONIE Of course he was. (*Sits on arm of sofa beside* WILL) Will, I rely on you. Don't let Paula brood. Can't she drop the sociology in the summer? I think in the fall you're much better—braced—for things like that. Keep her happy, Will.

WILL I'll do my best now that—thanks to you—I have the means.

LEONIE Oh. . . . (*Remembering*) Oh, you didn't mind, did you? I hope you didn't mind.

WILL (*Embarrassed*) Very generous of you.

LEONIE Generous! Please don't say that. After all—we who are in the embarrassing position nowadays of being rich must do something with our money, mustn't we? That's why I'm helping Boris to write this book. *Noblesse oblige.* Don't you think so, Will? Boris tells me that the Russians—the *present* Russians—

WILL You mean the Bolsheviks?

LEONIE Yes, I suppose I do. He says they don't like his father at all any more and won't read his works because in his novels he occasionally went on the assumption that rich people had souls and spirits too. You don't think like that too, do you, Will—that because I'm rich I'm just not worth bothering about at all— No, you couldn't!

(*The appeal is tremulous.* WILL *succumbs entirely*)

WILL (*Bluntly*) Mrs. Frothingham, I love you!

LEONIE (*Rises from arm of sofa and sits in sofa beside* WILL. *To* PAULA) Isn't he sweet? (*To* WILL) And I love you, Will. Please call me Leonie. Do you know how Mother happened to name me Leonie? I was born in Paris, you know, and I was to be called Ruhama after my father's sister. But Mother said no. No child of mine, she said, shall be called Ruhama. She shall have a French name. And where do you think she got Leonie?

WILL From the French version of one of those Gideon Bibles.

LEONIE (*As breathless as if it happened yesterday*) Not at all. From a novel the nurse was reading. She asked the nurse what she was reading and the nurse gave her the paper book and Mother opened it and found Leonie!

WILL   What was the book?

LEONIE   Everyone wants to know that . . . But I don't know. Mother didn't know. She kept the book to give to me when I grew up. But one day she met M. Jusserand on a train—he was the French Ambassador to Washington, you know—and he picked up the book in Mother's compartment and he read a page of it and threw it out of the window because it was trash! You see what I've had to live down.

WILL   Heroic!

LEONIE   I hope you stay all summer, Will. I won't hear of your going anywhere else.

WILL   Don't worry. I have nowhere else to go!

LEONIE   Tell me—that magazine you and Dennis want to start—will it be gay?

WILL   Not exactly.

LEONIE   Oh, dear! I know. Columns and columns of reading matter and no pictures. Tell me—your father is coming to dine, isn't he? I am so looking forward to meeting him. I love scientific men. They're usually so nice and understanding. Now, I've really got to go.
    (*Rises and starts out*)

PAULA   Dennis will be on that train.

LEONIE   Oh, good! I like Dennis. He makes me laugh and I like people around who make me laugh, but I do wish he'd dress better. Why can't radicals be chic? I saw a picture of Karl Marx the other day and he looks like one of those advertisements before you take something. I'll look after Dennis, Will—save you going to the station— (*To* PAULA) And Paula, tell Sam—

PAULA   Yes?

LEONIE   (*Forgetting the message to* SAM)   You know, I asked Dr. Rice if he would treat me professionally and he said I was uninteresting to him because I was quite normal. Isn't that discouraging? Really, I must cultivate something. Goodbye, darlings.
    (*She runs out*)

WILL   But what was the message to Sam?
    (*He sits*)

PAULA (*Helplessly*) I'll never know. Neither will she. (WILL *laughs*) What can you do with her? She makes me feel like an opinionated old woman. And I worry about her.

WILL Do you?

PAULA Yes. She arouses my maternal impulse.

WILL (*Who feels he can be casual about* LEONIE *now that she is gone*) She relies rather too much on charm!

PAULA (*Turning on him bitterly*) Oh, she does, does she! (*Goes over to sofa and sits right of* WILL) You renegade. You ruin all my discipline with Mother. You're like a blushing schoolboy in front of her . . .

WILL (*Protesting sheepishly*) Now, Paula, don't exaggerate!

PAULA You are! I thought in another minute you were going to ask her to the frat dance. And where was all that wonderful indignation about her leaving you the check? Where was the insult to your pride? Where was your starving brother in Seattle? Where? Where?

WILL I don't know but somehow you can't face your mother with things like that. It seems cruel to face her with realities. She seems outside of all that.

PAULA (*Conceding that*) Well, you're going to be no help to me in handling Mother, I can see that!

WILL (*Changing subject—a bit sensitive about having yielded so flagrantly to* LEONIE) This Russian—

PAULA What about him?

WILL (*Gauche*) Platonic, do you suppose?

PAULA Don't be naïve!
(*Enter* SAM FROTHINGHAM, PAULA'S *father, a very pleasant-faced, attractive man between forty-five and fifty*)

SAM Oh, hello.
(WILL *rises*)

PAULA (*Flying to him*) Darling!—

SAM (*They meet center and embrace*) Hello, Paula. Delighted to see you.

PAULA This is Will Dexter.

SAM (*Shaking hands with* WILL) How do you do?

WILL I'm delighted to meet you.

PAULA (*To* WILL)   Wait for me at the beach, will you, Will?

WILL   No, I'll run down to the station and ride back with the others.

PAULA   Okay.
  (SAM *nods to him.* WILL *goes out*)

SAM (*Crosses to front of sofa*)   Nice boy.
  (*Follows her*)

PAULA   Like him?

SAM   Do you?

PAULA   I think so.

SAM   Special?

PAULA   Sort of.

SAM   Very special?

PAULA (*Sits right end of sofa*)   Well—not sure.

SAM   Wait till you are. You've lots of time.

PAULA   Oh, he's not exactly impulsive.

SAM   Then he's just a fool.

PAULA   How are you, darling?

SAM   Uneasy.

PAULA   With me!

SAM   Especially.

PAULA   Darling, why?

SAM   I'll tell you. That's why I've come.

PAULA   Everything all right?

SAM   Oh, fine.

PAULA (*Mystified*)   Then . . . ?

SAM (*Switching off*)   How's Leonie?

PAULA   Fine. Delighted you were coming.

SAM   Was she?

PAULA   She really was. She's off to Ellsworth to meet a doctor.

SAM   Doctor?

PAULA   Psychoanalyst she's having up to massage her Russian's complexes.

SAM (*Laughing*)   Oh— (*With a sigh*) What's going to happen to Leonie?

PAULA   Why? She's on the crest!

SAM   She needs that elevation. Otherwise she sinks.

PAULA   Well—you know Mother . . .

SAM   Yes. (*A moment's pause*) Paula?

PAULA   Yes, Dad.

SAM   The fact is—it's ridiculous I should feel so nervous about telling you—but the fact is . . .

PAULA   What?

SAM   I've fallen in love. I want to get married. There! Well, thank God that's out! (*He wipes his forehead; quite an ordeal*) Romance at my age. It's absurd, isn't it?

PAULA   Selena Bryant?

SAM   Yes.

PAULA   She has a grown son.

SAM (*Smiling at her*)   So have I—a grown daughter.

PAULA   You'll have to divorce Mother.

SAM   Yes.

PAULA   Poor Leonie!

SAM   Well, after all—Leonie—you know how we've lived for years.

PAULA   Has Leonie hurt you?

SAM   Not for a long time. If this with Selena hadn't happened we'd have gone on forever, I suppose. But it has.

PAULA   You know, I have a feeling that, in spite of everything, this is going to be a shock to Leonie.

SAM   Paula?

PAULA   Yes.

SAM   Do you feel I'm deserting you?
   (*She turns her head away. She is very moved*)

PAULA   No—you know how fond I am of you—I want you to be . . .

SAM (*Deeply affected*)   Paula . . . !

PAULA   Happy.

(*A silence. She is on the verge of tears*)

SAM   I must make you see my side, Paula.

PAULA (*Vehemently*)   I do!

SAM   It isn't only that—you're so young—but somehow—
we decided very soon after you were born, Leonie and I,
that our marriage could only continue on this sort of basis.
For your sake we've kept it up. I thought I was content to
be an—appendage—to Leonie's entourage. But I'm not—do
you know what Selena—being with Selena and planning with
Selena for ourselves has made me see—that I've never had a
home. Does that sound mawkish?

PAULA   I thought you loved Bay Cottage.

SAM   Of our various menages this is my favorite—it's the
simplest. And I've had fun here with you—watching you
grow up. But very soon after I married Leonie I found this
out—that when you marry a very rich woman it's always
her house you live in.

(*A moment's pause*)

PAULA   I'm awfully happy for you, Sam, really I am. You
deserve everything but I can't help it I . . .

SAM   I know. (*A pause*) Paula . . .

PAULA   Yes, Dad?

SAM   You and I get on so well together—always have—
Selena adores you and really—when you get to know her . . .

PAULA   I like Selena enormously. She's a dear. Couldn't be
nicer.

SAM   I'm sure you and she would get on wonderfully together. Of course, Leonie will marry again. She's bound to.
Why don't you come to live with us? When you want to . . .

PAULA   Want to!

SAM   All the time then. Leonie has such a busy life.

PAULA   It's awfully sweet of you.

SAM   Sweet of me! Paula!

PAULA   Where are you going to live?

SAM   New York. Selena has her job to do.

PAULA   She's terribly clever, isn't she?

SAM   She's good at her job.

PAULA   It must be wonderful to be independent. I hope I shall be. I hope I can make myself.

SAM   No reason you can't.

PAULA   It seems to take so much—

SAM   What sort of independence?

PAULA   Leonie's independent, but that independence doesn't mean anything somehow. She's always been able to do what she likes.

SAM   So will you be.

PAULA   That doesn't count somehow. It's independence in a vacuum. No, it doesn't count.

SAM   Maybe it isn't independence you want then?

PAULA   Yes, it is. I want to be able to stand on my own feet. I want to be—justified.

SAM   (*Understandingly*)   Ah! That's something else. (*A little amused*) That's harder!

PAULA   I mean it, really I do— (*Pause*) It's curious—how —adrift—this makes me feel. As if something vital, something fundamental had smashed. I wonder how Mother'll take it. I think—unconsciously—she depends on you much more than she realizes. You were a stabilizing force, Sam, in spite of everything and now . . .

SAM   (*Seriously*)   *You* are the stabilizing force, if you ask me, Paula . . .

PAULA   I don't know.

SAM   What's worrying you, Paula? Is it this Russian?

PAULA   Oh, I think he's harmless really.

SAM   What then?

PAULA   That one of these days—

SAM   What?

PAULA   That one of these days—now that you're going— somebody will come along—who won't be harmless.—You know, I really love Leonie.

(LEONIE *comes running in just ahead of* DR. KENNETH RICE, DENNIS *and* WILL. LEONIE *is in the gayest spirits.* DR. RICE *is handsome, dark, magnetic, quiet, masterful. He is con-*

scious of authority and gives one the sense of a strange,
genius-like intuition. DENNIS *is a flamboyant Irishman, a*
little older than WILL, *gawky, black-haired, slovenly, in-*
finitely brash. SAM *and* PAULA *rise.* LEONIE *comes down*
to center with KENNETH *at her left.* WILL *remains back of*
sofa. DENNIS *follows down to right center*)

LEONIE   Oh, Sam, how perfectly . . . This is Dr. Rice—my
husband Sam Frothingham—and my daughter Paula! Sam,
Dennis McCarthy.

DENNIS   How do you do?
(*No one pays any attention to him.* DR. RICE *shakes hands*
with SAM *and* PAULA. LEONIE *keeps bubbling, her little*
laugh tinkling through her chatter)

LEONIE   It's courageous of me, don't you think, Dr. Rice,
to display such a daughter? Does she look like me? I'll be
very pleased if you tell me that she does. Sit down, sit down,
everybody.

DENNIS (*Holding up his pipe*)   You don't mind if I—?

LEONIE   No, no, not at all— (*She sits center chair,* PAULA
sits on right end sofa, DENNIS *sinks into chair, right, by*
table) Sam! How well you're looking! Are you staying at
Selena's? How is Selena?

SAM   She's very well.

LEONIE   Dr. Rice knows Selena.

KENNETH   Yes, indeed!

LEONIE   I envy Selena, you know, above all women. So brilliant, so attractive and so self-sufficient. That is what I envy
in her most of all. I have no resources—I depend so much
on other people. (*Turns to* RICE) Do you think, Dr. Rice,
you could make me self-sufficient?

KENNETH   I think I could.

LEONIE   How perfectly marvelous!

KENNETH   But I shouldn't dream of doing it!

LEONIE   But if I beg you to?

KENNETH   Not even if you beg me to.

LEONIE   But why?

KENNETH It would deprive your friends of their most delightful avocation.

LEONIE Now that's very grateful. You see, Sam, there are men who still pay me compliments.

SAM I can't believe it!

LEONIE You must keep it up, Dr. Rice, please. So good for my morale. (*To* PAULA) Oh, my dear, we've been having the most wonderful argument— (*To* DENNIS) Haven't we?

DENNIS Yes.

LEONIE All the way in from Ellsworth— (*To* RICE) Really, Doctor, it's given me new courage . . .

PAULA New courage for what?

LEONIE I've always been afraid to say it for fear of being old-fashioned—but Dr. Rice isn't afraid.

KENNETH (*Explaining to* SAM) It takes great courage, Mr. Frothingham, to disagree with the younger generation.

SAM It does indeed.

PAULA Well, what was it about?

LEONIE Yes—what *was* it about, Dennis?

DENNIS Statistics and theology. Some metaphysics thrown in.

SAM Good heavens!
    (*Sits*)

DENNIS Statistics as a symbol.

WILL Dr. Rice still believes in the individual career.

KENNETH I hang my head in shame!

DENNIS He doesn't know that as a high officer of the National Student Federation, I have at my fingers' ends the statistics which rule our future, the statistics which constitute our horizon. Not your future, Paula, because you are living parasitically on the stored pioneerism of your ancestors.

PAULA Forgive me, Reverend Father!

DENNIS I represent, Doctor, the Unattached Youth of America—

KENNETH Well, that's a career in itself!
    (*They laugh*)

DENNIS (*Imperturbable*) When we presently commit the folly of graduating from a benevolent institution at Amherst, Massachusetts, there will be in this Republic two million like us. Two million helots. (*Leaning over* LEONIE) But Dr. Rice pooh-poohs statistics.

LEONIE (*Arranging his tie*) Does he Dennis?

DENNIS He says the individual can surmount statistics, violate the graphs. Superman!

WILL Evidently Dr. Rice got in just under the wire.

KENNETH I'd never submit to statistics, Mr. Dexter—I'd submit to many things but not to statistics.

LEONIE Such dull things to submit to—

DENNIS You must be an atheist, Dr. Rice.

KENNETH Because I don't believe in statistics?—the new God?

LEONIE Well, *I'm* a Protestant and I don't believe in them either.

DENNIS Well, Protestant is a loose synonym for atheist—and I, as an Irishman—and a—

KENNETH Young man—

DENNIS Yes?

KENNETH Have you ever heard Bismarck's solution of the Irish problem?

DENNIS No. What?

KENNETH Oh, it's entirely irrelevant.

LEONIE Please tell us. I adore irrelevancies.

KENNETH Well, he thought the Irish and the Dutch should exchange countries. The Dutch, he thought, would very soon make a garden out of Ireland, and the Irish would forget to mend the dikes.
(*They laugh*)

LEONIE That's not irrelevant—

DENNIS It is an irrelevance, but pardonable in an adversary losing an argument.

KENNETH (*To* PAULA) Miss Frothingham, you seem very gracious. Will you get me out of this?

PAULA No, I'm enjoying it.

LEONIE Whatever you may say, Dennis, it's an exciting time to be alive.

DENNIS That is because your abnormal situation renders you free of its major excitement—

LEONIE And what's that, Dennis?

DENNIS The race with malnutrition.

KENNETH But that race, Mr.—?

DENNIS McCarthy.

KENNETH Is the eternal condition of mankind. Perhaps mankind won't survive the solution of that problem.

WILL (*With heat*) It's easy to sit in this living room—and be smug about the survival of the fittest—especially when you're convinced you're one of the fittest. But there are millions who won't concede you that superiority, Dr. Rice. There are millions who are so outrageously demanding that they actually insist on the right to live! They may demand it one day at the cost of your complacency.

LEONIE Will! We were just chatting.

WILL I'm sorry! The next thing Dr. Rice'll be telling us is that war is necessary also—to keep us stimulated—blood-letting for the other fellow.

KENNETH Well, as a matter of fact, there's something to be said for that too. If you haven't settled on a career yet, Mr. Dexter, may I suggest evangelism?

DENNIS But Dr. Rice—!

KENNETH And now, Mrs. Frothingham, before these young people heckle me too effectively, may I escape to my room?

LEONIE (*Rising*) Of course. Though I don't think you need be afraid of their heckling, Doctor. You say things which I've always believed but never dared say.

KENNETH (*As they walk out*) Why not?

LEONIE I don't know—somehow—I lacked the—the authority. I want to show you your rooms myself. (*Leaving the room, followed by* RICE) I'll be right back, Sam— (RICE *nods to them and follows her out. As they go out she keeps talking to him*) I am giving you my father's rooms—he built the wing especially so that when he wanted to work he'd be away from the rest of the house—you have the sea *and* the garden—

(*They are off. A moment's pause*)

PAULA   Well, that's a new type for Leonie!

DENNIS   There's something Rasputinish about him. What's he doing in Maine?

WILL   What, for the matter of that, are you and I doing in Maine? We should be in New York, jockeying for position on the bread-line. Let's go to the beach, Dennis. Pep us up for the struggle.

DENNIS   In that surf? It looks angry. I can't face life today.

PAULA   Swim'll do you good.

DENNIS (*Starting for garden*)   It's not a swim I want exactly but a float—a vigorous float. Lead me to the pool, Adonais—

WILL   All right.

(*As he starts to follow* DENNIS, DR. DEXTER, WILL'S *father, comes in ushered by* ROBERT. *He is a dusty little man with a bleached yellow Panama hat. He keeps wiping his perspiring face with an old handkerchief. He doesn't hear very well*)

DENNIS   Ah, the enemy—!

(PAULA *and* SAM *rise*)

WILL   Hello, Dad. You remember Paula?

DEXTER   Yes . `. . yes, I do.

WILL (*Introducing* SAM)   My father—Mr. Frothingham.

SAM   Very glad to see you.

DEXTER (*Shaking hands*)   Thank you.

DENNIS (*Pointing dramatically at* DEXTER)   Nevertheless I repeat—the enemy!

PAULA   Dennis!

WILL   Oh, he's used to Dennis!

DEXTER (*Wipes his forehead*)   Yes, and besides it was very dusty on the road.

PAULA   Won't you sit down?

(DEXTER *does so, in center chair. The others remain standing*)

WILL   How long did it take you to drive over, Dad?

DEXTER   Let's see—left New Brunswick at two. . . .

WILL (*Looks at watch*)   Three and one half hours—pretty good—the old tin Lizzie's got life in her yet.

DEXTER   You young folks having a good time, I suppose? (*He looks around him absent-mindedly*)

PAULA   Dennis has been bullying us.

DEXTER   He still talking? (*Mildly*)   It's the Irish in him.

DENNIS (*Nettled*)   You forgot to say shanty!

DEXTER (*Surprised*)   Eh? Why should I say that?

WILL   Dennis is a snob. Wants all his titles.

DENNIS   You misguided children don't realize it—but here—in the guise of this dusty, innocent-seeming man—sits the enemy.

DEXTER (*Turning as if stung by a fly—cupping his hand to his ear*)   What? What did he say?

DENNIS   The ultimate enemy, the true begetter of the fatal statistics—Science. You betray us, Paula, by having him in the house; *you* betray us, Will, by acknowledging him as a father.

DEXTER (*Wiping his forehead*)   Gosh, it's hot!

SAM (*Sensing a fight and urging it on—solemnly*)   Can all this be true, Dr. Dexter?

DEXTER   What be true?

SAM   Dennis's accusation.

DEXTER   I am slightly deaf and McCarthy's presence always fills me with gratitude for that affliction.

DENNIS   It's perfectly obvious. You've heard of technological unemployment. Well, here it sits, embodied in Will's father. Day and night with diabolical ingenuity and cunning he works out devices to un-employ us. All over the world, millions of us are being starved and broken on the altar of Science. We Catholics understand that. We Catholics repudiate the new Moloch that has us by the throat.

WILL   Do you want us to sit in mediæval taverns with Chesterton and drink beer?

(DEXTER *turns to* DENNIS; *as if emerging suddenly from an absent-minded daze, he speaks with great authority, casually but with clarity and precision*)

DEXTER The fact is, my voluble young friend, I am not the Moloch who is destroying you but that you and the hordes of the imprecise and the vaguely trained—are destroying me! I have, you will probably be pleased to learn, just lost my job. I have been interrupted in my work. And why? Because I am successful. Because I have found what, with infinite patience and concentration, I have been seeking to discover. From the elusive and the indeterminate and the invisible, I have crystallized a principle which is visible and tangible and —predictable. From the illimitable icebergs of the unknown I have chipped off a fragment of knowledge, a truth which so-called practical men may put to a use which will make some of your numbers unnecessary in the workaday world. Well—what of it, I say?—who decrees that you shall be supported? Of what importance are your lives and your futures and your meandering aspirations compared to the firmness and the beauty and the cohesion of the principles I seek, the truth I seek? None—none whatever! Whether you prattle on an empty stomach or whether you prattle on a full stomach can make no difference to anybody that I can see. (*To* PAULA *abruptly, rising*) And now, young woman, as I have been invited here to spend the night, I'd like to see my room!

PAULA (*Crossing to him*) Certainly! Come with me. I'll have Robert show you your room. (*They go to door back. She calls*) Robert! (ROBERT *enters*) Will you take Dr. Dexter to his room?

(DEXTER *follows* ROBERT *out*)

SAM Gosh! I thought he was deaf!

WILL He can hear when he wants to! (*To* DENNIS) Now will you be good!

DENNIS I'm sorry—I didn't know he'd lost his job or I wouldn't have . . .

WILL Oh, that's all right. Well, Dennis, how does it feel to be superfluous?

DENNIS (*Sourly*) The man's childish!
(*He goes out, door right through garden*)

PAULA Isn't he marvelous? Don't you love Will's father?

SAM Crazy about him. He's swell.

WILL He's a pretty good feller. He seems absent-minded but actually he's extremely present-minded. If you'll excuse me, I'm going out to soothe Dennis.
  (*He follows* DENNIS *out*)
  (*A pause*)

SAM That young man appears to have sound antecedents.

PAULA Oh, yes—Will's all right, but—oh, Sam—!

SAM What?

PAULA With you gone—I'm terrified for Leonie. I really am! When I think of the foolish marriages Leonie would have made if not for you!

SAM It's a useful function, but I'm afraid I'll have to give it up!

PAULA (*With new determination*) Sam . . .

SAM Yes, Paula.

PAULA If Leonie goes Russian—

SAM Well?

PAULA Or if she goes Freudian—?

SAM In any case you and this boy'll probably be getting married.

PAULA That's far from settled yet.

SAM Why?

PAULA Will's scared.

SAM Is he?

PAULA Of getting caught in Leonie's silken web.

SAM That's sensible of him.
  (LEONIE *comes back, half running, breathless*)

LEONIE Well! Isn't Dr. Rice attractive?

SAM (*Rising*) Very.

PAULA (*Rising*) And so depressed about himself!
  (*She goes out—door right*)

LEONIE Isn't it extraordinary, Dr. Rice having achieved the position he has—at his age? He's amazing. And think of it, Sam—not yet forty.

SAM Anybody under forty is young to me!

LEONIE How old are you, Sam?

SAM   Forbidden ground, Leonie.

LEONIE   I should know, shouldn't I, but I don't. I know your birthday—I always remember your birthday . . .

SAM   You do indeed!

LEONIE   It's June 14. But I don't know how old you are.

SAM   Knowledge in the right place—ignorance in the right place!

LEONIE (*Meaning it*)   You're more attractive and charming than ever.

SAM   You're a great comfort.

LEONIE   It's so nice to see you!

SAM   And you too!
    (*He is not entirely comfortable—not as unself-conscious and natural as she is*)

LEONIE   Sometimes I think Paula should see more of you. I think it would be very good for her. What do you think of her new friends?

SAM   They seem nice.

LEONIE   They're all poor and they're very radical. They look on me—my dear, they have the most extraordinary opinion of me . . .

SAM   What is that?

LEONIE   I'm fascinated by them. They think of me as a hopeless kind of spoiled Bourbon living away in a never-never land—a kind of Marie Antoinette . . . (*She laughs*) It's delicious!

SAM   Is Paula radical too?

LEONIE   I think she's trying to be. She's a strange child.

SAM   How do you mean?

LEONIE   Well, when I was a child I was brought up to care only if people were charming or attractive or . . .

SAM   Well-connected . . .

LEONIE   Yes . . . These kids don't care a hoot about that.

SAM   I think the difference between their generation and ours is that we were romantic and they're realistic.

LEONIE   Is that it?

SAM   I think so.

LEONIE   What makes that?

SAM   Changes in the world—the war—the depression. . . .

LEONIE   What did people blame things on before—the war?

SAM   (*Smiling*)   Oh, on the tariff and on the Republicans—and on the Democrats! Leonie—

LEONIE   Yes, Sam.

SAM   I—I really have something to tell you.

LEONIE   (*Looks up at him curiously*)   What?
   (*Pause*)

SAM   I am in love with Selena Bryant. We want to get married.

LEONIE   (*Pause—after a moment*)   Human nature is funny! Mine is!

SAM   Why?

LEONIE   I know I ought to be delighted to release you. Probably I should have spoken to you about it myself before long—separating. And yet—when you tell me—I feel—a pang. . . .

SAM   That's very sweet of you.

LEONIE   One's so possessive—one doesn't want to give up anything.

SAM   For so many years our marriage has been at its best—a friendship. Need that end?

LEONIE   No, Sam. It needn't. I hope truly that it won't.

SAM   What about Paula?

LEONIE   Did you tell Paula?

SAM   Yes. . . .

LEONIE   Did she . . . ?

SAM   (*Rising*)   Leonie . . .

LEONIE   (*Pauses*)   Yes, Sam.

SAM   A little while ago you said—you thought Paula ought to see more of me.

LEONIE   Yes . . . I did. . . .
   (*She is quite agitated suddenly. The thought has crossed her mind that perhaps* PAULA *has told* SAM *that she would*

prefer to go with him. This hurts her deeply, not only for the loss of PAULA *but because, from the bottom of her being, she cannot bear not to be loved*)

SAM   Don't you think then . . . for a time at least . . .

LEONIE (*Defeatist in a crisis*)   Paula doesn't like me!
(*It is a sudden and completely accepted conviction*)

SAM   Leonie!

LEONIE   She'd rather go with you!

SAM   Not at all—it's only that . . .

LEONIE   I know what Paula thinks of me. . . .

SAM   Paula adores you. It's only that . . .

LEONIE   It's only that what—

SAM   Well, for instance—if you should get married—

LEONIE   What if I did?

SAM (*Coming to stand close to her left*)   It would mean a considerable readjustment for Paula—wouldn't it? You can see that. . . .

LEONIE (*Rising*)   But it would too with you and Selena.

SAM (*Taking step toward her*)   She knows Selena. She admires Selena.

LEONIE (*Rising and walking down to front of sofa*)   What makes you think she wouldn't admire—whomever I married?

SAM (*After a moment, completely serious now*)   There's another aspect of it which I think for Paula's sake you should consider most carefully.

LEONIE   What aspect?

SAM (*Coming down to her*)   Paula's serious. You know that yourself. She's interested in things. She's not content to be a Sunday-supplement heiress—floating along—she wants to do things. Selena's a working woman. Selena can help her.

LEONIE   I know. I'm useless.

SAM   I think you ought to be unselfish about this.

LEONIE   Paula can do what she likes, of course. If she doesn't love me . . .

SAM   Of course she loves you.

LEONIE If she prefers to live with you and Selena I shan't stand in her way.

(*Her martyrish resignation irritates* SAM *profoundly. He feels that really* LEONIE *should not be allowed to get away with it*)

SAM You're so vain, Leonie.

LEONIE (*Refusing to argue*) I'm sorry.
(*This makes it worse.* SAM *goes deeper*)

SAM After all, you're Paula's mother. Can't you look at her problem—objectively?

LEONIE Where my emotions are involved I'm afraid I never know what words like that mean.

(*He blunders in worse, farther than he really means to go*)

SAM (*Flatly*) Well, this sort of thing isn't good for Paula.

LEONIE (*Very cold, very hurt*) What sort of thing? (*A moment's pause. He is annoyed with himself at the ineptitude of his approach*) Be perfectly frank. You can be with me. What sort of thing?

SAM Well—Leonie— (*With a kind of desperate bluntness*) You've made a career of flirtation. Obviously Paula isn't going to. You know you and Paula belong to different worlds. (*With some heat*) And the reason Paula is the way she is is that she lives in an atmosphere of perpetual conflict.

LEONIE . Conflict? Paula?

SAM With herself. About you.

LEONIE (*Rising*) That's too subtle for me, I'm afraid.

SAM Paula's unaware of it herself.

LEONIE Where did you acquire this amazing psychological insight? You never used to have it. Of course! From Selena. Of course!

SAM I've never discussed this with Selena.

LEONIE No?

SAM She's told me she'd be happy to have Paula but . . .

LEONIE That's extremely generous of her—to offer without discussion. . . .

SAM (*She has him there; he loses his temper*) It's impossible for you to consider anything without being personal.

LEONIE I am afraid it is. I don't live on this wonderful, rarefied, intellectual plane inhabited by Selena and yourself —and where you want to take Paula. I'm sorry if I've made Paula serious, I'm sorry she's in a perpetual conflict about me. I'm sorry I've let her in for—this sort of thing! I'm sorry!

(*She is on the verge of tears. She runs out*)

SAM Leonie . . . ! (*He follows her to door back, calling*) Leonie! (*But it is too late. She is gone. He turns back into room*) Damn!

(PAULA *comes in—from beach, door right*)

PAULA Where's Leonie?

SAM She just went upstairs.

PAULA I've been showing Dr. Rice our rock-bound coast.

SAM What's he like?

PAULA Hard to say. He's almost too sympathetic. At the same time—

SAM What?

PAULA At the same time—he is inscrutable! I can't tell whether I like him or dislike him. You say Selena knows him. What does she say about him?

SAM Selena isn't crazy about him.

PAULA Why not?

SAM Brilliant charlatan, she says—also a charmer.

PAULA I gather that, and I resent him. How'd you come out with Leonie?

SAM I've made a mess of it. I'm a fool!

PAULA My going with you, you mean?

SAM Yes.

PAULA Sam . . .

SAM Yes?

PAULA Will you mind very much . . .

SAM What?

PAULA If I don't go with Selena and you?

SAM But I thought you said—and especially if she marries somebody—

PAULA (*Slowly*) That's just what I'm thinking of—

SAM What's happened?

PAULA There's no way out of it, Sam—I've got to stay.

SAM But why?

PAULA (*Simply, looking up at him*) Somebody's got to look after Leonie. . . .
  (KENNETH *enters*)

KENNETH My first glimpse of Maine. A masculine Riviera.

PAULA It's mild now. If you want to see it really virile—come in the late fall.

KENNETH You've only to crook your little finger. I'll be glad to look at more of Maine whenever you have the time.
  (*Sits, facing her*)

PAULA Of course. Tomorrow?

KENNETH Yes. Tomorrow. (*To* SAM) You know, from Mrs. Frothingham's description— (*Looking back at* PAULA, *intently*) I never could have imagined her. Not remotely.
  (ROBERT *enters*)

SAM What is it, Robert?

ROBERT Mrs. Frothingham would like to see Dr. Rice in her study.

KENNETH (*Rising*) Oh, thank you. (*He walks to door back*) Excuse me.
  (*He goes upstairs.* PAULA *and* SAM *have continued looking front. As* KENNETH *starts upstairs they slowly turn and look at one another. The same thought has crossed both their minds—they both find themselves looking suddenly into a new and dubious vista*)

CURTAIN

SCENE: *The same.*

> *Time: Midsummer—late afternoon.*
>
> *At Rise:* KENNETH *is at a bridge table working out a chess problem. He hears voices and footsteps approaching. Gets up, unhurried, and looks off into garden. Sees* BORIS *and* LEONIE *approaching. As they come in he strolls off— they do not see him.* LEONIE'S *arms are full of flowers. She is looking for* KENNETH. COUNT MIRSKY *follows her in.*
>
> COUNT MIRSKY, *a Russian, is very good-looking, Mongoloid about the eyes. His English is beautiful, with a slight and attractive accent. He is tense, jittery—a mass of jangled nerves—his fingers tremble as he lights one cigarette after another. He is very pale—his pallor accentuated by a dark scarf he wears around his neck.*

BORIS (*Stopping center*) It appears he is not here either.

LEONIE He? Who?

> (*Crossing to table behind sofa to put some flowers in vase*)

BORIS When you're in the garden with me you think— perhaps he is in the house. When you are in the house you think perhaps he is in the garden.

LEONIE Boris, darling, you have the odd habit of referring to mysterious characters without giving me any hint who they are. Is that Russian symbolism? There will be a long silence; then you will say: He would not approve, or they can't hear us. It's a bit mystifying.

BORIS (*Crossing to stand near her*) You know who I mean.

LEONIE (*Going to table right to put flowers in vase*) Really, you flatter me. I'm not a mystic, you know, Boris. I'm a simple extrovert. When you say "he," why can't it refer to some-one definite—and if possible to someone I know.

BORIS (*Crossing to back of table, facing her across it*)   You know him, all right.

LEONIE   There you go again! *Really*, Boris!

BORIS (*Moving closer to her around table*)   You've been divorced now for several weeks. You're free. We were only waiting for you to be free—

LEONIE (*Moving away, sitting in chair, right*)   Now that I am free you want to coerce me. It's a bit unreasonable, don't you think?

(BORIS *walks to end of window-seat and sits*)
(*Enter* KENNETH, *door back*)

KENNETH (*Strolling across stage toward* LEONIE)   Hello, Leonie. Count Mirsky—

LEONIE   Kenneth—I haven't seen you all day.

KENNETH   I've been in my room slaving away at a scientific paper.

LEONIE   My house hums with creative activity. I love it. It gives me a sense of vicarious importance. What's your paper on?

KENNETH   Shadow-neurosis.

LEONIE   Shadow-neurosis. How marvelous! What does it mean?

KENNETH (*Looking at* BORIS)   It is a sensation of non-exist-ence.

LEONIE   Is it common?

KENNETH   Quite. The victim knows that he exists and yet he feels that he does not!

LEONIE   In a curious way I can imagine a sensation like that —do you know I actually can. Isn't it amusing?

BORIS   The doctor is so eloquent. Once he describes a sensa-tion it becomes very easy to feel it.

LEONIE   That's an entrancing gift. Why are you so antagonis-tic to Kenneth? He wants to help you but you won't let him. I asked him here to help you.

KENNETH (*To* BORIS)   Your skepticism about this particular disease is interesting. Count Mirsky, because, as it happens, you suffer from it.

BORIS (*Bearing down on* KENNETH)   Has it ever occurred to you that you are a wasted novelist?

KENNETH   Though I have not mentioned you in my article I have described you.

LEONIE (*Rising and crossing left to table behind sofa*)   You should be flattered, Boris.

BORIS   I am!

LEONIE   Another case history! I've been reading some of Kenneth's scientific text-books. Most fascinating form of biography. Who was that wonderful fellow who did such odd things—Mr. X.? You'd never think you could get so interested in anonymous people. I'd have given anything to meet Mr. X.—though I must say I'd feel a bit nervous about having him in the house.

KENNETH   How is your book getting along, Count Mirsky?

BORIS   Very well. Oh—so—

KENNETH   Far along in it?

BORIS   Quite.

LEONIE   I'm crazy to see it. He's dedicating it to me but he hasn't let me see a word of it!

KENNETH   For a very good reason.

LEONIE   What do you mean?

KENNETH   Because there is no book. There never has been a book.

LEONIE (*She lets flowers drop*)   Kenneth!

KENNETH   Isn't that true, Count Mirsky?

BORIS   It is not!

KENNETH   Then why don't you let us see a bit of it?

LEONIE   Oh, do! At least the dedication page.

KENNETH   A chapter—

BORIS   Because it isn't finished yet.

LEONIE   Well, it doesn't have to be finished. We know the end, don't we? The end belongs to the world.

KENNETH Let us see it, Count.

BORIS I can't.

KENNETH What are you calling the book?

BORIS I haven't decided yet.

KENNETH May I suggest a title to you—?

LEONIE Oh, do! What shall we call it, Kenneth?

KENNETH "The Memoirs of a Boy Who Wanted to Murder His Father."

LEONIE What!

BORIS (*Gripping arms of chair*) I am not a hysterical woman, Doctor—and I'm not your patient!

LEONIE But Kenneth—Boris worshipped his father.

KENNETH No, he hated him. He hated him when he was alive and he hates him still. He grew up under the overwhelming shadow of this world-genius whom, in spite of an immense desire to emulate and even to surpass—he felt he could never emulate and never surpass—nor even equal— Did you worship your father, Count Mirsky?

BORIS It's true! I hated him!

LEONIE Boris!

BORIS I hated him!

KENNETH Now you can let us see the book, can't you—now that we know the point of view—just a bit of it?

LEONIE I'm more crazy than ever to see it now. I can tell you a little secret now, Boris. I was afraid—I was rather afraid—that your book would be a little like one of those statues of an ancestor in a frock-coat. Now it sounds really exciting. You hated him. But how perfectly marvelous! I can't wait to see it now. Do run up to your study and bring it down, Boris—do!

BORIS No.

LEONIE That's very unpleasant of you.

BORIS You might as well know it then. There isn't any book. There never will be. Not by me.

LEONIE But I don't understand—every day—in your room working—all these months!

BORIS (*Facing her*)   One wants privacy! Possibly you can't realize that. You who always have to have a house full of people.

LEONIE (*Goes back to flowers at table*)   Boris!

KENNETH (*Rising*)   Why don't you write the book anyway, Count Mirsky? There is a vogue these days for vituperative biography.

BORIS   I am not interested in the vogue.

KENNETH   We are quite used nowadays to children who dislike their fathers. The public—

BORIS   To titillate the public would not compensate me for forcing myself to recall the atmosphere of saintly sadism in which my childhood was spent—I can still smell that living room, I can still smell those stinking, sexless pilgrims who used to come from all over the world to get my saintly father's blessing. I used to sit with my mother in a room no bigger than a closet to get away from the odor of that nauseating humanitarianism. There was no privacy in the Villa Mirskovitch. Oh, no—it was a Mecca—do you understand—a Mecca!

KENNETH   Yes, I think I understand.

BORIS   Well, I have been paying the haloed one back. I have been getting privacy at his expense at last.

LEONIE   Why have you never told me before that you felt this way about your father?

BORIS   I never said anything about him. It was you who did the talking. You always raved about the great man with that characteristic American enthusiasm for what you don't know.

LEONIE   Nevertheless, the world recognizes your father as a great man. The books are there to prove it. There they are. You can't write books like that without greatness—no matter what you say. You are a petulant child. Your father was a great man.

BORIS   It makes no difference how great he was—those pilgrims stank!

   (LEONIE *turns away*)

KENNETH   I suggest that to write that book, even if no one ever sees the manuscript but you, might amuse you—a kind of revenge which, when you were a boy, you were in no position to take.

BORIS   Are you trying to cure me, Doctor? Please don't trouble. I don't need your particular species of professionalism. I do not need any help from you.

(*He goes to door back, turns to* LEONIE. LEONIE *looks bewilderedly at* KENNETH. BORIS *goes out*)

LEONIE   How did you know? You're uncanny!

KENNETH   All in the day's work.

LEONIE   Why is it I always get myself involved with men weaker than myself? I certainly am no tower of strength.

KENNETH   Possibly not—but you are generous and impulsive. You have a tendency to accept people at the best of their own valuation.

LEONIE   I want to help them. I do help them. After they get used to my help, after they get to count on my help, I get impatient with them. Why, I ask myself, can't people help themselves?

KENNETH   And very natural.

LEONIE   I seem to attract people like that!

KENNETH   Leonie—you are the last woman on earth Count Mirsky should marry. He would only transfer his hatred of his father to you.

LEONIE   I don't think I understand you, Kenneth—really I don't—and I do so want to understand things.

KENNETH   Well—your charm, your gaiety, your position, your wealth, your beauty—these would oppress him. Again, he cannot be himself.—Or, if he is himself, it is to reveal his nonentity, his inferiority—again the secondary rôle—Leonie Frothingham's husband—the son of Count Mirsky—the husband of Leonie Frothingham. Again the shadow—again, eternally and always—nonexistence. Poor fellow.

(*Pause*)

LEONIE   I'm so grateful to you, Kenneth.

KENNETH   Nonsense. You mustn't be grateful to me because I—exercise my profession.

LEONIE   I want to express my gratitude—in some tangible form. I've been thinking of nothing else lately. I can't sleep for thinking of it.

KENNETH   Well, if it gives you insomnia, you'd better tell me about it.

LEONIE   I want to make it possible for you to realize your ambition.

KENNETH   Ambition? What ambition?

LEONIE   Ah! You've forgotten, haven't you? But you let it slip out one day—you pump me professionally—but I do the same to you—non-professionally.

KENNETH   You terrify me!

LEONIE   That night last winter when we went to dinner in that little restaurant where you go with your doctor friends . . . you told me your dream.

KENNETH   My censor must have been napping.

LEONIE   He was. Or she was. What sex is your censor?

KENNETH   That's none of your business.

LEONIE   I'm sorry.

KENNETH   Which of my dreams was I so reckless as to reveal to you?

LEONIE   To have a sanatorium of your own one day—so you can carry out your own ideas of curing patients.

KENNETH   Oh, that! Out of the question.

LEONIE   Why?

KENNETH   To do it on the scale I visualize would cost more than I'm ever likely to save out of my practice.

LEONIE   I'll give you the sanatorium. I've never given any-one anything like that before. What fun!

KENNETH   Will I find it all wrapped up in silver foil on Christmas morning?

LEONIE   Yes. You will! You will! We'll have a suite in it for Mr. X.—for all your anonymous friends—we'll entertain the whole alphabet!

KENNETH   You see, Leonie!

LEONIE   What do you mean? I thought you'd be—

KENNETH   Of course, it's terribly generous of you. I'm deeply touched. But . . .

LEONIE   But . . . ?

KENNETH   I'm a stranger to you.

LEONIE   Kenneth!

KENNETH   Outside of my professional relation—such as I have with scores of patients—little more than that.

LEONIE   I thought—

KENNETH   And yet you are willing to back me in a venture that would cost a sizeable fortune—just on that. Leonie! Leonie!

LEONIE   It would be the best investment I've ever made. Paula's always telling me I have no social consciousness. Well, this would be.—It would keep me from feeling so useless. I do feel useless, Kenneth. Please!

KENNETH   I'm sorry. I couldn't hear of it. Of course, it's out of the question.

LEONIE   It isn't. I can afford it. Why shouldn't I? It would be helping so many people—you have no right to refuse. It's selfish of you to refuse.

KENNETH   I distrust impulsive altruism. You will forgive me, Leonie, but it may often do harm.

LEONIE   How do you mean, Kenneth?

KENNETH   I gather you are about to endow a radical magazine for the *boys*—

LEONIE   Will and Dennis! I thought it would be nice to give them something to do!

KENNETH   Yes. You are prepared to back them in a publication which, if it attained any influence, would undermine the system which makes you and people like you possible.

LEONIE   But it never occurred to me anyone would read it.

KENNETH   There is a deplorably high literacy in this country. Unfortunately it is much easier to learn to read than it is to learn to think.

LEONIE   Well, if you don't think it's a good idea, Kenneth, I won't do it. But this sanatorium is different.

KENNETH   Why?

LEONIE   Because, if you must know it, it would be helping you—and that means everything in the world to me. There, I've said it. It's true! Kenneth—are you terrified?

KENNETH   You adorable child!

LEONIE   It's extraordinary, Kenneth—but you are the first strong man who's ever come into my life— (*Enter* PAULA, DENNIS, WILL, *door back*) Oh, I'm very glad to see you! Will! Hullo, Dennis. You all know Dr. Rice. Mr. Dexter. Mr. McCarthy. Sit down, everybody. Well, children, how is New York?

   (DENNIS *crosses down front of them to chair left by sofa and sits*)

WILL   Stifling, thank you.

LEONIE   Any luck yet?

WILL   I am available, but New York is dead to its chief opportunity.

LEONIE   Then you can stay here for a bit. You can both stay here.

DENNIS   That was all right when we were in college, Mrs. Frothingham. Can't do it now.

LEONIE   Oh, you're working. I'm so glad!

DENNIS   I beg your pardon. Did you say working?

LEONIE   Well, then! I don't see why you can't stay here and take a holiday.

WILL   From what?

LEONIE   Since none of you are doing anything in town, you might as well stay here and do nothing and be comfortable.

DENNIS   Yes, but it's an ethical question. When we're in New York doing nothing, we belong to the most respectable vested group going! The unemployed. As such we have a status, position, authority. But if we stay here doing nothing —what are we? Low-down parasites.

KENNETH   No jobs about anywhere, eh?

WILL   Extinct commodity.

DENNIS   I did pretty well last week.

LEONIE   Really?

DENNIS   I was rejected by seven newspapers—including the *Bronx Home News* and the *Yonkers Herald*—six magazines and trade papers—a total of twenty-eight rejections in all, representing a net gain over the previous week of seven solid rejections. I submit to you, gentlemen, that's progress—pass the cigars, Will.

LEONIE   Couldn't you stay here and be rejected by mail?

DENNIS   Doesn't give you that same feeling somehow—that good, rich, dark-brown sensation of not being wanted!

LEONIE   You know, Kenneth, in a curious way, Dennis reminds me a bit of Mr. X.

DENNIS   And who's X.?

LEONIE   A sporting acquaintance.

DENNIS   There's one thing I'd like to ask Dr. Rice. . . . Do you mind?

KENNETH   At your service.

DENNIS   (*Turning chair and facing* KENNETH *upstage*)   In the psychoanalytic hierarchy Freud is the god, isn't he?

KENNETH   Of one sect, yes.

DENNIS   Well, the original sect—

KENNETH   Yes. . . .

DENNIS   Now, every psychoanalyst has to have himself analyzed. That's true, isn't it, Doctor?

KENNETH   Generally speaking—yes.

DENNIS   As I understand it, the highest prices go to those nearest the Master himself.

KENNETH   This boy is irreverent . . .

DENNIS   I know whereof I speak. I prepared an article on the subject for *Fortune*.

WILL   Rejection number three hundred.

DENNIS   I am afraid, Will, that you are a success worshipper!

LEONIE   Dennis is an *enfant terrible,* and he exhausts himself keeping it up!

DENNIS   I have examined the racket with a microscopic patience and this I find to be true: at the top of the hierarchy is the Great Pan Sexualist of Vienna. To be an orthodox and accepted Freudian, you must have been analyzed by another of the same. Now, what I am burning to know is this: Who analyzed Sig Freud himself? Whom does he tell his repressions to? Why, the poor guy must be as lonely as hell!

LEONIE   What would you do with him, Kenneth? He has no repressions whatever!

KENNETH   He needs some badly.

LEONIE   I wonder what Dennis would confess to his psychoanalyst that he isn't always shouting to the world?

DENNIS   I'd make the psychoanalyst talk. (*To* KENNETH. *Beckoning*) Tell me, Doctor, what did you dream last night?

KENNETH (*Behind his cupped hand*)   Not in public.

DENNIS (*Rises and crosses straight right*)   You see—he's repressed! I tell you these psychoanalysts are repressed. They've got nobody to talk to! I'm going swimming. It's pathetic!
    (*He goes out*)

LEONIE   I'm going too. He makes me laugh. How about you, Kenneth?

KENNETH   Oh, I'll watch.

LEONIE (*To others*)   Come along with us. There's plenty of time for a swim before dinner.
    (KENNETH *starts out with* LEONIE—*stops on the way*)

KENNETH   I suppose you and your Irish friend edited the comic paper at college?

WILL   No, we edited the serious paper.

KENNETH   Just the same it must have been very funny.
    (*He goes out after* LEONIE)

WILL   Don't think that feller likes me much.

PAULA   You're psychic.

WILL   Well, for the matter of that I'm not crazy about him either.

PAULA   Don't bother him. Concentrate on me!

WILL   How are you, darling?

PAULA   Missed you.

WILL (*Pulls her to sofa and sits with her.* PAULA *left end sofa*) And I you. Pretty lousy in town without you.

PAULA   Oh, poor darling!

WILL   Although my star is rising. I did some book-reviews for the New York *Times* and the *New Masses*.

PAULA   What a gamut!

WILL   I made, in fact, a total of eleven dollars. The student most likely to succeed in the first four months since graduation has made eleven dollars.

PAULA   Wonderful!

WILL   My classmates were certainly clairvoyant. As a matter of fact, I shouldn't have told you. Now I'll be tortured thinking you're after me for my money.

PAULA   You'll never know!

WILL (*Putting arm around her shoulders and drawing her to him*) What've you been doing?

PAULA   Lying in the sun mostly.

WILL   Poor little Ritz girl.

PAULA   Wondering what you do every night.

WILL   Forty-second Street Library mostly. Great fun! Voluptuary atmosphere!

PAULA   Is your life altogether so austere?

WILL   Well, frankly no. Not altogether.

PAULA   Cad!

WILL   What do you expect?

PAULA   Loyalty.

WILL   I am loyal. But you go around all day job-hunting. You find you're not wanted. It's reassuring after that to find a shoulder to lean on, sort of haven where you *are* wanted. Even the public library closes at ten. You have to go somewhere. If I'm ever Mayor of New York, I'll have the public libraries kept open all night . . . the flop-houses of the intellectuals!

PAULA   Is it anyone special . . . ?

WILL   Just a generalized shoulder.

PAULA Well, you're going to have a special one from now on—mine! You know, the way you're avoiding the issue is all nonsense.

WILL You mean my gallant fight against you?

PAULA I've decided that you are conventional and bourgeois. You're money-ridden.

WILL Eleven dollars. They say a big income makes you conservative.

PAULA I don't mean your money. I mean—my money. It's childish to let an artificial barrier like that stand between us. It's also childish to ignore it.

WILL (*Rising*) I don't ignore it. That's what worries me. I count on it. Already I find myself counting on it. I can't help it. Sitting and waiting in an office for some big-wig who won't see me or for some underling who won't see me I think: "Why the Hell should I wait all day for this stuffed shirt?" I don't wait. Is it because of you I feel in a special category? Do I count on your money? Is that why I don't wait as long as the other fellow? There's one consolation: the other fellow doesn't get the job either. But the point is disquieting!

PAULA What a Puritan you are!

WILL (*Sitting beside her again*) Will I become an appendage to you—like your mother's men?

PAULA You're bound to—money or no money.

WILL (*Taking her into his arms*) I suppose I might as well go on the larger dole—

PAULA What?

WILL Once you are paid merely for existing—you are on the dole. I rather hoped, you know—

PAULA What?

WILL It's extraordinary the difference in one's thinking when you're in college and when you're out—

PAULA How do you mean?

WILL Well when I was in college, my interest in the—"movement"—was really impersonal. I imagined myself giving my energies to the poor and the downtrodden in my spare time. I didn't really believe I'd be one of the poor and downtrodden myself. In my heart of hearts I was sure I'd break through the iron law of Dennis's statistics and land a job somewhere. But I can't—and it's given a tremendous jolt to my self-esteem.

PAULA   But you'll come through. I'm sure of it. I wish you could learn to look at my money as a means rather than an end.

WILL   I'd rather use my own.

PAULA   You're proud.

WILL   I am.

PAULA   It's humiliating but I'm afraid I've got to ask you to marry me, Will.

WILL   It's humiliating but considering my feelings I see no way out of accepting you.

PAULA   You submit?

WILL   (*Kisses her hand*)   I submit.

PAULA   After a hard campaign—victory!

WILL   You *are* a darling.

PAULA   (*Getting up and crossing to center*)   I can't tell you what a relief it'll be to get away from this house.

WILL   Why?

PAULA   I don't know. It's getting very complicated.

WILL   Leonie?

PAULA   *And* Boris. *And* Dr. Rice. Funny thing how that man . . .

WILL   What?

PAULA   Makes you insecure somehow.

WILL   Supposed to do just the opposite.

PAULA   He answers every question—and yet he's secretive. I've never met a man who—who—

WILL   Who what?

PAULA   Really I can't stand Dr. Rice.

WILL   I believe he fascinates you.

PAULA   He does. I don't deny that. And I can't tell you how I resent it. Isn't it silly? (*The old lady* WYLER *in a wheel chair is propelled in by a nurse. The old lady is much wasted*

since the preceding summer; she is touched with mortality)
Granny!

MRS. WYLER Paula! How are you, my dear?

PAULA I came up to see you before, but you were asleep.

MRS. WYLER Nurse told me.

(*Exit* NURSE, *door left*)

PAULA You remember Will?

WILL How do you do, Mrs. Wyler?

MRS. WYLER Of course. How do you do, young man?

PAULA Well, this is quite an adventure for you, isn't it,
Granny?

MRS. WYLER You're the boy who was always so curious
about my youth.

WILL Yes.

MRS. WYLER I've forgotten most of it. Now I just live from
day to day. The past is just this morning. (*A moment's
pause*) And I don't always remember that very well. Aren't
there insects who live only one day? The morning is their
youth and the afternoon their middle age. . . .

PAULA You don't seem yourself today. Not as cheerful as
usual.

MRS. WYLER Can't I have my moods, Paula? I am pleased
to be reflective today. People are always sending me funny
books to read. I've been reading one and it depressed me.

PAULA Well, I'll tell you something to cheer you up, Granny
—Will and I are going to be married.

MRS. WYLER Have you told your mother?

PAULA Not yet. It's a secret.

(*Enter* KENNETH)

KENNETH Well, Mrs. Wyler! Wanderlust today?

MRS. WYLER Yes! Wanderlust!

KENNETH Paula, if you're not swimming, what about our
walk, and our daily argument?

MRS. WYLER What argument?

KENNETH Paula is interested in my subject. She hovers between skepticism and fascination.

PAULA No chance to hover today, Kenneth. Will's improving his tennis. Sorry.

KENNETH So am I.

MRS. WYLER I've a surprise for you, Paula.

PAULA What?

MRS. WYLER Your father's coming.

PAULA No!

MRS. WYLER Yes.

PAULA But how——! How do you know?

MRS. WYLER Because I've sent for him, and he wired me he's coming. He's driving from Blue Hill. He should be here now.

PAULA That's too——! Oh, Granny, that's marvelous! Will, let's drive out to meet him, shall we? Does Mother know?

MRS. WYLER I only had Sam's wire an hour ago.

PAULA Granny, you're an angel.

MRS. WYLER Not quite yet. Don't hurry me, child.

PAULA Come on, Will.
  (*Exit* PAULA *and* WILL)

MRS. WYLER I can see you are interested in Paula. You are, aren't you, Dr. Rice?

KENNETH Yes. She's an extraordinary child. Adores her father, doesn't she?

MRS. WYLER How would you cure that, Doctor?

KENNETH It's quite healthy.

MRS. WYLER Really? I was hoping for something juicy in the way of interpretation.

KENNETH Sorry!

MRS. WYLER What an interesting profession yours is, Dr. Rice.

KENNETH Why particularly?

MRS. WYLER Your province is the soul. Strange region.

KENNETH People's souls, I find are, on the whole, infinitely more interesting than their bodies. I have been a general practitioner and I know.

MRS. WYLER   These young people—don't they frighten you?

KENNETH   Frighten!

MRS. WYLER   They are so radical—prepared to throw everything overboard—every tradition—

KENNETH   Paula's friends have nothing to lose, any change would be—in the nature of velvet for them.

MRS. WYLER   What do you think of Will?

KENNETH   I'm afraid I've formed no strongly defined opinion on Will.

MRS. WYLER   Oh, I see— That is a comment in itself.

KENNETH   He's nondescript.

MRS. WYLER   Do you mean to point that out to Paula?

KENNETH   I don't think so. That won't be necessary.

MRS. WYLER   Why not?

KENNETH   Blood will tell.

MRS. WYLER   That's very gracious of you, Doctor. (*Pause*) And what do you think of Leonie?

KENNETH   Very endearing—and very impulsive.

MRS. WYLER   For example—I mean of the latter—

KENNETH   She offered to build me a sanatorium—a fully equipped modern sanatorium.

MRS. WYLER   Did she? Convenient for you.

KENNETH   Except that I refused.

MRS. WYLER   Wasn't that quixotic?

KENNETH   Not necessarily.
   (PAULA *and* SAM *enter, door back*)

PAULA   Here he is!

MRS. WYLER   Sam!

SAM   Louise!

PAULA   He wouldn't come if I'd ask him. He said so shamelessly. You know Dr. Rice?

SAM   Of course.

KENNETH   Excuse me.
   (KENNETH *goes out*)

SAM Well, Louise!

MRS. WYLER Hello, Sam.
  (SAM *kisses her*)

SAM How's she behaving?

PAULA Incorrigible. Dr. Prentiss tells her to rest in her room.
You see how she obeys him. She'll obey you though.

SAM Well, I'll sneak her away from Dr. Prentiss and take
her abroad.

MRS. WYLER I want to go to Ethiopia. Run along, dear. I
want to talk to Sam.

PAULA Keep him here, Granny. Pretend you're not feeling
well.

MRS. WYLER I'll try. (*Exit* PAULA *door back*) Well, Sam—

SAM I got your wire last night. Here I am.

MRS. WYLER It's nice of you.

SAM Oh, now, Louise. You know you're the love of my
life.

MRS. WYLER Yes, Sam, I know—but how is Selena?

SAM Flourishing.

MRS. WYLER You're all right then?

SAM Unbelievably.

MRS. WYLER I knew you would be.

SAM And you?

MRS. WYLER I'm dying, Sam.

SAM Not you—

MRS. WYLER Don't contradict me. Besides, I'm rather looking forward to it.

SAM Is Dr. Prentiss—?

MRS. WYLER Dr. Prentiss soft-soaps me. I let him. It relieves
his mind. But that's why I've sent for you.

SAM You know, my dear—

MRS. WYLER Yes, Sam. I know I can count on you. I'm
dying. And I'm dying alone. I have to talk to somebody.
You're the only one.

SAM Is anything worrying you?

MRS. WYLER   Plenty.

SAM   What, dear?

MRS. WYLER   The future. Not my own. That's fixed or soon will be. But Leonie's—Paula's—

SAM   Aren't they all right?

MRS. WYLER   I am surrounded by aliens. The house is full of strangers. That Russian upstairs; this doctor.

SAM   Rice? Are you worried about him?

MRS. WYLER   What is he after? What does he want? He told me Leonie offered to build him a sanatorium—

SAM   Did he accept it?

MRS. WYLER   No. He refused. But something tells me he will allow himself to be persuaded.

SAM   I don't think Rice is a bad feller really. Seems pretty sensible. Are you worried about this boy—Dexter, and Paula?

MRS. WYLER   Not in the same way. I like the boy. But Paula —I'm worried about what the money'll do to her. We know what it's done to Leonie. You know, Sam, in spite of all her romantic dreams Leonie has a kind of integrity. But I often wonder if she's ever been really happy.

SAM   Oh, now, Louise, this pessimism's unlike you—

MRS. WYLER   This money we've built our lives on—it used to symbolize security—but there's no security in it any more.

SAM   Paula'll be all right. I count on Paula.

MRS. WYLER   In the long run. But that may be too late. One can't let go of everything, Sam. It isn't in nature. That's why I've asked you to come. I want you to remain as executor under my will.

SAM   Well, I only resigned because—since I'm no longer married to Leonie—

MRS. WYLER   What has that got to do with it?

SAM   All right.

MRS. WYLER   Promise?

SAM   Certainly.

MRS. WYLER   I feel something dark ahead, a terror—

SAM   Now, now, you've been brooding.

MRS. WYLER   Outside of you—Will is the soundest person I'll leave behind me, the healthiest—but in him too I feel a recklessness that's just kept in—I see a vista of the unknown —to us the unknown was the West, land—physical hardship —but he's hard and bitter underneath his jocularity—he isn't sure, he says, what he is— Once he is sure, what will he do? —I want you to watch him, Sam, for Paula's sake.

SAM   I will.

MRS. WYLER   They're all strange and dark. . . . And this doctor. A soul doctor. We didn't have such things—I am sure that behind all this is a profound and healing truth. But sometimes truths may be perverted, and this particular doctor—how are we to know where his knowledge ends and his pretension begins? Now that I am dying, for the first time in my life I know fear. Death seems easy and simple, Sam—a self-indulgence—but can I afford it?

(*She smiles up at him. He squeezes her hand*)

SAM   Everything will be all right. Trust me.

MRS. WYLER   I do. (*A pause*) You'll stay the night?

SAM   Of course.

MRS. WYLER   Now I feel better.

SAM   That's right.
(*Pause*)

MRS. WYLER   I'd like to live till autumn.

SAM   Of course you will. Many autumns.

MRS. WYLER   Heaven forbid. But this autumn. The color— the leaves turn. (*Looking out window.* SAM *looks too*) The expression seems strange. What do they turn to?

SAM   (*Softly, helping her mood*)   Their mother. The earth.

MRS. WYLER   I'm happy now. I'm at peace.

SAM   (*Puts arm around her and draws her to him*)   That's better.

MRS. WYLER   (*Smiling up at him*)   It's very clever of me to have sent for you, Sam. I'm pleased with myself. Now, Sam, let 'em do their worst—

SAM   (*Smiling back at her and patting her hand*)   Just let 'em . . . !

CURTAIN

SCENE: *The same.*

Time: A few hours later—before dinner. LEONIE *is standing in doorway looking out.* BORIS *center; he is fatalistically quiet at first.*

BORIS What it comes to is this then! You're through with me. You want me to go!

LEONIE I'm no good to you! I can no longer help you.

BORIS Frustrated altruist!

LEONIE You hate me!

BORIS That would be encouraging!

LEONIE We have nothing more for each other.

BORIS Less than we had in the beginning!

LEONIE Less than I thought we had.

BORIS (*Walking toward her*) And the man of science?

LEONIE What?

BORIS (*Still bearing down on her*) This intricate man of science. You fluctuate so, Leonie.
  (*Facing her*)

LEONIE Please, Boris. I've failed. Can't we part—beautifully?

BORIS What do you want to do? Go out on the bay and say farewell before the villagers in a barge drawn by a flock of swans? Shall we have a little orchestra to play—with the strings sobbing—and the bassoon off key?

LEONIE You are bitter and cruel. Why? I've tried to help you. Why are you bitter?

BORIS (*Moving close to her*)   At least I'm honest. Can you say the same?

LEONIE (*Breaking away from him*)   I don't know what you mean by that.

BORIS (*Getting in front of her*)   Yes, you do.

LEONIE   You're eating yourself up. You're killing yourself. There's the great lovely world outside and you sit in your room hating—

BORIS   What do you recommend? Cold showers and Swedish massage? What does the man of science prescribe for me?

LEONIE   Why do you hate Kenneth so?

BORIS   I'm jealous, my dear!

LEONIE   Poor Boris. You're beyond a simple emotion like that, aren't you?

BORIS   I envy you, Leonie. All like you.

LEONIE   Do you?

BORIS   I envy all sentimental liars who gratify their desires on high principle. It makes all your diversions an exercise in piety. You're sick of me and want to sleep with the man of science. (LEONIE *turns away. He seizes her arms and turns her to him*) Does this suffice for you? No. It must be that you can no longer help me. (*Little silent laugh*) My sainted father was like that! God!

LEONIE   This is the end, Boris.

BORIS   Of course it is. I tell you this though: Beware of him, Leonie. Beware of him.

LEONIE   Your hatred of Kenneth—like all your hatreds— they're unnatural, frightening. I'm frightened of you.
  (*Turning from him*)

BORIS (*Crossing before her, closing door so she can't escape*) Much better to be frightened of him. You know what I think. What does he think? Does he tell you? Do you know?

LEONIE   Yes, I know.

BORIS   You know what he tells you. This clairvoyant who gets rich profoundly analyzing the transparent.
  (*Enter* KENNETH, *door back*)

KENNETH   Your mother would like to see you, Leonie.

LEONIE   Is she all right?

(BORIS *goes upstage to small table. Gets cigarette*)

KENNETH   Oh, very chipper. Mr. Frothingham is with her.

LEONIE   She sent for Sam, didn't she? I wonder why.

BORIS   Perhaps she felt the situation too complicated—even for *you,* Dr. Rice.

KENNETH   I don't think so.

BORIS   You are so Olympian, Dr. Rice. Would it be possible to anger you?

KENNETH   Symptoms, my dear Count, never anger me. I study them.

BORIS   Really, you are in a superb position. I quite envy you. One might cut oneself open in front of you—and it would be a symptom. Wouldn't it?

LEONIE   Boris, please—what's the good?

BORIS   (*Crossing slowly to* LEONIE)   You are quite right, my dear, no good—no good in the world. Give your mother this message for me. Tell her that under the circumstances I shall simplify the situation by withdrawing.

LEONIE   You make me very unhappy, Boris.

BORIS   How agreeable then that you have Dr. Rice here—to resolve your unhappiness.

(*Crosses quickly to table behind sofa and puts out cigarette*)

LEONIE   (*Following him*)   Where will you be in case I—in case you—Boris?

BORIS   Don't worry about me. A magazine syndicate has offered me a great deal for *sentimental* reminiscences of my father. Imagine that, sentimental! They have offered me—charming Americanism—a ghost-writer. It will be quaint—one ghost collaborating with another ghost. (*Raising hand like Greek priest*) My blessings, Leonie. (*Kisses her hand*) You have been charming. Dr. Rice—

(*He bows formally. Exit* BORIS)

LEONIE   Poor Boris—

(*She sinks into a chair, overcome*)

KENNETH   He's part of the past. You must forget him.

LEONIE   Poor Boris!

KENNETH   You will forget him.

LEONIE   I'll try.

KENNETH   Exorcised!

LEONIE   You know, Kenneth, I feel you are the only one in the world I can count on.

KENNETH   Not me.

LEONIE   Whom else?

KENNETH   Yourself!

LEONIE   Light reed! Fragile! Fragile!

KENNETH   Pliant but unbreakable.

LEONIE   No. Don't think much of myself, Kenneth. Really I don't. My judgment seems to be at fault somehow. Paula thinks so too. She's always lecturing me.
   (*Sits right end of sofa*)

KENNETH   Paula can't abide me.

LEONIE   It's not true!

KENNETH   You know, Leonie, I have an instinct in these matters—so, also, has your daughter.

LEONIE   Don't you like Paula?

KENNETH   I love her. Everyone connected with you.

LEONIE   Kenneth! How dear of you! Of course Paula and I are poles apart. Look at her friends!

KENNETH   Raffish!

LEONIE   (*A little taken aback by this*)   Oh, do you think so? All of them? Don't you like Will?

KENNETH   Nice enough. Clever in his way. With an eye to the main chance.

LEONIE   Really?

KENNETH   Naturally—penniless boy.

LEONIE   I've always encouraged Paula to be independent. I've never tried to impose my ideals or my standards on her. Have I done wrong to give her her own head this way? She's such a darling, really. She's killing, you know. So superior, so knowing. The other day—the other day, Kenneth . . . I took her to lunch in town and she criticized me—now what do you think about?

KENNETH (*Sitting on arm of chair*)   For once my intuition fails me.

LEONIE   About my technique with men. She said it was lousy. Isn't it delicious?

KENNETH   Not more specific than simply lousy?

LEONIE   She said I threw myself at men instead of reversing the process.

KENNETH   But I should think she would have approved of that. She makes such a fetish of being candid!

LEONIE   That's just what I said—exactly. I said I couldn't pretend—that I couldn't descend to—technique. I said that when my feelings were involved I saw no point in not letting the other person see it. I reproached her for deviousness. Strange ideas that child has—strange!

KENNETH   I'm afraid her generation is theory-ridden!
   (*Pause*)

LEONIE   Kenneth?

KENNETH   Yes, Leonie?

LEONIE   It's true of course.

KENNETH   What?

LEONIE   Paula's—criticism. I can't conceal my feelings. Least of all—from you.
   (*Slight pause*)

KENNETH   Why should you?

LEONIE   Oh, Kenneth, I'm so useless! You know how useless I am!

KENNETH   I know only that you are gracious and lovely— and that you have the gift of innocence.

LEONIE   I hate my life. It's been so scattered—emotionally.

KENNETH   Whose isn't?

LEONIE   You are such a comfort. Really it's too much now to expect me to do without you. Kenneth?

KENNETH   Yes . . . Leonie.

LEONIE   Will you be a darling—and marry me?

KENNETH   Leonie?

LEONIE (*Returning his gaze*)   Yes, Kenneth.

KENNETH   Have you thought this over?

LEONIE   It's the first time—the very first time—that I've ever been sure.

KENNETH   You are so impulsive, Leonie.

LEONIE   Kenneth, don't you think we'd have a chance—you and I—don't you think?

(*Enter* PAULA, *door back*)

PAULA   (*Realizes she has interrupted a tête-à-tête*)   Oh, sorry—!

LEONIE   Paula dear, have you been with Mother?

PAULA   Yes. Granny wants to see you, as a matter of fact.

LEONIE   Oh, I forgot! Is she all right? Cheerful?

PAULA   Oh, very.

LEONIE   I'll be right there. Stay and talk to Kenneth, Paula. He thinks you don't like him. Prove to him it isn't true. Do you think you could be gracious, Paula? Or is that too old-fashioned?

(*Exit* LEONIE *door back. In the following scene* PAULA *determines to get rid of the tantalizing and irritating mixed feelings she has about* KENNETH, *her sense of distrusting, disliking and simultaneously being fascinated by him— she feels he has something up his sleeve; she is playing a game to discover what it is and yet she becomes increasingly conscious that game is not unpleasant to her because of her interest in her victim*)

PAULA   Leonie's all a-flutter. What is it?

KENNETH   She was just telling me—she envies you your poise.

PAULA   Your intentions are honorable, I hope.

KENNETH   Old hat, Paula.

PAULA   I beg your pardon.

KENNETH   Undergraduate audacity. Scott Fitzgerald. Old hat.

PAULA   We don't like each other much, do we?

KENNETH   That's regrettable.

PAULA   And yet—I'm very curious about you.

KENNETH   What would you like to know?

PAULA   Your motive.

KENNETH   Ah!

PAULA   And yet even if you told me—

KENNETH   You wouldn't believe it?

PAULA (*Facing him*)   No. Now why is that? Even when you are perfectly frank your frankness seems to me—a device. Now why is that?

KENNETH   I'll tell you.

PAULA   Why?

KENNETH   Because you yourself are confused, muddled, unsure, contradictory. I am simple and co-ordinated. You resent that. You dislike it. You envy it. You would like such simplicity for yourself. But, as you are unlikely to achieve it, you soothe yourself by distrusting me.

PAULA   You say I'm muddled. Why am I muddled?

KENNETH   You've accepted a set of premises without examining them or thinking about them. You keep them like jewels in a box and dangle them. Then you put them back in the box, confident that they belong to you. But, as they don't, you feel an occasional twinge of insecurity—

PAULA   Do you mind dropping the parables—?

KENNETH   Not at all—

PAULA   Why am I muddled? For example—

KENNETH   You're a walking contradiction in terms—

PAULA   For example?

KENNETH   For example—for example—your radicalism. Your friends. Your point of view. Borrowed. Unexamined. Insincere.

PAULA   Go on.

KENNETH   You are rich and you are exquisite. Why are you rich and exquisite? (*Walking back to face her*) Because your forebears were not moralistic but ruthless. Had they been moralistic, had they been concerned, as you pretend to be, with the "predatory system"—this awful terminology—you'd be working in a store somewhere wrapping packages or waiting on querulous housewives with bad skins or teaching school.

Your own origins won't bear a moralistic investigation. You must know that. Your sociology and economics must teach you that.

PAULA   Suppose I repudiate my origins?

KENNETH   That takes more courage than you have.

PAULA   Don't be so sure.

KENNETH   But why should you? If you had a special talent or were a crusader there might be some sense in it. But you have no special talent and you are not a crusader. Much better to be decorative. Much better for a world starving for beauty. Instead of repudiating your origins you should exult in them and in that same predatory system that made you possible.

(Crossing to table behind sofa for cigarette)
(Pause)

PAULA   What were your origins?

KENNETH   *(Lighting cigarette)*   Anonymous.

PAULA   What do you mean?

KENNETH   I was discovered on a doorstep.

PAULA   Really?

KENNETH   Like Moses.

PAULA   Where were you brought up?

KENNETH   In a foundling asylum in New England. The place lacked charm. This sounds like an unpromising beginning but actually it was more stimulating than you might imagine. I remember as a kid of twelve going to the library in Springfield and getting down the *Dictionary of National Biography* and hunting out the bastards. Surprising how many distinguished ones there were and are. I allied myself early with the brilliant and variegated company of the illegitimate.

PAULA   You don't know who your parents were?

KENNETH   No.

PAULA   Did you get yourself through college?

KENNETH   *And* medical school.

PAULA   Did you practice medicine?

KENNETH   For a bit. I devoted myself—when the victims would let me—to their noses and throats. It was a starveling occupation. But I gave up tonsillectomy for the soul. The poor have tonsils but only the rich have souls. My instinct was justified—as you see.

PAULA You've gone pretty far.

KENNETH Incredible journey!

PAULA Having come from—from—

KENNETH The mud—?

PAULA Well—I should think you'd be more sympathetic to the under-dogs.

KENNETH No, why should I? The herd bores me. It interests me only as an indication of the distance I've traveled.

PAULA Will would say that you are a lucky individual who—

KENNETH Yes, that is what Will would say. It always satisfies the mediocrity to call the exceptional individual lucky.

PAULA You don't like Will?

KENNETH I despise him.

PAULA Why?

KENNETH I detest these young firebrands whose incandescence will be extinguished by the first job! I detest radicals who lounge about in country-houses.

PAULA You're unfair to Will.

KENNETH I have no interest in being fair to him. We were discussing you.

PAULA You are too persuasive. I don't believe you.

KENNETH My advice to you is to find out what you want before you commit yourself to young Mr. Dexter.

PAULA But I have committed myself.

KENNETH Too bad.

PAULA For him or for me?

KENNETH For both of you; but for him particularly.

PAULA Why?

KENNETH I see precisely the effect your money will have on him. He will take it and the feeling will grow in him that in having given it you have destroyed what he calls his integrity. He will even come to believe that if not for this quenching of initiative he might have become a flaming leader of the people. At the same time he will be aware that both these comforting alibis are delusions—because he has no integrity to speak of nor any initiative to speak of. Knowing they are lies he will only proclaim them the louder, cling to them the harder. He will hate you as the thief of his character—petty larceny, I must say.

PAULA (*Jumping up, taking several steps away from him*) That's a lie.

KENNETH Will is an American Puritan. A foreigner—Boris, for example—marries money, feeling that he gives value received. Very often he does. But young Dexter will never feel that—and maybe he'll be right.

PAULA You hate Will.

KENNETH You flatter him.

PAULA How did you get to know so much about people? About what they feel and what they will do?

KENNETH I began by knowing myself—but not lying to myself. (*A silence. He looks at her. He takes in her loveliness. He speaks her name, in a new voice, softly*) Paula—

PAULA (*She looks at him fixedly*) What?

KENNETH Paula—

PAULA What?

KENNETH Do you know me any better now? Do you trust me any better now?

PAULA I don't know.
     (*Enter* WILL)

KENNETH Paula, Paula, Paula— (PAULA *starts toward door back*) Don't go, Paula!

WILL Oughtn't you to be changing for dinner? (PAULA *stops upstage*) Hello, Doctor. What's the matter?

KENNETH May I congratulate him?

WILL What's he been saying?

KENNETH Paula told me she is going to marry you.

PAULA The doctor is a cynic.

KENNETH We were discussing the European and American points of view toward money marriages—There's a great difference. The European fortune-hunter, once he has landed the bag, has no more twinge of conscience than a big-game hunter when he has made his kill. The American—

WILL   Is that what you think I am, Doctor?

KENNETH (*To* PAULA *amiably*)   You see. He resents the mere phrase. But my dear boy, that is no disgrace. We are all fortune-hunters—

PAULA (*Pointedly*)   Not all, Kenneth—!

KENNETH   But I see no difference at all between the man who makes a profession of being charming to rich ladies—or any other—specialist. The former is more arduous.

PAULA   Are you defending Will or yourself?

KENNETH   I am generalizing. (*To* WILL) Congratulations! I admit that to scatter congratulations in this way is glib, but we live in a convention of glibness. Good God, we congratulate people when they marry and when they produce children—we skim lightly over these tremendous hazards—Excuse me.

(*Exit* KENNETH)

WILL   God damn that man!

PAULA   Will!

WILL   I can't stand him—not from the moment I saw him—because he's incapable of disinterestedness himself, he can't imagine it in others. He's the kind of cynical, sneering— He's a marauder. The adventurer with the cure-all. This is just the moment for him. And this is just the place!

PAULA   I've never seen you lose your temper before, Will.

WILL   You know why, don't you?

PAULA   Why?

WILL   Because he's right! While he was talking I felt like hitting him. At the same time a voice inside me said: Can you deny it? When I came in here he was saying your name. He was looking at you—it seems he hasn't quite decided, has he?

PAULA   I'm worried about him and Leonie—

WILL   He's got Leonie hook, line and sinker. That's obvious.

PAULA   She mustn't! Will, she mustn't!

WILL *You* can't stop it—you can't do anything for Leonie. Nobody can do anything for anybody. Nobody should try.

PAULA Will—you mustn't go back to New York. You must stay and help me.

WILL Sorry. Nothing doing.

PAULA Will!

WILL I have a feeling you'll rather enjoy saving Leonie from the doctor.

PAULA Will! That's not fair, Will!

WILL It may not be fair but it is obvious. Also, it is obvious that the doctor won't mind being saved.

PAULA It's lucky for both of us that one of us has some self-control.

WILL No, I won't stay here. I hate the place, I hate Dr. Rice, I hate myself for being here!

PAULA Don't let me down, Will—I need you terribly just now—

WILL (*At white heat*) I haven't quite the technique of fortune hunting yet—in the European manner. Which of the two is he after—you or Leonie? Will he flip a coin?

PAULA I hate you! I hate you!

WILL Well, we know where we are at any rate.

PAULA Yes. We do!
   (LEONIE *comes running in. She wears an exquisite summer evening frock. She is breathless with happiness*)

LEONIE Paula! Why aren't you dressed? I want you to wear something especially lovely tonight! Do you like this? It's new. I haven't worn it before. (*She twirls for them*) I've a surprise for you, Will. You'll know what it is in a minute. I was thinking of you and it popped into my mind. You know, Will, I'm very, very fond of you. And I think you are equally fond of me. I can't help liking people who like me. I suppose you think I'm horribly vain. But then, everybody's vain about something. (BUTLER *comes in with cocktails and sandwiches, to table right of fireplace*) If they're not, they're vain about their lack of vanity. I believe that's a mot! Pretty good for a brainless— Here, Will, have a cocktail— (WILL *takes cocktail*) Paula—what's your pet vanity? She thinks mine's my looks but it's not. If I had my way I shouldn't look at all the way I look.

(*Enter* DR. DEXTER, *door back. He wears a sea-green baggy dinner-suit; he looks as "hicky" and uncertain as ever*)

DEXTER Good evening, Mrs. Frothingham.

LEONIE Dr. Dexter—how good of you to come. Delighted to see you.

DEXTER Good evening. Hello, Will.

WILL Dad!

DEXTER Mrs. Frothingham invited me. Didn't you know?

LEONIE (*Takes* DEXTER'S *arm and goes to* WILL) You told me you had to leave tomorrow to visit your father in Brunswick so I just called him up in Brunswick—

DEXTER She sent the car all the way for me. Nice car. Great springs.

LEONIE (*To* WILL) Now you won't have to leave tomorrow. You can both spend the week-end here.

WILL (*Walking away a little right*) Awfully nice of you, Leonie.

LEONIE (*Following him*) (DEXTER *sits on sofa*) You see, Will, I leave the big issues to the professional altruists. I just do what I can toward making those around me happy. And that's *my* vanity!

(*Enter* DENNIS, *door back*)

DENNIS Well! Well! Fancy that now, Hedda!

LEONIE Oh, hello, Dennis, just in time for a cocktail.
(LEONIE *leads him over to sofa.* WILL *is isolated down right center*)

DENNIS (*To* DEXTER) How are you?

DEXTER (*Not friendly*) I'm all right.

DENNIS Complicated week-end! You and the Healer! Faraday and Cagliostro. That'll be something.

LEONIE (*Takes* DENNIS'S *arm*) Everybody tells me to like you, Dennis. I'm in such a mood that I'm going to make the effort.

DENNIS I've been waiting for this. I'm thrilled!

LEONIE (*Strolling with him across stage front*)   Something tells me you could be very charming if you wanted to. Tell me, Dennis, have you ever tried being lovable and sweet?

DENNIS   For you, Mrs. Frothingham, I would willingly revive the age of chivalry!

LEONIE   But there's no need of that. I just want you to be nice. Here, have a cocktail. Give you courage.

DENNIS   Just watch me from now on, Mrs. Frothingham.

LEONIE   I will. Passionately. (*Hands him cocktail*) I'll be doing nothing else.
(BUTLER *crosses back of sofa, offers* DEXTER *and* PAULA *cocktails.* DR. RICE *comes in*)

DENNIS (*Stage sigh*)   Ah-h-h! The doctor! Just in time to look at my tongue, Doctor.

KENNETH   That won't be necessary, young man. I can tell— It's excessive.

LEONIE (*Crossing to* KENNETH)   Kenneth—you remember Will's father—Dr. Dexter.

KENNETH   How do you do?
(*They shake hands. A second* BUTLER *has come in and he and* ROBERT *are passing cocktails and hors d'œuvres.* LEONIE *keeps circulating among her guests.* KENNETH *and* DEXTER *are in the center—*DENNIS, *obeying a malicious impulse, presides over them. Announces a theme on which he eggs them on to utter variations*)

DENNIS   A significant moment, ladies and gentlemen—the magician of Science meets the magician of Sex—The floating libido bumps the absolute! What happens?

DEXTER (*Cupping his hand to his ear*)   What?
(WILL *crosses to door and looks out moodily*)

DENNIS   The absolute hasn't got a chance. Isn't that right, Dr. Rice?

KENNETH   I shouldn't venture to contradict a young intellectual. Especially a very young intellectual.

LEONIE (*Crosses front of* KENNETH, *to* DENNIS)   There, you see, I'm afraid, after all, I'll have to give you up, Dennis. You can't be lovable. You can't be sweet.

DENNIS   But I didn't promise to be winsome to everybody, only to you.

LEONIE   You really must treat him, Kenneth. He has no censor at all.

DENNIS   My censor is the Catholic tradition. We Catholics anticipated both Marx and Freud by a little matter of nineteen centuries. Spiritually, we have a Communion in the Holy Ghost—Communion. As for Dr. Rice, he offers confession without absolution. He is inadequate.

(LEONIE *returns with tray of canapés*)

LEONIE   It seems such bad taste to discuss religion at cocktail time. Try a stuffed olive.

DEXTER   By the time you get your beautiful new world, true science will have perished.

LEONIE   Aren't you too pessimistic, Dr. Dexter? Too much science has made you gloomy. Kenneth, the depression hasn't stopped your work, has it? Depression or no depression—

(WILL *springs up*)

WILL   (*Tensely*) That's right, Leonie. (*Everyone faces* WILL) Depression or no depression—war or peace—revolution or reaction—Kenneth will reign supreme!

(KENNETH *stares at him.* WILL *confronts him*)

LEONIE   Will!

WILL   Yes, Leonie. His is the power and the glory!

LEONIE   Dennis, this is your influence—

WILL   I admire you unreservedly, Doctor. Of your kind you are the best. You are the essence.

KENNETH   You embarrass me.

WILL   Some men are born ahead of their time, some behind, but you are made pat for the instant. Now is the time for you—when people are unemployed and distrust their own capacities—when people suffer and may be tempted—when integrity yields to despair—now is the moment for you!

KENNETH   (*Strolling closer to him so they are face to face*) When, may I ask, is the moment for you—when if ever?

WILL   After your victory. When you are stuffed and inert with everything you want, then will be the time for me.

(*He goes out*)

PAULA (*Running after* WILL)   Will . . . Will . . . Will . . .
(*She follows him out*)

LEONIE (*Devastated by this strange behavior*)   What is it?
I don't like it when people stand in the middle of the floor
and make speeches. What's the matter with him? Dennis, do
you know?

DENNIS (*With a look at* KENNETH)   I can guess.

LEONIE   Has he quarreled with Paula? Paula is so inept.
She doesn't know how to . . . At the same time, if he had
a grievance, why couldn't he have kept it until after dinner?
(*Enter* ROBERT)

ROBERT   Dinner is served.
(*Exit* ROBERT)

LEONIE   Well, we'll do what we can. Sam is dining with
Mother in her room. Boris has a headache. Dennis, you and
Dr. Dexter—

DENNIS   You've picked me, Dr. Dexter. I congratulate you.

DEXTER   Thank God, I can't hear a word you say.
(*Exit* DEXTER, *door back*)

DENNIS (*Sadistically*)   Oh, yes, he can. And we'll fight it out
on these lines if it takes all dinner.
(*He follows* DEXTER *out*)

LEONIE   What extraordinary behavior! What do you suppose,
Kenneth—shall I go after them?

KENNETH   I wouldn't. It's their problem. Give them time.

LEONIE (*Reassured*)   You are so wise, Kenneth. How did I
ever get on without you? I have that secure feeling that you
are going to be my last indiscretion. When I think how
neatly I've captured you—I feel quite proud. I guess my
technique isn't so lousy after all.
(*She takes his arm and swings along beside him as they
waltz in to dinner*)

                                                    CURTAIN

ACT THREE

SCENE: *The same.*

Time: Late that fall. The trees have turned. The sumach have put out the brilliant red flowers of autumn.

At Rise: WILL *and* DENNIS *have just arrived, and are standing at fireplace, back.* LEONIE *comes in to greet them.* SAM *strolls in with her.*

LEONIE I'm so glad to see you! (*She shakes hands with each of them warmly*) Will! How are you? (*To* DENNIS) It's so good of you to come.

SAM (*Shaking hands with* WILL) Very glad to see you.

WILL Thanks.

(SAM *shakes hands with* DENNIS)

LEONIE Sam drove over for a few hours from Blue Hill to talk business to me. He hasn't had much luck so far. It's simply wonderful having you boys here—it's like old times. I didn't tell Paula. (*To* SAM) I did all this on my own. It's a surprise for Paula.

DENNIS She'll be overcome when she sees me. Maybe you should prepare her.

WILL Where is Paula?

LEONIE Isn't it provoking! She and Kenneth went for a walk. They should have been back long before this. (*Turning back to them*) Paula hasn't been at all herself, Will. I thought you would cheer her up.

DENNIS I will be glad to do what I can, of course. Several very stubborn cases have yielded to my charm.

LEONIE I'm sure! Do sit down.

(*She sits*)

350

DENNIS (*Taking out his pipe*) Do you mind?
  (WILL *sits*)

LEONIE Oh, please—I can't tell you how I appreciate your coming—

DENNIS (*The harassed businessman*) Well, as a matter of fact, Leonie, it wasn't easy to get away from the office—

LEONIE Are you in an office?

DENNIS Sometimes as many as fifteen in a day. (LEONIE *laughs*) But when I got your appealing letter—*and* the return tickets—I'm chivalrous at heart, you know, Leonie—

LEONIE I know you are!

SAM How's town?

WILL Very hot.

SAM I'm just on my way down. Stopped by to go over several things with Leonie—

LEONIE Poor Sam's been having an awful time with me. He keeps putting things in escrow. Where is escrow?

DENNIS It's where squirrels put nuts in the winter-time.

LEONIE I see! Dennis is much more lucid than you, Sam.

DENNIS I have a knack for making the abstruse translucent. Especially in economics. Now, would you like to know why England went off gold?

LEONIE No, I wouldn't.

DENNIS I shall yield to your subconscious demand and tell you.

LEONIE (*To others*) Help!

DENNIS I see that there is no audience for my peculiar gift.

LEONIE You know, Will, I've thought perhaps you were angry with us.

WILL Why?

LEONIE You haven't been here for so long. (*To* SAM) Since Granny died—none of them have been here. Did Paula write you about Granny's funeral?

WILL No. She didn't.

LEONIE Of course I hate funerals—I can't bear them—but this was so—natural. Mother wanted to live till the fall and she did. It was a dreaming blue sky and there was that poignant haze over the hills and over the bay, and the smell of burning wood from somewhere. Burning wood never smells at any other time the way it does in Indian summer. And the colors that day! Did you ever, Sam, see such a day?

SAM   It was beautiful.

LEONIE   They say the colors of autumn are the colors of death, but I don't believe that. They were in such strength that day. I cried—but not on account of Mother—that kind of day always makes me cry a little bit anyway. You couldn't cry over consigning anyone you loved to an earth like that—on a day like that. I put some blazing leaves over her, but when I passed there the other day, they were withered and brown—

SAM (*Chiding her*)   Now Leonie—

LEONIE   Sam thinks I shouldn't talk about Mother. But I don't see why. She doesn't depress me. I think of her with joy. She had a wonderful life.

SAM   She was a wonderful woman.

LEONIE (*To* WILL)   Imagine, Will—when Sam was here last time—you were here that week-end—she *knew*. She asked Sam to be executor of her will.

SAM (*Very annoyed at her for bringing this up*)   Leonie—

LEONIE   Why didn't you tell me, Sam, then?

SAM   Seemed no point.

LEONIE   She didn't want me to know, did she?

SAM   No. She didn't want to distress you.
  (*A moment's pause*)

LEONIE   What can be keeping Paula? (*She glances out of the window*) Sam, do you want to talk business to me some more?

SAM   I'd like to talk to Will a minute.

LEONIE   Oh—yes. Well, Dennis, wouldn't you like me to show you to your room?
  (*She rises, goes to door into hallway.* DENNIS *follows*)

DENNIS   Thanks. I've got to answer a chain letter.

LEONIE   I've given you a room you've never had. The tower room.

DENNIS   Is it ivory? I won't be comfortable if it isn't ivory.

LEONIE   Well just this once you're going to be uncomfortable—and like it!

(*She goes out*)

DENNIS (*Tragically*)   And for this I gave up a superb view of the gas-house on 149th Street.

(*He goes out*)

SAM (*Rises and goes up toward fireplace*)   Will—

WILL   Yes, Mr. Frothingham.

SAM   Oh—call me Sam.

WILL   All right.

SAM   I'll have to be pushing off in an hour or so. I rather wanted to talk to you.

WILL   Yes—

SAM (*Wipes his forehead*)   Gosh, Leonie's a difficult woman to talk business to.

(*Sits*)

WILL   I can imagine that. She's not interested in business.

SAM   *She—is—not!!!*

WILL   What do you want to speak to me about?

SAM   Paula.

WILL   What about Paula?

SAM   As I'm her father—I hope you won't think me—

WILL   Of course not—

SAM   It's not altogether easy—

WILL   Do you want me to help you?

SAM   Yes. I wish you would!

WILL   You're worried about Paula and me, aren't you? So was her grandmother. You think me irresponsible. Less responsible for example— (*As if making a random comparison*) than Dr. Rice?

SAM   Well, as a matter of fact, I've rather gotten to know Dr. Rice, and in many respects, he's a pretty sound feller. (*Rising and going to stand above* WILL) Hang it all, Will, I like you, and I don't like to preach to you, you know.

WILL   Go on.

SAM   Well, there are—from my point of view at least—a lot of nonsensical ideas knocking about. I'd like to point out just one thing to you. Your radicalism and all that—Well, the point is this—if you marry Paula—and I hope you do, because I like you—and, what is more important, Paula likes you—you'll have responsibilities. Paula will be rich. Very rich. Money means responsibility. Now, I shouldn't, for example, like you to start radical magazines with it. I shouldn't like you to let the money drift through your fingers in all sorts of aimless, millennial directions that won't get anywhere.

WILL   Who told you that was my intention?

SAM   A little bird.

WILL   With a black moustache?

SAM   Does that matter?

WILL   No.

SAM   (*Putting hand on* WILL'S *shoulder*)   As a matter of fact, I'm not worried about you at all. Money, I expect, will do to you what getting power does to radical opposition, once it gets office—

WILL   Emasculate me, you mean?

SAM   Well, hardly. Mature you. Once you're rich yourself, I have no doubt you'll be—

WILL   Sound.

SAM   Yes. Sound. But your friends—this McCarthy boy—

WILL   Well, I can easily cut Dennis—all my poor and unsound friends—

SAM   (*Quietly*)   I'm sorry you're taking this tone with me, Will. I'm the last person in the world to ask you to drop anybody. I'd be ashamed of you if you did. Only—

WILL   Only?

SAM   I must tell you that I am in position—by virtue of the will left by Mrs. Wyler—to keep Paula's money from being used for any purpose that might be construed as—subversive.

WILL   From whose point of view?

SAM (*Quietly*) From mine.

WILL   I see.

SAM   Possibly you may not believe this—but I trust you, Will. Mrs. Wyler trusted you.

WILL   You needn't worry. Paula seems to have other interests apparently.

SAM   What do you mean?

WILL   Sounder interests—
(DENNIS *enters, through door back*)

DENNIS   The tower room lets in light on four sides, but nothing to look at. Just the sea and the landscape.

SAM   What did you do with Leonie?

DENNIS   She's gone to her mother's room to potter around.

SAM   Maybe I can get her attention while she's pottering. Excuse me.
(SAM *goes out*)

DENNIS   Poor Leonie—she's the last of the lovely ladies. The inheritance taxes'll get 'em soon. You know we were by way of getting our magazine from Leonie when Dr. Rice spiked our guns. So I'm leaving. My time is too valuable. But the Healer won't last forever, and when he goes, I shall return. Take heart, my good man. I know you feel a little tender about doing this, but remember, my lad, it's the Cause that counts. Remember what Shaw says: "There is no money but the devil's money. It is all tainted and it might as well be used in the service of God." (*A moment*—WILL *is obviously thinking of something else*) What's the matter?

WILL   Nothing.

DENNIS (*Bringing down chair to sit left of* WILL *he imitates* RICE'S *manner*) Now you must speak, young man—how can I sublimate your subconscious troubles, if you won't speak? Are you unhappy about Paula, my lad? (*No answer*) Tell me what's happened between you—relieve your soul, and, as a reward, I may make you co-editor of our magazine. (*No response. He rises and walks to opposite side of table*) No? Assistant editor you remain. I may even fire you. Yes, I think I will fire you. (*Crossing in front of* WILL *to fireplace*) Dexter—you're through. Go upstairs and get your check.

(*Rubs his hands together in glee*) God, it gives me a sense of power to fire a man—especially an old friend!

(PAULA *and* KENNETH *come in door right from the garden*)

PAULA (*Amazed to see them*) Will! But how—! Dennis!

WILL (*Rather coolly*) Hello, Paula.

DENNIS We came to surprise you. Now that we have surprised you, we can go home.

WILL Leonie asked me to come.

PAULA Oh. Well, it's very nice to see you.

WILL Thanks.

PAULA When I wired you to come a few weeks ago, you were too busy. It takes Leonie, doesn't it?

DENNIS You should have tried me, Paula. Hello, Dr. Rice. How's business? Any suppressions today?

KENNETH (*Significantly*) Apparently not.

DENNIS Well, come on up to my room, Doctor, and we'll play Twenty Questions.

(*He goes out*)

WILL Hello, Dr. Rice.

KENNETH How are you?

PAULA Will—I'm awfully glad to see you. I was just going to write you to thank you for the sweet letter you sent me after Granny died.

KENNETH I'm afraid it's my fault, Dexter. I do my best to keep Paula so busy that she finds no time to write letters.

WILL I was sure I could count on you, Doctor.

(WILL *goes out*)

PAULA You enjoy hurting Will, don't you?

KENNETH When there is an obstacle in my path, I do my best to remove it.

PAULA What makes you think it is only Will that stands between us— That if left to myself I—

KENNETH Because it is true. Were it not for the squids of idealistic drivel spouted around you by Will and his friends, there would be no issue at all between us. I resent even an imputed rivalry with someone I despise.

PAULA Rivalry?

KENNETH Paula— There's no reason any longer why I shouldn't tell you the truth.

PAULA What is it, Kenneth?

KENNETH (*After a moment—slowly*) Do you know what I feel like? I feel like a man on a great height, irresistibly tempted to jump over. Do you want the truth really? (*She says nothing. Somehow his words, his voice, his attitude make her feel that really now he may reveal something which before he wouldn't have revealed. He is in a trance-like state almost; she feels it; she is rather horribly fascinated—somehow, though she distrusts him utterly, some instinct tells her that, at this moment actually he is tempted by a force, disruptive to himself, to tell her the truth*) Don't you know it? Don't you feel it? (*Pause*) Haven't you known it? Haven't you felt it? (*A moment's pause*) I love you.

PAULA What?

KENNETH I love you.
(*A pause. She is too stupefied to speak. She too is under a spell. She is fascinated by him—by the enormity of this. She rises, walks away from him to stand by sofa*)

PAULA I suppose I should be afraid of you. I'm not afraid of you.

KENNETH I am afraid of you. You tempt me to venture the impossible. That is impractical. And I have always been eminently practical.

PAULA I'm sure you have.
(*She feels herself talking automatically, as if out of a hypnotic state—at the same time some vanity and shrewdness keeps pounding inside her: "See how far he will go —see how far he will go!"*)

KENNETH I have lived by a plan. The plan has matured. But I have yearned for a face that would give me joy, for the voice that would soothe me. It is your face. It is your voice.
(PAULA *is fighting not to scream; at the same time she is caught in a nightmarish fascination*)

PAULA (*Very faintly*) Don't you love Mother?

KENNETH No. (*A moment's pause*) You are the youth I have never had, the security I have never had—you are the home I have hungered for. (*Moves toward her—stands over her and a little back*) That I am standing near you now, that I have achieved a share in your life, that you are listening to me, that you are thinking of me and of what I am, to the exclusion of everything else in the whirling universe —this is a miracle so devastating, that it makes any future possible—Paula—

PAULA What?

KENNETH Paula!

PAULA What *is* it!

KENNETH (*Bending over her*) Paula . . . (*It is as if he got a sexual joy from saying her name*) I love your name. I love to say your name.

PAULA I *am* afraid of you. I'm sorry for you.

KENNETH Do you think me insane?

PAULA Yes.

KENNETH Because I am ambitious, because I am forthright, because I deal scientifically with the human stuff around me —you think me insane. Because I am ruthless and romantic, you think me insane. This boy you think you love—who spends his time sniveling about a system he is not strong enough to dominate—is he sane?

PAULA I don't expect you to—

KENNETH When I hear the chatter of your friends, it makes me sick. While they and their kind prate of co-operative commonwealths, the strong man takes power, and rides over their backs—which is all their backs are fit for. Never has the opportunity for the individual career been so exalted, so infinite in its scope, so horizontal. House-painters and minor journalists become dictators of great nations. (*With puckish humor—leaning on arm of her chair*) Imagine what a really clever man could do! See what he has done! (*He smiles, makes a gesture of modest self-assertion, indicating the room as part of his conquest. She laughs, rather choked and embarrassed. He goes on*) And this I have done alone. From an impossible distance—I have come to you, so that when I speak, you can hear. What might we not do together, Paula—you and I—

(*To her surprise,* PAULA *finds herself arguing an incon-*

ceivable point. She loathes the strange fascination she feels in this man, and yet is aware that it might turn to her advantage)

PAULA We don't want the same things.

KENNETH You want what everyone wants who has vitality and imagination—new forms of power—new domains of knowledge—the ultimate sensations.

PAULA You *are* romantic, aren't you?

KENNETH Endlessly. And endlessly—realistic. (*Staring at her*) What are you thinking?

PAULA (*Shrewd against him—against herself*) I keep thinking—what you want now—what you're after now?

KENNETH (*Moving toward her*) You don't believe then—that I love you?

PAULA (*Leaning back in chair—not looking at him*) You are a very strange man.

KENNETH I am simple really. I want everything. That's all!

PAULA And you don't care how you get it.

KENNETH Don't be moralistic, Paula—I beg you. I am directly in the tradition of your own marauding ancestors. They pass now for pioneers—actually they fell on the true pioneers, and wrested what they had found away from them, by sheer brutal strength. I am doing the same thing—but more adroitly.

PAULA Why are you so honest with me?

KENNETH (*With his most charming smile*) Perhaps because I feel that, in your heart, you too are an adventurer.
    (*A pause. During these half-spell-bound instants a thought has been forming slowly in* PAULA'S *mind that crystallizes now. This man is the enemy. This man is infinitely cunning, infinitely resourceful. Perhaps—just the possibility— he really feels this passion for her. If so, why not use this weakness in an antagonist so ruthless? She will try*)

PAULA I shouldn't listen to you—
    (*A moment. He senses her cunning. He looks at her*)

KENNETH You don't trust me?

PAULA Have I reason to trust you?

KENNETH   What reason would you like? What proof would you like?

PAULA   Aren't you going to marry Mother?

KENNETH   Only as an alternative.

PAULA   Will you—tell her so? Will you give up the alternative?

KENNETH   And if I do?

PAULA   What shall I promise you?

KENNETH   Yourself.

PAULA (*Looks at him—speaks*)   And if I do?

KENNETH   Then . . .

PAULA (*Taking fire*)   You say you love me! If you feel it —really feel it— You haven't been very adventurous for all your talk! Taking in Mother and Sam! Give up those conquests. Tell her! Tell Mother! Then perhaps I will believe you.

KENNETH   And then?

PAULA   Take your chances!

KENNETH (*Quietly*)   Very well.

PAULA   You will?

KENNETH   I will.

PAULA   You'll tell Mother—you love me?

KENNETH   Yes.

PAULA (*Going to the foot of the stairs, calls*)   Mother! Mother!

LEONIE (*Offstage*)   Yes, Paula. I'm coming right down! I've the most marvelous surprise for you! Wait and see!
(PAULA *walks to end of sofa—looking at* KENNETH. LEONIE *comes in. She is wearing an exquisite old-fashioned silk wedding-dress which billows around her in an immense shimmering circle. She is a vision of enchantment*)

LEONIE (*In a great flurry of excitement*)   Children, look what I found! It's Mother's. It's the dress she was married in. I was poking around in Granny's room while Sam was talking to me about bonds, and I came upon it. Do you like it, Kenneth? Isn't it adorable? Have you ever . . . What's the matter? Don't you like it?

PAULA   It's very pretty.

LEONIE   (*Overwhelmed by the inadequacy of this word*) Pretty! Pretty! (*She hopes for more from* KENNETH) Kenneth . . . ?

KENNETH   It's exquisite.

LEONIE   Isn't it? (*She whirls around in the dress*) Isn't it? Yes. Exquisite. Can you imagine the scene? Can you imagine Granny walking down the aisle—and all the august spectators in mutton-chop whiskers and Prince Alberts? We've lost something these days—a good deal—oh, I don't miss the mutton-chops—but in ceremony, I mean—in punctilio and grace. . . .

PAULA   (*Cutting ruthlessly through the nostalgia*)   Mother!

LEONIE   What is it, Paula?

PAULA   Kenneth has something to tell you.

LEONIE   Kenneth?

PAULA   Yes. He has something to tell you.

LEONIE   Have you, Kenneth?

KENNETH   Yes.

LEONIE   What is it?

KENNETH   (*Quietly*)   I love Paula. I want to marry Paula. (*A pause. Granny's wedding-dress droops*)

LEONIE   Do you mean that, Kenneth?

KENNETH   Yes.

LEONIE   (*Piteously*)   This isn't very nice of you, Paula.

PAULA   I had nothing to do with it. I loathe Kenneth. But I wanted you to know him. Now you see him, Mother, your precious Lothario—there he is! Look at him!

LEONIE   These clothes are picturesque, but I think our modern ones are more comfortable. I think—I feel quite faint—isn't it ridiculous?

(*She sways*)

PAULA   I'm sorry, Mother. I had to. But I love you. I really do.

LEONIE   (*Very faint*)   Thank you, Paula.

PAULA   You'd better go up and lie down. I'll come to you in a moment.

LEONIE   Yes. I think I'd better. Yes.
(*She begins to sob; she goes out, hiding her face in the lace folds of her dress.* PAULA, *having gone with her to the door, rings bell for* ROBERT, *turns to* KENNETH)

PAULA   I suppose you're going to tell me this isn't cricket. Well, don't, because it will only make me laugh. To live up to a code with people like you is only to be weak and absurd.

KENNETH   (*His voice is low and even but tense with hate*) You, Miss Frothingham, are my *last* miscalculation. I might even say my first. Fortunately, not irreparable!
(ROBERT *enters*)

PAULA   Robert.

ROBERT   Yes, Miss Frothingham.

PAULA   (*Still staring fixedly at* KENNETH)   Dr. Rice is leaving. Will you see that his bags are packed, please?

ROBERT   Yes, Miss.
(*He goes out*)

KENNETH   Forgive me—for having over-estimated you.
(*He goes out door right.* PAULA *comes slowly down and sits on sofa. She gets a reaction herself now from all she has been through; this game hasn't been natural to her; she is trembling physically; she is on the verge of tears.* WILL *comes in*)

PAULA   Will—Will darling—
(*She clings to* WILL)

WILL   (*Worried*)   Paula!

PAULA   Put your arms around me, Will—hold me close—
(WILL *obeys*)

WILL   What's happened?

PAULA   I've tricked him. I made him say in front of Mother that he loved me, that he wanted to marry me. Poor Leonie! But it had to be done! And do you know, Will—at the end I felt—gosh, one has so many selves, Will. I must tell you—for the—well, for the completeness of the record—

WILL   (*Curious*)   What?

PAULA   At the end I felt I had to do it—not only to save Leonie—but to save myself. Can you understand that? I felt horribly drawn to him, and by the sordid thing I was doing— But it's over. Thank God it's over. Will, darling, these six weeks have been hell without you. When I got your letter about Granny, I sat down and cried. I wanted to go right to New York to be with you. And yet I couldn't. How could I? But now, Will—I don't want to wait for you any longer. I've done what I can. It's cost me almost— Will—I need you terribly—

WILL   And I you, Paula. But listen, darling—I've decided during the weeks I've been away from you— I can't marry you now— I can't face what I'd become—

PAULA   But Will, I— (*Springing up*) But Will, I'll give up the money. I'll live with you anywhere.

WILL   I know that, Paula. But I mustn't. You mustn't let me. I've thought it all out. You say you'd live with me anywhere. But what would happen? Supposing I didn't get a job? Would we starve? We'd take fifty dollars a week from your grandmother's estate. It would be foolish not to. Taking fifty, why not seventy-five? Why not two hundred? I can't let myself in for it, Paula. (*A long pause*) Paula, darling—do you hate me?

PAULA   No.

WILL   Supposing you weren't rich? Is it a world in which, but for this, I'd have to sink? If it is, I'm going to damn well do what I can to change it. I don't have to scrabble for the inheritance of dead men. That's for Kenneth—one robber baron—after the lapse of several generations—succeeding another. I don't want this damn fortune to give me an unfair advantage over people as good as I am who haven't got it. (*Torn with pity for her*) Paula—my dearest—what can I do?

PAULA   I see that you can't do anything. I quite see. Still—

WILL   I love you, Paula, and I'll be longing for you terribly, but I can't marry you—not till there's somebody for you to marry. When I've struck my stride, I won't care about Sam, or the money, or anything, because I'll be on my own. If you feel the way I do, you'll wait.

PAULA   (*Very still voice*)   Of course, Will. I'll wait.

WILL   (*Overcome with gratitude and emotion—seizes her in his arms passionately*)   Darling—darling—
       (LEONIE *comes in.* WILL, *overcome with emotion, goes out*)

LEONIE   It's easy to say "lie down." But what happens then?
Thoughts assail you. Thoughts . . .

PAULA   Mother . . .

LEONIE   Kenneth's going. He's leaving. I suppose you're
happy. It's the end—the end of summer.

PAULA (*Herself shaken with emotion*)   Mother—
    (*She wants to talk to* LEONIE, *to tell her what has hap-
    pened, but* LEONIE *is lost in her own maze*)

LEONIE   It's cold here. I hate this place. I'm going to sell it.
(*She sits, in chair, right of fireplace*) I've always wanted
things around me to be gay and warm and happy. I've done
my best. I must be wrong. Why do I find myself this way?
With nothing. With nothing.

PAULA (*Running to her mother and throwing herself on her
knees beside her*)   Mother—Mother darling—

LEONIE (*Not responding, reflectively*)   I suppose the thing
about me that is wrong is that love is really all I care about.
(*A moment's pause*) I suppose I should have been interested
in other things. Good works. Do they sustain you? But I
couldn't somehow. I think when you're not in love—you're
dead. Yes, that must be why I'm . . .
    (*Her voice trails off rather.* PAULA *drops her head in her
    mother's lap and begins to cry*)

LEONIE (*Surprised*)   Paula—what is it? What's the matter?
Are you sorry? It's all right, child.

PAULA (*Through her tears*)   It's Will—

LEONIE   Will?

PAULA   He's going away.

LEONIE   Why don't you go with him?

PAULA   He doesn't want me.

LEONIE   That's not true. It must be something else.

PAULA   The money.

LEONIE   Oh, the money. Yes, the money. The money won't
do anything for you. It'll work against you. It's worked
against me. It gives you the illusion of escape—but always
you have to come back to yourself. At the end of every journey—you find yourself.

PAULA   What shall I do, Mother?

LEONIE   You and Will want the same things. In the end you will find them. But don't let him find them with someone else. Follow him. Be near him. When he is depressed and discouraged, let it be your hand that he touches, your face that he sees.

PAULA   (*Breathless*)   Mother—you're right—he told me last summer—"you must have a shoulder to lean on"—

LEONIE   Let it be your shoulder, Paula; follow him. Be near him.

PAULA   Thank you, Mother.

LEONIE   (*Ruefully*)   I am telling you what *I* should do. It must be bad advice.

PAULA   (*Gratefully*)   Darling!
   (DENNIS *and* WILL *come in*)

DENNIS   Here you are! We're off to the boat! Thirty minutes! Why don't you and Paula come too? What do you say, Leonie?

LEONIE   You know, all these years I've been coming up here, and I've never been on the Bar Harbor boat.

DENNIS   It may be said, Mrs. Frothingham, if you have never been on the Bar Harbor boat, that you have not lived!

LEONIE   Really! I'd always heard it was poky.

DENNIS   Poky! The *Normandie* of the Kennebec poky! Mrs. Frothingham!

LEONIE   It's fun, is it? But doesn't it get into New York at some impossible hour?

DENNIS   At seven A.M.

LEONIE   Seven!
   (*She shudders*)

DENNIS   (*The brisk executive*)   Seven! Yes, sir! At my desk at nine! All refreshed and co-ordinated and ready to attack my South American correspondence.

LEONIE   I must learn not to believe him, mustn't I?

DENNIS   I am my own master, Leonie. All day for nine mortal hours I grind out escape fiction for the pulp magazines. But one day I shall become famous and emerge into the slicks and then I doubt very much whether I shall come here.

LEONIE   I shall miss you.

DENNIS   Then I'll come.

LEONIE   I hate to have you go, Dennis. You cheer me up. Why don't you stay?

DENNIS   Impossible, Leonie. I must go to New York to launch the magazine. But for the moment, good-bye, Leonie. As a reward for your hospitality I shall send you the original copy of one of my stories. Would you like to escape from something?

LEONIE   (*Smiling wanly*)   I would indeed!

DENNIS   Think no more about it. You're as good as free. The story is yours, typed personally on my Underwood. Those misplaced keys—those inaccuracies—how they will bemuse posterity!
   (*He goes out*)

WILL   (*Awkwardly*)   Good-bye, Leonie.

LEONIE   Good-bye, Will.
   (*He goes out without looking at* PAULA. *In pantomime,* LEONIE *urges* PAULA *to go after him.* PAULA *kisses her quickly and runs out after* WILL. *Left alone,* LEONIE *walks to the chair in which her mother sat so often—she looks through the glowing autumn at the darkening sea.* KENNETH *comes in. There is a pause*)

KENNETH   Leonie—

LEONIE   Yes, Kenneth.

KENNETH   I don't expect you to understand this. I shall not try to make you understand it.

LEONIE   Perhaps I'd better not.

KENNETH   Really I am amused at myself—highly entertained. That I should have almost had to practice on myself what hitherto I have reserved for my patients—that I who have made such a fetish of discipline and restraint so nearly succumbed to an inconsistency. I must revise my notion of myself.

LEONIE   And I too.

KENNETH   Why? Why you?

LEONIE   I seem to be a survival—Paula's directness—and your calculations—they are beyond me.

KENNETH Nevertheless, it's curious how you and Paula are alike—no wonder that, for a moment at least, you seemed to me—interchangeable.

LEONIE Did you know it from the beginning—that it was Paula?

KENNETH I was attracted by her resemblance to you—for exercising this attraction I hated her. She felt it too—from the beginning and she must have hated me from the beginning. Between us there grew up this strange, unnatural antagonism—

LEONIE What?

KENNETH This fused emotion of love and hate. It had to be brought out into the open. It's a familiar psychosis—the unconscious desire of the daughter to triumph over the mother.

LEONIE But I don't understand—

KENNETH There is so much in these intricate relationships that the layman can't understand—

LEONIE You mean that you—felt nothing for Paula?

KENNETH No, I don't mean that at all. But I saw that what I felt for her was some twisted reflection of what I felt for you. And I saw there was only one way out of it—to let her triumph over you. I told her that I loved her. But this was not enough. I must repeat it in front of you. You must witness her triumph. I made it possible. I gave her her great moment. Well, you see what it's done. It freed her so beautifully that she was able to go to Will. They've gone away together. Perfect cure for her as well as for myself.

(*A moment's pause*)

LEONIE It all sounds almost too perfect, Kenneth.

KENNETH I said I didn't expect you to understand it—you have lived always on your emotions. You have never bothered to delve beneath them. You are afraid to, aren't you?

LEONIE I know this, Kenneth. I heard you say that you loved Paula. I heard your voice. No, I can't accept this, Kenneth! It's not good enough. I've never done that before. I'd only think now that everything you did, everything you said, was to cover what you felt. And I'd end by telling myself that I believed you. I'd end by taking second best from you. No, I must guard myself from that. I felt this a month ago—that's why I sent for Will.

KENNETH   Some day, Leonie, you will learn that feeling is not enough.

LEONIE   But I trust my instinct, Kenneth.

KENNETH   That, Leonie, is your most adorable trait—

LEONIE   What?

KENNETH   That trust—that innocence. If it weren't for that, you wouldn't be you—and everyone wouldn't love you—

LEONIE   Oh, no, Kenneth—
  (DENNIS *comes in*)

DENNIS   Oh, excuse me. But I left my brief-case. Oh, here it is. (*He picks it up*) Without my brief-case I am a man without a Destiny. With it I am—

KENNETH   A man with a brief-case.

LEONIE   (*Crossing rather desperately to* DENNIS—*this straw in the current*)   What's in it—your stories?

DENNIS   Stories—no, that wouldn't matter. I am fertile; I can spawn stories. But the plans for the magazine are in here—the future of Young America is here—

LEONIE   Will you stay and have a whiskey and soda?

DENNIS   Thanks, but if I do, I shall miss the boat.

LEONIE   Suppose you do?

KENNETH   Leonie—that would delay the millennium one day.

DENNIS   The doctor's right. That would be selfish.

LEONIE   Be selfish. Please stay.

DENNIS   No. Once you are enlisted in a cause, you can't live a personal life. It is a dedication.

LEONIE   Kenneth is leaving. I shall be lonely, Dennis. I can't bear to be alone.

KENNETH   Your need for people is poignant, isn't it, Leonie?

LEONIE   Stay for dinner. After dinner we can talk about your magazine.

DENNIS Oh, well—that makes it possible for me to stay. Thank you, Kenneth.

(*He goes to sofa, sits, busying himself with brief-case*)
(*She goes to console to make highball*)

KENNETH Send me your magazine, Dennis. I shall be honored to be the first subscriber.

DENNIS I'll be glad to. Your patients can read it in the waiting-room instead of the *National Geographic*.

KENNETH Your first subscriber—and very possibly your last. (*He crosses to door and turns back*) Good-bye, Leonie. Good luck, Dennis. We who are about to retire—salute you.

(*She does not look at him. He bows formally to* DENNIS'S *back, makes a gesture of "good luck" and exits*)

DENNIS Trouble with that fellow is—he lives for himself. No larger interest. That's what dignifies human beings, Leonie —a dedication to something greater than themselves.

LEONIE (*Coming down to hand him his highball*) Yes? Here's your whiskey and soda. I envy you, Dennis. I wish I could dedicate myself to something—something outside myself.

DENNIS (*Rising to sit beside her*) Well, here's your opportunity, Leonie—it's providential. You couldn't do better than this magazine. It would give you a new interest—impersonal. It would emancipate you, Leonie. It would be a perpetual dedication to Youth—to the hope of the world. The world is middle-aged and tired. But we—

LEONIE (*Wistfully*) Can you refresh us, Dennis?

DENNIS Refresh you? Leonie, we can rejuvenate you!

LEONIE (*Grateful there is someone there—another human being she can laugh with*) That's an awfully amusing idea. You make me laugh.

DENNIS (*Eagerly selling the idea*) In the youth of any country, there is an immense potentiality—

LEONIE You're awfully serious about it, aren't you, Dennis?

DENNIS Where the magazine is concerned, Leonie, I am a fanatic.

LEONIE I suppose if it's really successful—it'll result in my losing everything I have—

DENNIS   It'll be taken from you anyway. You'll only be anticipating the inevitable.

LEONIE   Why—how clever of me!

DENNIS   Not only clever but graceful.

LEONIE   Will you leave me just a little to live on—?

DENNIS   Don't worry about that—come the Revolution— you'll have a friend in high office.

(LEONIE *accepts gratefully this earnest of security. They touch glasses in a toast as the curtain falls*)